Engendering the social

Feminist encounters with sociological theory

D1634995

Engendering the social

Feminist encounters with sociological theory

Edited by
Barbara L. Marshall and Anne Witz

Open University Press

Open University Press
McGraw-Hill Education
McGraw-Hill House
Shoppenhangers Road
Maidenhead
Berkshire
England
SL6 2QL

email: enquiries@openup.co.uk
world wide web: www.openup.co.uk

and Two Penn Plaza, New York, NY 10121-2289, USA

First published 2004

A catalogue record of this book is available from the British Library

ISBN 0 335 21269 7 (pb)   0 335 21270 0 (hb)

Library of Congress Cataloging-in-Publication Data
CIP data has been applied for

Typeset by RefineCatch Limited, Bungay, Suffolk
Printed in the UK by Bell and Bain Ltd, Glasgow

Contents

Notes on contributors

Lisa Adkins is Senior Lecturer in Sociology at the University of Manchester, UK. Her research interests include social and cultural theory, and the sociologies of economy, gender and sexuality. She is the author of *Gendered Work* (1995, Open University Press) and *Revisions: Sexuality and Gender in Late Modernity* (2002, Open University Press).

Caroline Arni is a historian and sociologist working at the University of Berne, Switzerland. Her research interests include the history of the heterosexual couple and love, the historical sociology of humanities and social sciences, and the historical sociology of feminist thought. Her work includes 'Jenny P. d'Héicourt. Weibliche Modernität und die Prinzipien von 1789' (co-authored with Claudia Honegger), in *Frauen in der Soziologie*, edited by Claudia Honegger and Theresa Wobbe (1998), ' "La toute-puissance de la barbe". Jenny P. d'Héicourt et les novateurs modernes', in *CLIO* (2001). She is now completing a book on the crisis of marriage and the couple around 1900.

Ute Gerhard is Professor of Sociology and Director of the Cornelia Goethe Centre for Women's and Gender Studies at the University of Frankfurt/Main in Germany. She specializes in the study of law, social sciences and history and has published widely on women's rights, social policy, the history of women and the women's movement, and feminist theory. She is author of the following books: *Verhältnisse und Verhinderungen. Frauenarbeit, Familie und Rechte der Frauen im 19. Jahrhundert* (*Women's Work, Family and Women's Rights during the 19th Century*) (1978); *Gleichheit ohne Angleichung. Frauen im Recht* (*Equality Without Assimilation, Women in Law*) (1990); *Unerhört. Die Geschichte der deutschen Frauenbewegung* (*History of the German Women's Movement*) (1990); *Frauen in der Geschichte des Rechts. Von der Frühen Neuzeit bis zur Gegenwart* (*Women in the History of Law. From Early Modern Times to the Present*) (1997); *Atempause. Feminismus als demokratisches Projekt* (*Breather: Feminism as a Democratic Project*) (1999); *Debating Women's Equality. Toward a Feminist Theory of Law from a European Perspective* (2001).

Anne Kovalainen previously held the professorship in women's studies at the Swedish School of Economics and Business Administration, Finland. She is currently Professor at the Department of Management at Turku School of Economics and Business Administration. An economic sociologist by training, she has researched on women's employment, self-employment, labour markets and economy. Her authored and co-authored books include *At the Margins of the Economy* (1995) and *Working Europe: Reshaping European Employment Systems* (co-edited, 1999). Recent journal articles and book chapters include those in *Northern Lights* (2003) and *Organizational Behaviour Reassessed: the Impact of Gender* (2001).

Barbara L. Marshall is Professor of Sociology at Trent University, Peterborough, in Canada. She is the author of *Engendering Modernity* (1994) and *Configuring Gender* (2000) as well as co-editor (with Austin Harrington, UK, and Hans-Peter Mueller, Germany) of the forthcoming Routledge *Encyclopedia of Social Theory*.

Lois McNay is a Reader in Politics and Fellow of Somerville College, Oxford University. She is the author of *Gender and Agency* (2000).

Charlotte Müller is Director of the Institute of Teacher Training, Department of Primary and Elementary Education at the State and University of Berne in Switzerland. A historian and sociologist, her recent publications include ' "Die Galanterie wich dem Kampf" – Frauen an Schweizer Universitäten im 19. Jahrhundert' (co-authored with Claudia Crotti), in *Occasional Papers for Swiss Studies* (2001); 'Paradigmenwechsel in der Genderforschung – Welche Lehren hat die Schulforschung daraus gezogen?', in *Sonderheft: Genderfragen in der Lehrerinnen- und Lehrerbildung* (2001); 'Normative Grundlagen und institutionalisierte Leitbilder in den Curricula der Berner Lehrer- und Lehrerinnenbildung 1798–2001', in *Professionalisierung der bernischen Primar- und Sekundarlehrkräfte 1798–2001* (2002), edited by Claudia Crotti and Jürgen Oelkers.

R.A. Sydie is Professor and Chair of the Department of Sociology at the University of Alberta, Edmonton, Canada. She is the author of *Natural Woman/ Cultured Man: A Feminist Perspective on Sociological Theory* (1987) and co-author (with Bert Adams) of *Classical Sociological Theory* (2001) and *Contemporary Sociological Theory* (2001).

Anne Witz is Reader in Sociology at the University of Leicester and author of *Professions and Patriarchy* (1992), co-author of *Gender, Careers and Organisations* (1997) and co-editor of *Gender and Bureaucracy* (1992) and *For Sociology: Legacies and Prospects* (2000).

Theresa Wobbe is Professor of Sociology at Erfurt University, Germany. A historian and sociologist, she is author of *Wahlverwandtschaften. Die Soziologie und die Frauen auf dem Wege zur Wissenschaft* (1997) and co-editor with Claudia

Honegger of *Frauen in der Soziologie* (1998). Together with Bettina Heintz she is currently preparing an introduction to *Gender Sociology* (2003).

Eileen Janes Yeo is Professor of Social and Cultural History and Director of the Centre in Gender Studies at the University of Strathclyde. She has written *The Contest for Social Science: Relations and Representations of Gender and Class* (1996). Her work on the history of empirical investigation includes a chapter on 'Mayhew as a Social Investigator', in *The Unknown Mayhew*, which she co-edited with E.P. Thompson, and a chapter on 'Social Surveys in the Eighteenth and Nineteenth Centuries' in Volume 7 of the *Cambridge History of Science* (forthcoming).

Acknowledgements

This book has its origins in an international network of scholars from North America and Europe that since 1998 has convened for a series of meetings on feminism and sociological theory. The editors would like to especially thank the organizers of two meetings that were instrumental in advancing the work published here: Ute Gerhard, Director of the Cornelia Goethe Centre for Women's and Gender Studies at the University of Frankfurt/Main in Germany, who organized and hosted the 1999 meeting where the editors met, and Eileen Janes Yeo, Director of the Centre for Gender Studies at Strathclyde University in Glasgow, which sponsored the 2002 meeting at Ross Priory which gave final shape to this volume. We would also like to thank all of the contributors for their amazing work and cheerful responses to nagging emails, Louise Dobbie for her assistance in organizing the Ross Priory meeting, Claire Houston for her assistance in producing the bibliography and Lucy Marshall-Kiparissis for all her help and support.

An earlier version of Chapter 2, R.A. Sydie's 'Sex and the Sociological Fathers', was published in the *Canadian Review of Sociology and Anthropology*, (volume 31, 1994) and we are grateful for permission granted by that journal to include a revised version of this essay here.

Thanks go as well to Justin Vaughan and Miriam Selwyn, both formerly of Open University Press, for their part in making this book happen.

Finally, we particularly thank each other for the unflagging mutual support and inspiration as this volume made its way to reality through a sea of other commitments.

Introduction: feminist encounters with sociological theory

Anne Witz and Barbara L. Marshall

> For consider once more the procession of the sons of educated men; ask yourself once more, where is it leading us?
>
> (Woolf 1938)

The sociological canon is patrilineal. It is a procession of men, of 'founding fathers' who, joined by their sons, have made their way from the nineteenth through the twentieth and into the twenty-first century as the canonized 'masters' (Coser 1977a) of sociological thought. If we round up the usual suspects, then it appears that it is largely straight white men who get to do the abstract, universally generalizable thinking that counts as sociological theory with a big T (Kimmel 1990).

In this book we critically interrogate this tradition of sociological theorizing from a feminist standpoint, taking up Janet Wolff's (2000) call for a feminist politics of interrogation that strategically interrogates texts in order to expose how masculinity has operated as a core constitutive category of the social. The aim is to encourage critical reflection on the sociological tradition as a way of opening up new avenues of working more productively at the interface between sociological and feminist concerns. But a necessary precursor to such a reconstructive project must entail a critical unpacking of the gendered inclusions and erasures that have functioned to privilege both the male subject and the male knower in the history of sociological thought. A critique of the partial, androcentric nature of the discipline is the starting point for all feminist interventions into sociology. Feminist sociology insists on gender as a fundamental dimension of social life and as a central analytic category within the discipline, without which the key interests of the discipline (such as work, politics, education, religion and 'culture') cannot be adequately understood. The result has been a rich body of work bringing women's lives and experiences into the purview of the social.

Feminist sociologists have often regarded theory with a capital T as a quintessentially male discourse (Smith 1987a, b; Stanley and Wise 1993), and instead have prioritized *doing* sociology in new ways, by pioneering new methodologies and foci of sociological investigation, as well as redefining and expanding the conventional male-centred, sociological problematic. Broadly speaking, feminist sociologists have focused their energies on corrective strategies seeking to displace sociology's exclusive focus on the lives and interests of men. While such work has sometimes been portrayed as merely 'additive', effectively 'stirring in' the missing pieces to produce 'better' or more complete accounts of the social, this does not do justice to the impact of feminist sociology on sociology more generally.

While the sociological gaze has certainly been opened up to 'areas of social life and experience which to date have been obscured by the partial perspective and particular bias of mainstream sociology' (Wolff 2000: 45), the job of pulling women into the sociological gaze has fundamentally *altered* that gaze. The problem, it seems, was not just the subject matter of the discipline but how sociology itself was *thought*. As Millman and Kanter charged in their programmatic statement for a feminist sociology nearly 30 years ago, feminist sociologists have had to:

> reassess the basic theories, paradigms, substantive concerns and methodologies of sociology and the social sciences to see what changes are needed to make social theory and research reflect the multitude of both female and male realities and interests.
>
> (Millman and Kanter 1975: viii)

As part of this far-reaching project, feminists have engaged critically with the foundations of the discipline via an interrogation of the canon. In doing so, they have uncovered the extent to which 'the exclusion of women from the heart of the classical project has resulted in a skewed picture of social life, of the very subject matter of sociology' (Marshall 1994: 9). Feminist engagements with the canon are thus integral to the feminist challenge to androcentric sociology more generally. As Wolff recommends, we need to immerse ourselves in the dominant sociological discourse represented by the procession of sociological men, 'in order to explore – and perhaps explode – its strategies and its contradictions' (Wolff 2000: 34).

Feminism confronts the canon

Canonization, as a collective and highly selective representation of a discipline to itself, is an ongoing process. The sociological canon provides 'a symbolic focus, a shared language, and some kind of identity, for academics and students in sociology' (Connell 1997: 1544). As Stacey d'Erasmo wryly notes: 'Like its military homonym, the canon is a machine: a form. Its main function is to place, to order, to establish things (texts) in relation to one another . . . Like Spam, the canon is resilient and, for planners of curricula, cheap' (cited in Winders 1991: 3).

Because the 'canon' is a man-made edifice (Connell 1997; Smith 1999; Wolff 2000; Pedersen 2001) we need to ask who recommends these texts, who controls their circulation and who speaks for them (Winders 1991). Becoming schooled in the canon requires a tremendous personal investment of time and results in many tacit understandings or ways of thinking sociologically. It should come as no surprise then that it also comes to be regarded as 'the heart, soul, and viscera' of a field of intellectual enquiry (Winders 1991). It should also come as no surprise that feminist critique of received ways of thinking is most likely to be ignored by those working at the canonical core of the discipline. But is feminist critique necessarily fatal to the canon? Is it the case, as Winders (1991: 12) suggests, that 'to take feminist arguments seriously would be to say farewell to the canon . . .'? Or is it the case that, as Turner (1996) maintains, feminist theory has impacted on the classical tradition in a purely additive way, latching gender differences onto class differences and renovating the classical tradition at the same time as preserving its explanatory strategies? Feminist arguments about the canon take a number of forms, requiring perhaps different sorts of reconstructive responses. But all, we think, demand a potentially radical rethink of the disciplinary core.

As a heuristic device, we might identify four main ways of critically engaging with the sociological canon, although we stress that these are neither mutually exclusive nor exhaustive. Different analytical strategies, however, point up different lacunae in the classical corpus and, perhaps more significantly, in its subsequent interpretation.

The first strategy is to mine the canon for a theory of women, asking explicitly what classical theorists had to say about women. For example, we might include here the surveys of canonical texts by Sydie (1987) and Kandal (1988). As Sydie (1987) makes clear, however much analyses of the social diverged or converged during the nineteenth and early twentieth centuries, the social is defined in terms of the public sphere in which men interact. Kandall (1988) in turn reveals that it is not entirely true to say that classical theory omitted women; it did (somewhat spasmodically) include women but in a distorted fashion. Sociological commentaries on women, which were generally fleeting, often revealed more about sociological men's vision of what woman and her place should be than about the problematic impact of modernity on women's lives. They were, in other words, prescriptive and normative. Modernity was seen as primarily problematic for men and the overriding concern was with how *men* were to live under the new, troubling and challenging condition of the modern. Of course, Durkheim is the prime example here as various contributions to this volume confirm (see Chapters 1, 2 and 6).

The second strategy of feminist critical engagement with the canon is located more in the field of the sociology of knowledge, or intellectual history, and takes on the question of the biographical, political and historical context of particular theories. For example, Jean Pedersen (2001) and Janet Shope (1994) have written on the relationship between Durkheim's theories and the sexual politics of France at the time, while Mike Gane (1993) has explored a range of theorists' views on gender in relation to their personal relationships with women. As Bill Ramp notes, classical theorists were 'caught up in a web of meanings and practices' through which they were 'compelled to make political choices and to construct meaning . . . with ambivalent consequences' (Ramp 2001: 110). Such approaches to the canon recognize texts as not just descriptive, but prescriptive, normative, interested and positioned – although not always consciously so (Gane 1993).

A third mode of engagement is the examination of the process of canonization itself, asking what and who gets included and excluded (Connell 1997; Pedersen 2001). Here we would also include those attempts to recuperate within the sociological tradition neglected women theorists (McDonald 1994, 1997; Lengermann and Neibrugge-Brantley 1998). Feminists (although not necessarily sociologists) have long been interested in the work of the feminist writer Charlotte Perkins Gillman, whose books sold phenomenally well during her lifetime, and who was influenced by the sociologist Lester Frank Ward, who in turn held her in great esteem (Lengermann and Neibrugge-Brantley 1998; Adams and Sydie 2001). Within sociology itself, the work of Harriet Martineau is now being recognized by some as comparable to that of Durkheim and Toqueville, particularly in terms of pioneering the distinct methods of observation and social commentary that were features of the nascent sociological tradition (Chapter 4, see also Rossi 1973; Drysdale 1992; Lengermann and Neibrugge-Brantley 1998; Adams and Sydie 2001). Yet canonization is, after all, a process of selective remembering and theoretical histories, like all histories, tend to be told from the perspective of the victors. Certainly, the national and international contexts within which sociological communities have formed, reformed or been undone since the nineteenth century have created a very complex picture of the slow and uneven institutionalization of sociology (Connell 1997). Yet by 1950 the fate of women thinkers had been sealed by male scholars, who had written them out of the sociological storyline (Adams and Sydie 2001). Pederson (2001) usefully calls our attention to the influential canonizers – most notably Durkheim – whose selective remembering includes silencing feminist voices, some of whom are directly challenging lines of argument that are to directly influence the nascent sociological tradition (see Chapter 4 for an account of Jenny d'Héricourt's public fury with prominent French male thinkers).

Although valuable in their own right, all of these strategies implicitly call forth a fourth mode of engagement: immanent critique that unmasks the masculinity of sociological theory (Bologh 1990; Lehmann 1994; Morgan

1992; Felski 1995; Smith 1999; Wolff 2000). This is a politics of *interrogation* of sociological texts that seeks to render explicit how *masculinity* operated as a core constitutive category of the social. This is a strategy tacitly implied by all feminist engagements with the classics, and frames our discussion here. The gendered erasures and inclusions of sociological texts have functioned both canonically *and* discursively. We thus trace a shifting emphasis from mapping the exclusions generated by the male standpoint from which sociology was written to consideration of the context, implications and textual strategies that sustain the masculinity of social theory.

Artemis March (1982), in a relatively neglected yet pioneering feminist critique of classical sociological theories, uses the term 'androcentric domain assumptions' to describe how 'the implicit Ego or centre from which the theories are elaborated, the implicit experiences and interests on which they are based, are male' (p. 99). Although on the whole invisible, women are by no means completely absent, they exhibit varying degrees of 'absence'. March distinguishes between 'exclusion' where women are completely ignored (as in Weber); 'pseudo-inclusion' where women are momentarily pulled into view but then dismissed (as in Durkheim); and 'alienation' where women are momentarily glimpsed in specific locations, such as 'the family', but otherwise elided within central organizing concepts such as social class (as in Marxism).

Sydie's (1987) analysis of the representations of men and women within sociological texts relies on a critique of the embedded naturalism in these texts – the constant deployment of a dualistic conceptual framework, which counterposed 'natural woman' and 'cultured man'. Sydie argues that it was the founding fathers' inability to think beyond this gendered dualism that accounts for what she sees as a failure of the sociological imagination to pull women into its purview.

Kandal (1988) catalogues classical theory's pronouncements on women, seeing these as linked to their political responses to the 'woman question'. Kandal's book alerts us to the fact that 'the question of the position of women in society is more important in classical sociological theory than one would gather from a reading of most of the existing literature on the classical theorists' (1988: 246). It also raises questions about the nostalgic autobiography of social theory – that which understands itself as born out of social upheaval and as intimately connected to the political and intellectual currents of the post-Enlightenment – given its stubborn refusal to recognize modern feminism as one of the most significant of these currents.

Whereas Sydie locates classical sociologists' thoughts on women within the Western European tradition of dualistic metaphysics, and Kandal locates this within national political contexts within which the 'woman question' was being debated, with Lehmann (1994) and Bologh (1990) there is a discernible shift away from locating women in the texts to interrogating these texts with a view to excavating their gendered subtextual strategies. Lehmann notes, for example, that when women appear in Durkheim's text, they do so as a disruption to the central categories of his analysis, and thus must be made to disappear in order for him to re-establish and maintain the internal consistency of his theory. With Bologh the focus shifts more explicitly to the masculinity of the text in her interrogation of Weber's sociology as an imaginary landscape of modernity animated by masculine forms of social action – as a no-woman's land. Her re-reading of Weber hints at how 'manliness' inheres in sociological concepts and functions as a metaphor of modernity.

Gane's (1993) and Seidler's (1994) discussions of the links between masculinity and social theory suggest some of the reasons for the obliteration of women from the sociological imaginary. Gane's analysis of the textual strategies of classical social theorists explores the links between male social theorists' personal strategies of masculinity – how they negotiated their own lived masculinity and relationships with women – and masculinity as a theoretical strategy in the texts they wrote. Lurking beneath the textual or theoretical strategies of classical social theory there are sexual strategies and, together, these constitute a largely unconscious formation of a structure of desire. Women as objects of desire thus appear as 'virtual objects' in textual strategies and, although 'he is reflected in the virtual images that he has desired' (Gane 1993: 203), 'he' disappears. At the same time, many male theorists have believed that 'their own masculinity, their own being as men, is born in love, in homage to, in the arms of, a woman . . . Out of this awakened masculinity comes the strength to go out into the world; but in the end this strength creates a world where the feminine is a secondary agency' (1993: 8). Thus, 'in its theoretical strategy masculinity is rendered invisible, for everything happens in the domain of men themselves, or only in the realm of pure logic' (1993: 8).

Vic Seidler (1994) has similarly exposed the masculinist theoretical strategy of social theory and locates this in sociology's Enlightenment ancestry:

> Within an Enlightenment vision of modernity, to lack reason is to lack humanity . . . As reason is defined in fundamental opposition to nature within our moral lives, so culture is set up in opposition to nature . . . The relationship of masculinity to modernity becomes a crucial point of investigation because of the identification of masculinity with reason.
>
> (Seidler 1994: ix–x)

Thus reason, progress and civilization were explicitly aligned with male faculties and potentialities, saturating men with both mindfulness and rationality. As Seidler (1994: 14) says 'It is men who think. It is men who are conceived of in our Western philosophical tradition as the rational sex, for they alone can take their reason for granted and so can escape from the demands of nature'.

There is no doubt, then, that sociology, and in particular social theory, has been written from a male standpoint. As Dorothy Smith summarizes the import of this insight:

> The frames of reference which order the terms upon which inquiry and discussion are conducted originate with men . . . And even before we become conscious of our sex as a basis of an exclusion (they are not talking about us), we nonetheless do not fully enter ourselves as the subjects of its statements, since we must suspend our sex, and suspend our knowledge of who we are as well as who it is that in fact is speaking and of whom.
>
> (Smith 1987a: 91)

Smith, here, is speaking as a woman[1] and addressing the woman reader. Smith's point then, is that women readers of sociological texts cannot find themselves there, even though their subject is ostensibly genderless. How, though, might a man enter the same text *as a man*? Or might he even think of looking for himself as a man? Reflexive accounts of male sociologists who have tried to do this are instructive in revealing the extent to which the same textual strategies that 'marked women as gendered beings . . . made gender invisible to men' (Kimmel 1990: 93). Writing as a man, Kimmel reflects upon how 'that which privileges us is rendered invisible by the very process that constructs that privilege' (Kimmel 1990: 93).

Similarly, David Morgan has recalled his own coming to awareness that taking *gender* into account meant taking *men* – and his own masculinity – into account: 'Men . . . have to work against the grain – their grain – in order to free their work from sexism, to take gender into account. The male researcher needs, as it were, a small voice at his shoulder reminding him at each point that he is a man' (Morgan 1981: 95). Morgan revisits some canonical texts – including Max Weber's *The Protestant Ethic and the Spirit of Capitalism* – and finds that re-reading these with an awareness of the masculinity of the text generates new insights about the interplay of gender with other key social processes (for example, rationality, capitalism and Protestantism) (Morgan 1992: 64).

For both Kimmel and Morgan, explicitly recognizing their own masculinity shifted their relationships to sociological texts, highlighting the extent to which 'the reader both activates the text and is responding to it' (Smith 1999: 145). There is considerable room for further interrogation of the relationship that Smith (1999) discerns between the 'standpoint within the text' and the 'social within the text'. For Smith, the social is the 'virtual object' of sociology inscribed in texts by actual subjects – male subjects. Smith's critique of sociology prompts further interrogation of how the standpoint within the text affects its own erasures in these seemingly positionless accounts. At the same time, this standpoint constructs an imaginary architecture of the social that both presumes and erases the masculine. The issue then becomes one of the consequences of recognizing the partiality of sociological accounts and perspectives, where masculinity is presumed yet negated, as he assumes a gender-neutral universality. If sociological writings are replete with a presumed yet unmarked masculinity, then does this render them useless for feminist purposes or mean that feminists cannot 'think the gendered social' within the parameters of extant theoretical frameworks such as those offered by sociology? This is clearly not the case methodologically, as there has been a mutual growth and accommodation of feminist and sociological methodological procedures over the past 30 years. But it is still a moot point as far as the sociological canon is concerned and the ways in which sociology forms and reforms its core problematics with reference to this canon. Clearly, many feminists work within non-feminist intellectual lineages, often becoming advocates, while simultaneously engaging in immanent critique, of a particular theorists, such as Habermas, Foucault, Durkheim, Marx and so on, or school of thought. Nonetheless, Iris Marion Young (1998), reflecting upon her own engagement of Merleau-Ponty's phenomenology to analyse specifically female gendered styles of embodiment, asks whether that means she is making an implicit claim that there are equally specific masculine modalities (as yet unspecified) or whether to specify female modes of embodiment implicitly recognizes that 'it is the case in male-dominated society [that] humanly universal standards of freedom and creativity are coincidental with masculine standards?' (Young 1998: 288). Otherwise, Young (1994) is happy to advocate acting like a 'feminist bandita', raiding the coffers of philosophy and social theory for the useful bits and using them to further specifically feminist analysis.[2]

Retrenchments and reconfigurations

If a strategy of interrogation focuses on the cultural work that texts do, in the sense that sociological discourse constitutes one way of imagining the modern (Felski 1995) and that, by representing gender relations, sociological texts also *constitute* them, then we need to consider the extent to which mainstream sociological texts *still* perform this cultural work in the present (Winders 1991).

Attempts to assess the impact of feminist insights over the years have consistently indicated that the relationship between feminism and sociology remains problematic (Stacey and Thorne 1985a; Oakley 1989; Maynard 1990; Alway 1995; Roseneil 1995; Franklin 1996; Marshall 2000). On the one hand, gender is quite firmly established as a legitimate focus of sociological investigation. On the other hand, it has tended to develop most notably as a subsection of the discipline ('sociology of gender') or within some feminized subareas (for example, 'sociology of the family') rather than transforming the theoretical core. In a review of introductory sociology textbooks, Marshall (2000: 32–4) found that 'gender' still points to places where women are present in the text. That is, when sociologists talk about gender, they are, for the most part, talking about 'women'. With few exceptions, social phenomena as diverse as bureaucracies, motorcycle gangs and language can be discussed without reference to gender, unless women are anchoring the reference. In its sharpest form, this is represented by indexes that, at the end of the entry on 'gender' instruct us to 'see also, women', yet have no entry for 'men' in the index at all.

Joan Alway argues that sociological theory has been particularly resistant to the transformation demanded by feminism because 'gender not only challenges the dichotomous categories that frame sociological thought, it also displaces sociology's founding problematic – the problematic of modernity' (1995: 211). She goes on to suggest that it is because they both share 'modernity' as a 'discursive centre', that postmodern theory has been taken up to a greater extent than feminist theory (p. 220). Certainly, 'modernity' remains central to sociological theory's self-understanding in a way that 'gender' does not. Perhaps, though, it is not so much a displacement of that problematic that a serious consideration of gender prompts, but a radical rethinking of the way 'modernity' has been constructed as a sociological problematic.

It is useful to recognize 'modernity', as it continues to frame sociological theory, as an 'ideal type' in the most Weberian of terms:

> An ideal type is formed by the one-sided accentuation of one or more points of view and by the synthesis of a great many diffuse, discrete, more or less present, and occasionally absent concrete individual phenomena, which are arranged according to those one-sidedly emphasized viewpoints into a unified analytical construct
>
> (Weber 1994: 263–4)

The papers in this volume go a long way towards illustrating the 'one-sidedness' of these accentuations, and in pointing up the 'absent' phenomena. As Weber goes on to insist, however, an ideal type is a 'utopia', not an empirical reality; it does not exist. Yet theory text after theory text begins with 'modernity' as a universalized and often reified entity. Those same texts might admit 'women', en masse, or 'feminism' as a critical voice, in small doses, but only in carefully contained ways that do little to disturb the ideal type of modernity (or even to reveal it as such) that frames them. There is certainly no indication that modernity, that central problematic of sociology, is a thoroughly gendered construction. Nigel Dodd, for example, in *Social Theory and Modernity* (1999), finds feminist theory, and even sexuality itself (here elided with gender), only relevant in his discussion/assessment of Foucault. In Gerard

Delanty's *Social Theory in a Changing World: Conceptions of Modernity* (1999) gender warrants even less mention. In these texts, as is standard practice in the discipline, gender-neutral terms are used throughout – 'the individual', 'the subject' and so on. But as Derek Sayer pointed out some time ago, simply de-gendering the language of classical theory obscures, rather than illuminates, the masculinity of modernity:

> That, for the most part, they universalize under the sign of the modern the social experience of men should, to my mind, be highlighted, not swept under a unisex carpet. When they say 'Man', that is precisely who they usually mean . . . To imagine this deficiency can be remedied by changing the gender of pronouns is to efface even more thoroughly that world of feminine experience sociology has so conspicuously neglected.
>
> (Sayer 1991: 5)

A heightened awareness of the gendered erasures and inclusions that operated in classical theorizations of the social is urgently needed in the current climate, where retrenchment and reconfiguration are curiously overlapping strategies in sociology. There are signs of retrenchment as sociologists seek to protect the contours of their discipline, for example by re-asserting the continued salience of its classical heritage in the face of an alleged cultural turn towards a merely 'decorative sociology' (Rojek and Turner 2000), or by recuperating the works of classical sociologists in order to develop a distinctly sociological perspective on the body (Shilling 2001) to resist its discursive colonization by cultural studies. While we are not antipathetic to arguments that insist upon the continued salience of the sociological tradition, we are deeply troubled by the relatively unreflexive recuperation of these texts and the attendant dangers of reinstating the privileged masculine subject of classical theory.

Happily there are also signs of reconfiguration of the problematic bequeathed by the classical canon. Larry Ray's *Theorizing Classical Sociology* (1999) recuperates the theme of nature and gender, which ran so heavily through classical texts yet later got erased from the institutionalized, canonized core of the discipline. Ray argues that classical theorists were well aware of the transformations of gender relations wrought by capitalism and modernity, even if they generally misunderstood them, and he ties this through his discussions of the different theorizations of the social that emerged in classical sociology. A similar exercise is engaged in by Adams and Sydie (2001) in their text *Classical Sociological Theory*, where there is not only a discussion of class, gender and race in relation to every theorist they discuss, but also a recuperation of key feminist social theorists in their own right. Such reconfigurations of the classical heritage represent a considerable advance on more conventional texts, which at best might latterly add a separate chapter on feminist theory and/or feminist theorists (often written by someone other than the main author of the text). This more conventional (and unfortunately more common) approach has the effect of preserving other chapters as gender-free zones, and suggests that a concern with gender is something produced only recently by a separate breed of academics (feminists).

In the case of more recent theory, it is not necessarily the case that the privileged masculine subject is simply being *reinstated*. Rather, as Adkins (2002 and Chapter 7, this volume) argues, the exclusions and inclusions that operate in relation to the reflexive subject of much contemporary theory may serve to re-engender in new ways the concept of the 'post-structural social', even as the dissolution of gender is claimed. A feminist politics of interrogation and reconstruction within sociology demands, then, that we grapple with the ambivalent legacy of classical sociology, insofar as it continues to shape how we come to think sociologically. A focus on the problematic engendering of classical *and* contemporary sociological theory is a necessary precursor to a politics of reconstruction, which works both critically and creatively at the interface between mainstream sociological theory and feminist concerns.

Overview of the volume

Three key themes organize the contributions to this volume. In Part I, papers explore how the foundations of social theory were shaped by an implicit masculinity, suggesting that classical sociology actively constructed theories of difference.

Anne Witz and Barbara Marshall (Chapter 1) explore the manner in which gender differentiation was integral to classical sociological conceptions of modernity, arguing that as the epistemic core of sociology – the 'social' – was delineated in these accounts, women were metaphysically exiled from the social. They re-read key texts of Durkheim and Simmel through the conceptual grid of corporeality, embodiment and sociality to show how the very concept of the social presupposed specifically masculine forms of individualization, action and agency. Witz and Marshall go beyond asking 'where are the women' in these accounts, to also demand that men *qua* men be accounted for. What emerges is a deeply gendered ontology of 'the social' – the *masculinity* of modernity – rooted in a skewed conception of embodiment and agency. They then consider the implications of this legacy for more adequately apprehending the 'gendered social'.

Rosalind Sydie (Chapter 2) explores early sociological pronouncements on sexuality, treating sociology as part of that great nineteenth-century 'discursive explosion' on sex. She locates classical sociology's concern to 'place' sexuality *in* society against the backdrop of debates about citizenship, family, heterosexual desire and practice. Focusing on the work of Auguste Comte,

Emile Durkheim and Max Weber, she argues that 'the description of the modern world offered by the sociological fathers was compromised by their inability to recognize that sexual desire and expression was just as much a cultural construction for women as for men'. This resulted in a problematic – indeed, contradictory – understanding of embodiment and individualization which saw women anchored in a natural, pre-social sexuality which was nonetheless potentially threatening to the rational control over desire demanded of the disciplined male citizen and worker. Sydie suggests that the sociological fathers were themselves embodied, and thus construed eroticism – displaced onto women – as a potential threat to male autonomy and hence social order.

Theresa Wobbe (Chapter 3) addresses the relationship between Georg Simmel's and Marianne Weber's analyses of individuation, social differentiation and gender difference. Both were centrally concerned with the question of social integration in modernity – a problematic which, of course, was central to the founding moments of sociology more generally. Simmel and Weber were both engaged in drawing out the gendered nature of individuation in relation to this problematic, but with very different results. While both were 'centrally concerned with the problematic status of women in what they . . . recognized as man-made modernity', Weber was more successful in recognizing the cultural potential of the 'new woman'. Simmel's concern was with the fragmented male subject in modernity, and he was, in the end, unable to provide a sociological analysis of women's individuation, instead discounting its very possibility. Wobbe deftly draws out both the points of affinity and difference in Weber's and Simmel's accounts, suggesting that it was their respective feminist and masculinist standpoints that either provided or blocked access to a fully social account of gender differentiation in modernity.

In Part II, the relationship between feminism and sociology is explored. Papers here both recount histories of this relationship and consider their consequences. In particular, the question of how alternative accounts of the social were suppressed in sociology's founding moments is pursued.

Eileen Yeo (Chapter 5) interrogates the founding moments of British sociology, drawing out important differences between this tradition and its continental counterparts. She recounts how, rather than excluding women from the realm of the social and of citizenship, there was a determined attempt to counter constructions of the egotistical male individual of political economy by insisting that qualities heretofore associated with women – for example, altruism and care for others – were integral to good citizenship. A 'communion of labour', where men and women would bring their respective virtues to divided tasks in all spheres, both public and private, was seen as the best route to the good society. While this certainly posed limits on women's roles, what Yeo terms the 'feminization of the citizen in Britain' also opened opportunities for education and professional careers. But the 'communion of labour' formula held contradictory consequences for women who took advantage of these opportunities. By way of illustration, Yeo probes the marriages of a number of female social science professionals and their pioneer sociologist husbands, demonstrating that both patterns of the institutionalization of sociology as a discipline and the reassertion of a biological foundation for gender-differentiated tasks effaced the role of women in those critical moments of reforming the citizen.

Caroline Arni and Charlotte Müller (Chapter 4) provide a fascinating account of how two neglected women theorists – Harriet Martineau in Britain and Jenny d'Héricourt in France – contested the masculinist foundations of sociology in its founding moments. Martineau as both a prolific author and well-known translator (most notably of Comte's *Cour de philosophie positive*) contributed greatly to the development and documentation of a systematic method for sociology. Emile Durkheim, who most famously elaborated on sociological method, ignored her contribution while duplicating many of her basic insights on systematic and comparative observations. Martineau's social analysis emerges as not only prescient, but more consistently and rigorously sociological – unlike Durkheim, she does not retreat into pseudo-biological explanation for sex inequalities, but keeps her gaze firmly directed on the social production of difference and inequality. The Frenchwoman Jenny d'Héricourt, in her spirited – and often public – engagements with such thinkers as Proudhon and Comte, exhibited both a sharp wit and an astutely sociological analysis. Her devastating critique of what she termed the 'annihilation' of women in masculinist accounts cuts to and contests their core assumptions, exposing the faulty ontology of sexual difference that lay at their heart. Ontological assumptions of natural difference, she contended, were unscientific and purely speculative, and she directed attention instead to manifest phenomena of difference as that which deserved a genuinely social analysis. Arni and Müller make a forceful case for the consideration of Martineau and d'Héricourt as 'classics'. It seems clear, though, that these women were not just excluded from the sociological tradition because of their sex, but because of the disruption their interventions posed to the emerging conceptual apparatus of the new discipline of sociology.

Ute Gerhard (Chapter 6) explores the relationship between sociology and feminism in Germany by considering how issues raised in 'first wave' feminism at the turn of the twentieth century, and 'second wave' feminism since the 1960s have intersected with what have become understood within socio-logical theory as the 'first' and 'second' crises of modernity. In a highly original analysis, she locates feminism as a *sign* of crisis in modernity, demonstrating the intimate relationship between theoretical and political debates. She first reviews how gender was taken up in classical sociological theory – here, via an analysis of Tönnies, Durkheim, Weber and Simmel – and argues that the 'gender problematic' was integral to the crisis of 'first modernity'. The 'woman question' was openly discussed and debated by sociologists, despite some rather dubious answers proffered. By contrast, her review of more recent interchanges between feminism and sociology reveals a different picture. As feminist concerns were deemed to be 'unscientific and partisan' by institutionalized sociology, and as feminist theory itself assumed the character of a more interdisciplinary project, questions about gender have assumed far less importance to mainstream sociological theory than they did a century ago. As Gerhard argues, the relationship between feminism and sociology is more, rather than less, problematic than ever.

Chapters in Part III focus on contemporary sociological theory, asking whether the masculine subject still lurks beneath the supposedly generic individual, and in what ways feminist theory and sociological theory can inform one another.

Lisa Adkins' chapter (Chapter 7) begins with an assessment of the classical legacy, recognizing the exclusion of women from the social that has been elaborated in previous chapters, and she then moves to a consideration of how this legacy has shaped contemporary social theory. Reviewing theories of reflexive and aesthetic modernity, as well as theories of sexuality and gender, a shift from traditional dualisms, such as traditional/modern, to more contemporary dualistic formations of modernity/late modernity, or social/postsocial, is traced. In a strikingly original analysis, she argues that, rather than simply reinstating the privileged masculine subject and continuing to 'naturalize' women as a means of excluding them, significant strands of contemporary social theory have constructed a more novel gendered narrative. She focuses here on recent theory that emphasizes the decline of social structure in late modern societies – what she terms theories of the 'post-structural social'. Integral to this theoretical shift has been a reconceptualization of the conditions of agency – a freeing of agents from structure, releasing them to become mobile and reflexive subjects – and that these are conditions to which women are granted far less access. As she summarizes it: 'while in classical social theory women were excluded from sociality, here woman is *overdetermined* by the social, indeed cannot escape the social'. Her conclusions prompt us to think about *why* such theories contain women within the problematic of an earlier modernity.

Anne Kovalainen (Chapter 8) tackles a body of contemporary work that appears to have remained particularly immune to feminist insights, but which has become influential in both sociology and economics in recent years – theories of social capital and trust. She explores some of the reasons social capital and trust have become such widely circulated concepts, and probes beneath their intuitive appeal to expose a range of theoretical, methodological and epistemological problems in their deployment. Her analysis demonstrates that discussions of such wide-ranging issues as the nature of the rational actor, the family as a model for civic virtues, the putative decline of civic engagement and the transmission of social capital are shot through with gendered assumptions that cannot be sustained either theoretically or empirically. A feminist critic might ask, for example, whether Mrs Putnam is doing the washing up and minding the children while Mr Putnam bowls alone?

In a departure from the approach taken by other contributors to this volume, Lois McNay (Chapter 9) looks at a particular impasse in contemporary feminist theory – the debates between materialist and cultural feminisms – and suggests that a critical engagement with the work of Habermas and Bourdieu may be valuable in developing a social theory of gender. Specifically, she develops the concept of *situated intersubjectivity* as a sociological alternative to what she sees as shortcomings in both cultural and materialist feminist approaches, arguing that 'the idea of intersubjectivity provides a category through which the intertwinement of symbolic and material power relations can begin to be thought'. She demonstrates this intertwining through an examination of marriage as a form of situated intersubjectivity – one which illustrates the complex, shifting and often unstable relationships between the symbolic and the material, and which implicates a range of gendered power relations. McNay's analysis acts as a brilliant example of the potential of a creative interplay between feminist theory and sociological theory, enriching each and bringing them into full dialogue.

In sum, each of the chapters makes a distinctive contribution to expanding the range of feminist interrogation and reconstruction within sociology as we grapple with the ambivalent legacy of classical sociology. Taken together, they provide a rich resource for a critical and constructive rethinking of sociological theory.

Notes

1 As Smith has recounted in a retrospective account of her career (1992: 133), she experienced acute anxiety trying to write sociology as a woman.

> I used to drink a glass or so of brandy to get going. Looking back, I see that as the mark of the profound alienation of my located subjectivity and the mode in which I had to write. I had no ground from which to write into the objectified male-grounded textual ordering of sociology.

As an editorial note, we find gin to be equally effective!

2 The papers collected in this volume represent the work of an expanding network of feminist scholars, who have been developing their individual interests through network meetings over the past few years. As is evident from the structure of the book, individual interests cohere in different clusters – broadly

feminist interrogations of the canonical classical sociologists, of the relationship between feminist and sociological concerns historically and of contemporary sociological theorists. The absence of a chapter on feminism and Marxism reflects the simple fact that no network member was working in this area. It should not be taken to indicate a lack of engagement with Marxism. Indeed there has been a longstanding engagement, both productive and critical, between feminism and Marxism. Particularly in the early days of the emergence of feminism in the academy, there were intense interrogations of the potential of Marxism to provide a paradigm for feminist social scientific analysis (see Barrett 1980). The development of a distinctive materialist feminism (see Delphy 1984) represents one early wing of European sociological feminist critical engagement with Marxism, and has re-emerged recently in the United States, combined with discourse analysis (Hennessy and Ingraham 1997).

PART I
Interrogating the classical canon

1 The masculinity of the social: towards a politics of interrogation

Anne Witz and Barbara L. Marshall

In this chapter we interrogate sociological texts with a view to excavating the masculinity that inheres in these texts and saturates the concept of the social. Taking up Janet Wolff's call for a feminist politics of interrogation that 'immerses itself in that dominant masculinist discourse in order to explore – and perhaps explode – its strategies and contradictions' (Wolff 2000: 34), we explore how masculinity has operated as a core constitutive category of the social, securing both the metaphysical exile of women (Marshall 1994, 2000) and a masculine ontology of the social (Witz 2000, 2001). We focus on the problematic engendering of classical and contemporary sociological theory, arguing that there is a deeply gendered ontology of the social that underpins sociological conceptions of individualization, agency and action. The texts of two classical sociologists – Durkheim and Simmel – are interrogated in order to demonstrate some of the conceptual manoeuvres that undergirded the erection of masculine modernity in sociological discourse. We then go on to consider the different ways in which gender – the possibility of understanding both men and women as socially constructed – *might* have been thought within classical sociological discourse, and ponder the ambivalent legacy that the failure to do so has left us.

Modernity, masculinity and the social

Sociology has been simultaneously concerned with and produced by 'modernity'. In its construction of itself as a discipline, 'modernity' has functioned as its *leitmotif*. Moreover, 'the discourse of sociology has affected the ways in which all of us envisage the modern' (Felski 1995: 36). Yet women have always occupied a contradictory and ambivalent position in relation to the 'modern' as it has been sociologically interpreted, particularly in the sense of modernity as representing a gradual liberation of the individual from the bonds of tradition. Cast as unable to fully transcend these bonds, and hence incapable of becoming fully agentic, women could not take their place in the landscape of the 'social' as modern individuals.

As we will demonstrate with reference to Durkheim and Simmel, gender differentiation was explicitly identified as integral to modernity. For Durkheim, it is a 'morphological' difference – a categorical difference in classification – that marks the inequality of men and women. For Simmel, it is a metaphysical difference that grounds 'modernity' as explicitly masculine. For both, if the experience of modernity was encapsulated, for men, by their self-consciousness of differentiation and change, then women, quite simply, could not experience this.

Modernity was also represented by a series of institutional reconfigurations. Most significant here were increasingly distinct boundaries between the public and private realms, with most sociological interest directed towards the former. This is well-illustrated by the overwhelming emphasis on capitalism, industrialization, secularization and urbanization as the hallmarks of modernity. But the public/private distinction was (and continues to be) conflated with a masculine/feminine distinction, so that women were not seen to participate in, or even experience the effects of, the institutional dimensions of modernity that were of such interest to sociology. And yet these institutional transformations were profoundly gendered, creating newly gendered characters (such as workers, citizens and consumers). Nonetheless, sexual difference was regarded as absolute, located in the domestic/private, and hence in women. This is the familiar dualism of universal/particular – with the public world of universalized 'humanity' (read men) counterposed to the private world of particularity (read women). Given that the starting point for classical sociology was to theorize the individual as social – that is as constituted only within society and social relations – it should have been able to embrace both public and private spheres as wholly social in their constitution, but it did not. Women's very subjectivity was construed as being of a fundamentally different order than men's and it certainly wasn't that of the 'modern' subject. As Denise Riley suggests, the 'differing temporalities' of the category of 'women', in relation to the emerging categories of 'body', 'soul', 'society' and 'the social' in the post-Enlightenment may be read as a 'history of an increasing sexualization, in which female persons become held to be virtually saturated with their sex' (Riley 1988: 8).

This has had profound consequences for how sociology developed its understandings of itself and of the 'modern' world – and these two understandings are intricately interrelated. Here we argue that, because early sociology was remarkably resistant to a fully sociological understanding of women, neither by extension could it understand men *qua* men. Furthermore, far from simply 'reflecting' the prevailing sentiments about women's nature of the time, classical social theory actively *constructed* a theory of sexual difference, ultimately rooted in 'nature' and its variable relationship to the 'social'. Classical theorists mobilized the 'natural' in strategic ways to epistemologically carve out the distinctive contours of the social. This strategy effected the invisibilization of men *qua* men in classical sociological texts and the construction of a masculine ontology of the social that metaphysically secured women's exile from the social. This masculine ontology of the social was undergirded by a *deep ontology of difference* which overloaded woman with corporeality, while evacuating man of his and, in the process, delineated the terrain of the social as the terrain of the masculine. This is, we think, something that has been underappreciated in feminist reassessments of classical sociology, which have tended to focus on its faulty constructions of women and their resulting absence from the canon. To a large extent we have misrecognized and failed to adequately interrogate the utter and explicit *masculinity* of modernity, and the legacy of this with which we continue to struggle as theorists.

Women figured most frequently as a *strategic absence* in classical sociology – that is, we can glean as much or more about conceptualizations of women in the classical project by their dis-locations or absences from specific contexts as we can from the bits where they are present. Masculinity, by contrast, figures as an *absent presence* – always there, but largely unarticulated. Our interrogation of sociological texts is particularly concerned with exposing the ways in which virtual men and women are conjured up in these texts in the process of delineating the epistemic core of sociology – the social – and with how the supposedly generic players who animate the social – those individuals, social actors or agents – are essentially male. It is masculinity that animates and energizes the social as constituted within these texts, classical as well as contemporary. This is why we may speak of a masculine ontology of the social (Witz 2001) as indicative of the 'deep gendering' (Alway 1995) of the very concept of the social.

Interrogating the relation between sociology and modernity in this way allows us to focus on the metaphysical exclusion of women from 'the social' as distinct from their institutional exclusion from 'society' – here understood as particular historical instantiations of 'the social'. Distinguishing the social from society induces a more astute distinction between the metaphysical and institutional exile of women from modernity and assists us in avoiding the tendency, apparent in some earlier feminist engagements with classical sociology, to conflate the absence of sociological representations of women with their absence from historical configurations of the public sphere. Classical sociologists were not only describing men and women, but were deeply engaged in public and, as Jean Pedersen (2001) has noted, often noisy debates about the political reconfiguration of gender relations, while at the same time deploying specific discursive and textual strategies which inscribed particular forms of masculinity and femininity as they made the social emerge.

Sociological texts themselves become the sites for the constitution rather than simply the passive representations of gender difference and gender relations.

One strategy for interrogating the masculinity of modernity is to re-read sociological texts through the conceptual grid of corporeality, embodiment and sociality.[1] In this way we can explore the textual strategies whereby masculine individuals could be released from corporeality, and granted the sort of embodiment that allowed them to transcend their particularity and become *social* agents. Textual strategies are constitutive practices that accomplish an object in the process of its textual inscription (Smith 1990: 216). Writing sociological texts produces the social in texts organizing sociology as a discourse, hence the social is one of 'the virtual realities of sociological discourse' (Smith 1999: 52).[2] For us then, as for Smith, the social is 'the discursively constituted object of sociology's inquiry' (1999: 6).

We begin, then, by reconstructing the masculine ontology of Durkheim's and Simmel's embodied agents as a means of demonstrating the pitfalls of mistaking a specifically gendered construction for the generic 'social'. We show how in both the very concept of the social presupposes specifically masculine forms of individualization, action and agency. Simmel and Durkheim give us radically different, yet eerily similar accounts of the emergence of the social in modernity, with its individualized men and body-bound women. Despite their radically different epistemological commitments, they bequeath a masculine ontology of the social.

Durkheim: *homo duplex* and *femina simplex*

Beginning with the *Division of Labour in Society*, where he posits an increasing differentiation between women and men as integral to the development of societies, Durkheim never works with a generic conception of *human* individuals. He is clear that men and women are naturally differentiated, and on the basis of this, differentially incorporated into the expansion of the social in modernity. Even in his more optimistic moments, when he imagines that women might someday become more social, Durkheim conceived of this as a socialization of that pre-existing, pre-social difference – a slow evolutionary process whereby 'these differences will become of greater social use than in the past' (Durkheim 1964b: 385).

As a number of commentators have noted,[3] Durkheim's original assertion that women and men were alike in primitive societies, and evolved to become more different, is revised in light of his anthropological reading of primitive societies, most notably in his work on the incest taboo (Durkheim 1963) and in the *Elementary Forms of Religious Life* (Durkheim 1995). Here he finds that, far from being sexually egalitarian, primitive societies were structured by a rigid division between the sexes. Thus sexual difference is taken to be one of the most basic of divisions, akin to, and frequently aligned with, the distinction between sacred and profane. Women, as ritually profane, were prohibited from participation in collective ceremonies, and were required to segregate themselves from the collective more generally during specific times when their bodies were most particularly female – for example, during menstruation or parturition. Initiation rituals for men differentiated them from women and children, and in doing so initiated them into *social* life.

How, then, are we to read women into Durkheim's more general argument about the sources of the social? Denied entry into collective ritual, or access to the representation of the social via totemic symbols, women's bodies mark them as *not*-social. Man is located in, yet transcends his body in religious ecstasy, substituting a collective sentiment for his own sense-perceptions. Woman is less imbued with religious dignity; less able to go beyond herself, denied the capacity to substitute collective sentiment for particularism. Her body is less a source of connection *to* the social than a source of exile *from* the social. She is *corporealized*, he is *embodied*.

In *Elementary Forms*, Durkheim crucially distinguishes between the individual and the personality, suggesting that they have different sources: 'The first are made of impressions and images that come from every part of the body; the others consist of ideas and feelings that come from the society and express it'. It is the personality that 'represents society in us' and is 'not directly subordinate to the organic factor' (1995: 274), and it is the development of personality – derived from the collective – that is 'the only means we have of liberating ourselves from physical forces' (1995: 274): '. . . the more emancipated we are from the senses, and the more capable we are of thinking and acting conceptually, the more we are persons' (1995: 275).

He elaborates on this 'constitutional duality' in his essay on the 'dualism of human nature' (Durkheim 1960). 'Man' is both body and soul, engaged in a struggle between 'sensory appetites', which are necessarily egoistic, and 'moral activity', which is socially derived and impersonal. As Shilling (2001) has argued, Durkheim's conceptualization of 'man' as '*homo duplex*', or the 'body doubled' – that is, as an individual who is both embodied and social – accords agency to the embodied individual. It is in this way that, for Durkheim, embodied experience can be treated as a 'crucial medium for the constitution of society' (Shilling 2001: 332).[4] As Durkheim summarizes the '*homo duplex*' with its 'double center of gravity': 'On the one hand is our individuality – and more particularly, our body in which it is based; on the other is everything in us that expresses something other than ourselves' (1960: 328). That something 'other than ourselves' is, of course, society, the source of all that is moral and conceptual. As Durkheim explores throughout all his major works, the development of society furnishes men with that which makes them *men*: 'Man is man only because he is civilized' (Durkheim 1960). And when Durkheim says 'man', that is exactly who he means.

Women are denied that 'liberation from the senses' which would truly make them 'persons'.

Durkheim assumes, and builds his theory on, the veracity of accounts of absolute sexual difference drawn from such 'sciences' as craniometry, as well as biological accounts of 'drives' and 'instincts'. This is 'nature' – that which is 'under the exclusive influence of physical and organic-psychic forces' (Durkheim [1933] 1964a: 387 fn7). It is this 'nature' with which the 'social' emerges in tension, and whose domination is a measure of civilization: 'the progress of conscience is in inverse ratio to that of instinct' (p. 346). Conscience, or that morality which is derived from the social, fills the space that, in the civilizing process, 'instinct leaves free' (p. 387) in men. But woman, he tells us, 'has had less part than man in the movement of civilization' ([1933] 1964a: 247), is a more 'instinctive creature' (1964b: 272), and is less 'penetrated' by the social (1964b: 215). Not *homo duplex*, but *femina simplex*.[5] In fact, in *Suicide* (Durkheim 1951), he uses women's (and children's and 'primitives'') *lack* of a doubled nature and their consequently lower rates of suicide, as evidence in 'confirming' his explanation of egoism as a cause of suicide in men (1964b: 215–16).

In *Suicide* we can find an explicit rendering of the 'man problem' in classical theory. Here, it is only the male body that is rendered sociologically problematic, precisely because it is, unlike the female body, unmoored from nature through its sociality. While this valorizes the masculine agent and grants him exclusive access to the terrain of 'the social', it also renders the masculine body far more vulnerable to disruption. Quite simply, the greater degree of civilization, the greater risk there is of disturbance in negotiation of the mind/body relationship. For Durkheim, this is demonstrated by varying rates of mental disorders and suicides with variations in degrees of 'civilization'. Thus, he tells us in *The Division of Labor in Society* ([1933] 1964a) that, 'it is not without cause that mental diseases keep pace with civilization, nor that they rage in cities rather than in the country, and in large cities more than small ones' ([1933] 1964a: 273). Suicide, too, increases with civilization, as evidenced by higher rates among urban-dwellers and professionals than among agricultural workers. Woman, who 'has had less part than man in the movement of civilization' and 'recalls certain characteristics of primitive natures' has only one-quarter the suicide rate of man ([1933] 1964a: 273).

As men become 'civilized', their sexual appetites are no longer governed by instinct, and sexual desire 'no longer has the regular, automatic periodicity which it displays in animals . . . social regulation becomes necessary' (1964b: 270). Monogamous marriage is necessary to 'regulate the life of passion' (1964b: 270). The dangers of weak marital regulation are sharply posed by the sad case of the unmarried man, who lives in a state of 'chronic sexual anomy', who 'aspires to everything and is satisfied with nothing' (1964b: 271). The result is a 'strong suicidal tendency', which is aggravated in unmarried men between the ages of 20 and 45, 'just when sexual feelings are most aroused' (1964b: 274).[6] Thus, the male body requires ongoing and active social regulation, precisely because it is, unlike the female body, unmoored from nature through its sociality, rendering it far more vulnerable to disruption and dysfunction.[7] The routinization of male sexuality through monogamous heterosexual marriage thus becomes an imperative.[8]

In his discussion of sex education in his writings on moral education, Durkheim is concerned with how to educate the 'young man' about the 'moral aspects' of sexual intercourse (Durkheim 1979). Insistent that sex was not just a 'biological function, comparable to that of digestion and circulation', he draws here on the very nature of *homo duplex* that creates, in men, a tension between the 'sensory appetite' and 'moral life', which can only be mediated by recognizing the ultimately sacred character of sexual acts. He thus describes marital coitus as the 'communion of the most intimate kind possible between two conscious beings', erasing the boundaries between them and creating a new ethical unity (1979: 147). Sexuality thus civilized by a socially sanctioned, permanent union represents the transcendence of mere bodily imperatives.

While it might well be argued that Durkheim provides an embodied conception of agency (Shilling 2001), it is most certainly not a generic, ungendered conception of agency. To mistake it for such not only ignores the strategies by which Durkheim explicitly recognizes (however mistakenly) sexual difference, but also deflects attention from the interesting sociological questions of how bodies are socially recognized in ways which may produce fundamentally different experiences of embodiment – experiences which may indeed connect us to the collective, but which might also alienate us.[9]

Simmel's masculine ontology of the social[10]

Simmel was unique in his explicit identification of modernity as masculine, rendering both transparent and immutable the metaphysical exile of women from modernity that characterized sociological theory. However, whereas Durkheim works with what Simmel would term a 'naive' form of relativist dualism, defining women relative to man (as *lacking* sociality, morality, civility and so on), Simmel makes a determined bid to retrieve woman from the ravages of such naive dualistic thinking and to establish 'the autonomy of the female principle' (Simmel 1984b: 105). Simmel *metaphysically* crafts the meaning of woman, re-authenticating her within a deep ontology of difference. Here he fatefully fractures 'human being' into two absolute, incommensurate kinds: being-a-man and being-a-woman. It is because Simmel cheerfully abdicates the problem of defining woman to the realm of 'metaphysical presupposition' (Simmel 1984b: 128–9) that we can refer to his 'deep ontology of gender' (Witz 2001), which is crafted within his *philosophical* rather than his *sociological* imagination (Oakes 1984b; Lichtblau 1989/90; van Vucht Tijssen 1991; Felski 1995; Witz 2000, 2001). Simmel's deep ontology of difference creates an undertow that is too strong to permit a full instantiation of woman into his ontology of the social as she is perpetually dragged back under into the stagnant waters of the metaphysical.

Simmel constructs a masculine ontology of the social. Although the meanings of 'man' and 'woman' are essentially configured within Simmel's philosophical imagination via a deep ontology of a priori female and male modes of being, it is man and man alone who is re-configured as a masculine subject, animating and energizing the social and cultural forms of modernity. For Simmel, eroticism and sexuality *exhaust* the meaning of woman, it is 'the self-contained absolute of her nature' (Simmel 1984b: 109). She is nothing else, nothing less and, most crucially, nothing *more*. The ultimate essence of being-a-woman is intrinsically, absolutely sexual and erotic – she simply 'is-a-woman'. Man, however, 'is' in ways that are *more* than simply 'being-a-man', which is but a fleeting moment of his 'becoming'. Because she is so absolutely sexual and erotic, being-a-woman is not defined relatively through 'the relationship to the man' (Simmel 1984b: 109). Simmel underscores this point by evoking the image of 'the old woman' who, as she gets older:

> passes beyond the upper threshold of erotic attraction, in the active as well as the passive sense . . . All her sexuality that is oriented to the man is extinguished. Nevertheless, the distinctively female quality of her total being remains unchanged. Everything in her that, until that point, seemed to derive its purpose and meaning from her erotic relationship to the man is now revealed as lying completely beyond this relationship, a self-determined possession of her own nature with its own central locus.
>
> (Simmel 1984b: 109–10)

Woman's existence is wholly centred on itself and does not reach outside or beyond itself. Woman is existentially unproblematic. She is self-contained or concentric and exists in a 'state of pure repose in the inner centre' (Simmel 1984b: 115), 'a substantial and static self-contained completeness, in a sense prior to the division into subject and object' (Simmel 1984b: 132). Hence 'the metaphysical nature of the [=her] psyche is not oriented in the dualistic-objectivistic direction, but is rather conclusively defined in a consummate state of being and life itself' (Simmel 1984a: 101). Woman is 'at home' within herself, where man's 'home' is beyond himself (Simmel 1984b: 116). Here we have the crucial difference between female and male being, which is that being-a-woman is devoid of 'the dualism that splits the roots of human existence' (Simmel 1984b: 115) whereas, by contrast, man's being is *dualistic* – the masculine self strives to transcend itself and to live creatively.

Simmel transmutes his fractured ontology of human being into a masculine ontology of the social. Specifically, he ontologically roots the capacities for *differentiation* and *objectification* in a male mode of being. Hence the male mode of being transmutes via these exclusive capacities of his, as he differentiates 'self' from 'being' (differentiation) and turns his subjective energy towards the world and produces objects within it (objectification), into the masculinity of objective social and cultural forms, or forms of life and knowledge. Simmel sums this up neatly in his essay 'Female culture', where he describes:

> two modes of existence that have a completely different rhythm. One is dualistic, oriented to becoming, knowledge and volition [=male]. As a result, it objectifies the content of its life out of the process of life in the form of a cultural world. The other [=female] lies beyond this subjectively constituted and objectively developed dichotomy. For this reason, the contents of its life are not experienced in a form that is external to them.
>
> (Simmel 1984a: 100–1)

Simmel does not stop at ontologically grounding in a male mode of being the capacity to externalize the contents of his life in forms, but goes on to deny women any capacity for creating a 'world' at all. Playing his trump card, he declares 'the female consciousness may not constitute a "world" at all, because a "world" is a form of the contents of its consciousness' (Simmel 1984a: 101). Effectively woman can be neither full of life nor form-creating; she can neither energize nor inhabit the landscape of social and cultural forms.

By means of this contrary logic between modes of male and female being Simmel, like Durkheim, locates the distinctive trajectory of 'modernity' in an essentially masculine agentic capacity for *individualization*, which is in turn rooted in the capacity for differentiation of 'self' from 'being'. Like Durkheim, Simmel links individualization to the increasingly specialized division of labour in modern society, which is a division of labour between men, who become individualized and 'one-sided'. Men are differentiated *from* women sexually, as well as *from each other economically*. For women, however, there is no difference that *makes* a difference.

Corporeality, embodiment and agency

In Simmel and Durkheim, a masculine ontology of social being is secured on the back of a *deep ontology of difference* that is evoked in order to render man as social and society as male. This deep ontology inheres in the metaphysical or philosophical shadowlands that provide the underbelly of the emerging sociological imaginary in the nineteenth century. This moment of difference *between* men and women, in other words, an *ontology of human being*, transmutes into a moment of differentiation *of* men *from* women, in other words, an *ontology of social being*. In the course of this transmutation women are locked into and overwhelmed by their corporeality, while men rise above it and are defined, determined and distinguished by their sociality. It is in this moment of difference that male corporeality is presumed *and* negated to establish their difference *from* women in order to secure the first moment in the 'individuation' of man, who then assumes his role as the agentic core of modernity and dons the mantle of sociality.

This masculine ontology of the social, then, relies on the counter-positioning of *female corporeality* and *male sociality* (Witz 2000). The very concept of the social, as it comes to be articulated in the sociological imaginary, relies on the simultaneous exclusion of the corporeal and of women. At the same time, man is divested of his corporeality in order to establish his exclusive claim to sociality. But what happens to *his* body as he arrogates sociality to himself? Male bodies must necessarily occupy an ambiguous space in the classical sociological texts, as these simultaneously saturate her with corporeality while refusing his – they must *necessarily* appear for a fleeting moment *for they are the bodies that are not-women's bodies and that qualify them to animate the social.* Indeed, precisely because the boundary between the natural and the social must be slippery and unstable, male bodies are *abject* as they disappear at the unstable boundary between 'the corporeal' and 'the social'. It is in that borderland, then, between female corporeality and male sociality that, for a fleeting conceptual moment, male bodies appear, only to effect their immediate disappearance through an implicit notion of male embodiment – an always, already mediate and approximate fleshiness, as distinct from the immediate, proximate fleshiness of female corporeality.

Hence, it is the masculine heterosexual body that grounds most of the disciplinary corpus, but is rarely explicitly named as such. Yet, while male bodies may well slide out of view at that slippery boundary of the corporeal and the social, *they always threaten to re-appear as a disruption*.[11] These abject male bodies always threatened to reappear as a disruption, precisely because such a chronic burden of socialization and rationalization was placed on their shoulders (or other body parts?). Male bodies lurked only ever so slightly beneath the veneer of sociality with which the masculine self was saturated within the sociological discourse of modernity. Indeed, it is *male sexuality* that is rendered most precarious by the motif of 'civilization' that underpins this discourse because it is men's sexuality that is critical to the project of rational mastery over nature: 'The nature which man [sic] struggled to know and master was not merely outside himself – associated with women and with the alien (and often colonized other) – but also nature within himself' (Jackson and Scott 1997: 55).

Woman figures strategically in sociological texts, because it is by mobilizing the spectre of 'woman', overloading her with corporeality, as in Durkheim, and saturating her with sexuality, as in Simmel, that permits the delineation of the very concept of the social itself. Female corporeality serves as the constant foil against which a masculine ontology of the social was constructed and the qualities of sociality became synonymous with those of masculinity. Furthermore, the spectre of corporealized woman also served to mark her as *collectively particular*, while he arrogated the generic status of *universally individual* to himself, yet without naming himself as such. Paradoxically, then, adopting the terms of a twentieth-century discourse of gender, classical sociological man, unlike classical sociological woman, assumed a gender yet remained unmarked *as* a gender. Hence, masculinity remains an absent presence, lurking invisibly beneath at the same time as animating the social.

While for Simmel, the masculine *homo duplex* is in many ways the tragedy of modernity, for Durkheim he represents the triumph of culture over nature. For both, however, to populate the social requires a form of individualization that enables men to be different from one another, a first step that corporealized woman is unable to take. In Durkheim and Simmel we have two renderings of the *femina simplex* – as compared to the *homo duplex*. Simmel's is metaphysical, while Durkheim's is more sociologized. This hints perhaps that Durkheim's project is more easily rehabilitatable from a feminist sociological perspective – in that by thinking through his 'unthought' we might render it intelligible within the terms of his project. To accept Simmel's analysis one would need to buy into the argument of a radical alterity of woman that is difficult to sustain sociologically. It condemns one to recuperating woman by authenticating her in and through her difference, which is effectively what Simmel tries to do.

Gendering the social

We now open up further questions concerning the relation between ways of thinking the social and ways of gendering the social. This turns upon the question of the intimate relation between ways of making meaning and ways of thinking gender within the Western tradition of logical thought. Ramp (2001) takes up Foucault's question of the relation between the thought and the unthought in sociological theory. We might ask then to what extent does thinking about social agency rest upon an unthought sex/gender matrix? That it does so in key classical renderings of the problem of individualization and agency has been demonstrated through our readings of Durkheim and Simmel, but we would argue that this was not a problem unique to classical theorists. As Adkins (Chapter 7) suggests in her discussion of contemporary theories of the 'post-structural social', even as the conditions for agency appear to shift in late modernity, differentially gendered access to those conditions is assumed, but never fully theorized.

We might also ask, as Ramp does of Durkheim, whether or not the 'failure to recognize and reconcile a discourse about gender is to be taken as a failure of a *particular* modernist project, or as an example of the failure of modernism *itself*' (Ramp 2001: 105). That it is a failure of modernism itself is suggested by much feminist theory, and by feminist philosophy in particular, where dichotomous thinking is invariably associated with the deep inscription of gendered meanings into all disciplinary logics (Hekman 1990; Gatens 1991). However, a feminist interrogation of the 'gendering' of the social might profit from being alert to the *form* assumed by gender dichotomies and the consistency or lack thereof between gender distinctions, both stated and unstated, and other distinctions operating within the logic of the social.[12]

Nancy Jay (1981) engages in an astute discussion of the relation between gender and dichotomies and whether these take the form of contrary distinctions (A/B) or logically contradictory ones (A/not-A):

> Thus men and women may be conceived as men and not-men, or women and not-women, between which there is logically not continuity, or as two forms (A/B) of the class 'human' which may be supposed to have a good deal in common. Furthermore, in A/B distinctions both terms have positive reality. In A/Not-A dichotomies only one term has positive reality; Not-A is only the privation or absence of A.
>
> (Jay 1981: 44)

Simmel clearly sought to escape the grip of an Aristotelian logic – A/not-A – where woman is conceptualized as a deformed or 'misbegotten' man, defined in terms of a lack. As we have seen above, he explicitly refused such a relativist dualism. He works with an A/B contrary distinction, yet this is articulated within a metaphysical ontology of being. He repeatedly attempts to think woman into society and culture but is forced by the power of his own metaphysics of gender to admit defeat. Simmel's (1984a) question of whether a 'female culture' is possible, given that objective culture is shaped by a male principle is, of course, an apothetic or unanswerable question which cannot be pursued without encountering major contradictions and antinomies that must necessarily emerge from his dualistic gender metaphysics (Lichtblau 1989/90; see also Oakes 1984b; van Vucht Tijssen 1991; Witz 2001). Hence 'the question itself must be considered inappropriate on the basis of Simmel's own presuppositions' (Lichtblau 1989/90: 95) as the very concept of a female culture 'is vitiated by his basic ontological assumptions' (Oakes 1984b: 45). Simmel is eventually prompted to 'think the gendered unthought' (Ramp 2001) precisely because he is unable to think women into the social (Witz 2001). In this he differs from Durkheim, whose thoughts on women are sporadic and only dealt with in an explicit manner when they threaten to disrupt the central categories of his sociological thought (Lehmann 1994). Simmel, however, ties himself up in all sorts of neo-Kantian knots, irreparably rooting the capacities for objectification, differentiation and individualization exclusively in a male mode of being, and rendering them singularly absent from a female mode of being. It is uniquely male capacities, then, which energize the social, generating and animating the social content and cultural forms of modernity. Simmel explicitly recognizes that the constant threat of desubjectification that is the tragedy of modern culture is a gender-specific tragedy – it is a tragedy of *masculinity*.

However, as Jay (1981) points out, Durkheim used only two logically contradictory A/not-A distinctions – sacred/profane, man/woman – and these had a direct existential reference – 'real religion' within which 'real' women become categorically embedded within the profane, while 'real' men, unmarked by profanity, become embedded in the sacred. In contrast to Simmel, by Durkheim's own sociological logic, we *could* think gender into his theory. If we accept that Durkheim was empirically mistaken in accepting uncritically the biological inferiority of women (as demonstrated, for example, through his reiteration of LeBon's craniometry) then we can begin from the premise that women have the same sensory capacities as men. What stunts their capacity to think beyond their particularity, and their own sense-experience of corporeality, is their *social* exclusion from collective sentiments, collective ritual and collective representation. Deploying bodily criteria to mark them as not-men, women's social segregation denies them access to the very capacities that Durkheim defines as social. Just as men are deemed sacred, not by their individual, but by their socially derived character, so could women be understood as profane by their exclusion from the social, not by biological fiat.[13] They are profane *in relation to men*. In other words, we could do what Durkheim insisted upon, but could not himself do when it came to gender – explain social facts with reference to social facts.

Jay contrasts Durkheim's approach with Weber's sociology of religion, where he used contrary, A/B distinctions between innerworldly/outerworldly, mysticism/asceticism and so on. In line with Weberian methodological injunctions concerning conceptual thinking through ideal types, these have no direct existential references. They are 'ways of thinking', 'ideal types' deployed to clarify elements of religious phenomena, not exhaustively or directly describe them. Hence these distinctions are 'clear enough conceptually', yet 'fluid in actuality' (Weber, cited in Jay 1981: 50).

This raises the interesting question of whether an 'ideal typical', contrary masculine/feminine distinction constitutes a distinctive sociological 'way of thinking' about gender phenomena, hence 'socializing' both woman and man. It also raises the question of whether such an analysis might contain the germs of a distinctive sociological apprehension of 'masculine' and 'feminine' that is 'clear enough conceptually' yet 'fluid in actuality'. A feminist strategy of interrogation needs to confront the issue of the 'gendered unthought' not simply by exposing the masculinity that inheres in sociological texts, but also by considering the different ways in which gender – the possibility of men and women acquiring elements of their being men and women through social forces – *might* have been thought within sociological discourse. How *could* one think about 'men' and 'women' through the conceptual grids of 'feminine' and 'masculine', which are effectively ideal-typical constructs that identify some of the elements that go to make up actually existing 'men' and 'women'?

As a number of other chapters in this volume make clear, suggestions for such an approach were already present at the time of sociology's formation. Jenny d'Héricourt, for example, with access to the same 'scientific' data on sex difference available to Comte, insisted on the unknowability of a priori difference, focusing instead on its social production. Likewise, Harriet Martineau outlined an approach to the study of society which was remarkably similar to Durkheim's, but she applied it more consistently. She was thus able to understand gender difference and inequality as a social phenomenon in a manner that eluded Durkheim (see Chapter 4, this volume). Wobbe (Chapter 3) notes how Gertrud Simmel was impatient with her husband's gender metaphysics, as was Marianne Weber. Although both Georg Simmel and Max Weber were alive to the complexity of the problem of gendered individualization and modernity, only Weber, like Martineau, deployed a historically sensitive, comparative methodology to specify the ambivalent position of women in relation to the social forces of rationalization and individuation. Weber works with a concept of culture that allowed for the possibilities of both men's and women's individualization but, most significantly, insists that family life is not beyond, but part of, the social. By subjecting manifest sex difference to newly forged standards of sociological understanding these women were, as Arni and Müller (Chapter 4) put it 'more sociological than the sociologists'. It is only by taking seriously men's and women's own understandings of their positioning within historical and social processes that we begin to see how gender is implicated in the 'mobile and shifting meanings of the modern' (Felski 1995: 8).

Revisiting the sociological classics after 30 years of modern feminism we must, in all fairness, enquire as to the options available to all of us, dead and alive, in 'thinking the gendered unthought'. To do this within a sociological paradigm means saturating the categorical distinction men/women with socially constructed meaning. It entails an analysis of *how* the social does its work in order to 'fit' those held within the categories 'men' and 'women' into those categories as they are lived. This would have demanded (and indeed still demands) a radical epistemological break with the Western European tradition of metaphysics in order to find a way of thinking outside of extant ontologies of human being. As we have contended, those extant ontologies of human being, already fatefully fractured into dualistic ontologies of dichotomous modes 'male' and 'female' being, are transformed into an ontology of social being that is equally as fractured. This is a 'masculine ontology of the social' (Witz 2000, 2001) where man, and man alone, was qualified to animate, energize and inhabit 'the social' – the epistemic core of the new discipline, sociology. It is the qualities of manhood that have saturated sociological conceptions of the individual and of agency as, to cite Lehmann (1994), 'man becomes social and society becomes male'.

Conclusions: the ambivalent legacy

We have argued for a more sustained interrogation of how a masculinist ontology of the social was built into classical texts. The value of such an exercise is not simply a revelatory one – a sort of 'once you didn't see men and now you do' exercise. Re-readings of classical texts should also function as salutory exercises in reading *all* sociological texts, sniffing out the *presumptions* of masculinity and masculine agency, as well as both the erasures of femininity and the truncation of female agentic capacities.

As we have demonstrated, male embodiment is deeply sedimented in the sociological imaginary as the very condition of social action and the constituent of social agency. Paradoxically then, the work which we call upon the concept of 'gender' to do as feminist sociologists has always been done with respect to the masculine, as he disappeared his corporeality, assumed his embodiment and rendered himself fully social. And sociological theorists are still letting him get away with it; assuming his own sociality as 'generic', while occasionally mobilizing the concept of gender to name she who is not contained within the generic understanding of the social. Thus abstract categories that attempt to catch trajectories of social change – reflexive individualization and de-traditionalization, for example, *still* tend to be more easily 'energized' by typically masculine forms of identity and action. For example, in Giddens' (1991) *Modernity and Self-Identity*, special qualifying clauses have to be inserted about women experiencing the openness of late modernity in a fuller yet more contradictory way than men. It is only when women enter the text, already marked, that men become marked as *men*.

An integral part of feminist sociology's aim to rethink – and perhaps reshape – the social must be to excavate the gendered erasures and inclusions that shaped the concept of the social in the first place. A feminist politics of interrogation also necessitates that we rework the concept of the social in such a way that it erases less and includes more, rather than simply reasserting its continued salience. To begin making explicit the masculinity of sociological conceptions of the social in modernity – including its 'late' and 'post' variants – and the skewed conceptions of individualization and agency on which these rest, requires that we grapple more directly with the ambivalent legacy of classical sociology.

Notes

1 The term corporeality is used to evoke immanence or a proximate fleshiness, while the term embodiment evokes more of a mediate fleshiness – an embedded sociological sense of the body as the necessary condition and constituent of action. By sociality we mean the enactment of that capacity for action.

2 Smith refers sometimes to 'methods of *writing the social* into texts' (1999: 46) and sometimes to 'methods of writing *society* into texts' (1999: 54). Yet, it is important to be clear that the 'virtual reality' of sociological discourse is 'the social', *not* 'society'.

3 See, for example, Gane (1993).

4 However, as we have elaborate elsewhere (Witz and Marshall 2003) Shilling fails to recognize the explicitly gendered nature of Durkheim's construction of embodied agency.

5 We elaborate on this in Witz and Marshall (2003).

6 Again, this only applies to men. 'No such acceleration' appears in women, confirming Durkheim's belief that women are 'naturally' regulated, 'instinctual' and so on.

7 For an extended discussion of this theme, including its representation in the sexual science of the time, see Marshall (2002).

8 For an alternative reading, see Sydie (Chapter 2) who suggests that it was the regulation of women's sexuality that was central in Durkheim's analysis of marriage.

9 Given the differential ways in which embodiment is socially experienced, it is not surprising that 'critical issues for twenty-first century female citizens continue to revolve around women's sexual and reproductive rights and capacities' (Sydie, Chapter 2).

10 Here, we focus on Simmel's metaphysics of gender as elaborated in his essays 'Female culture' (1984a) and 'The relative and absolute in the problem of the sexes' (1984b). Wobbe and Gerhard in Chapters 3 and 6 deal with other of Simmel's writings, and Wobbe touches on the relation between what we are calling his 'sociological' and his 'philosophical' imaginaries.

11 As David Morgan so pithily put it: 'The erection is the jester in the wings of the civilizing process' (1993: 76).

12 Gerhard (Chapter 6) shows how gender dualism operates in subtly different ways in different classical theorizations of the social, and of particular interest is Tönnies 'strong thesis' linking gender dualism and forms of community and society.

13   As Nancy Jay (1981: 43) has argued, 'Durkheim himself could not have made this analysis because he took rigidly dichotomous gender distinction for granted, a biological given, and never looked at it sociologically.' A parallel might be drawn here to Christine Delphy's argument that gender (a social division) precedes and provides the framework of meaning for sex (a biological distinction) (Delphy 1993).

2 Sex and the sociological fathers

R.A. Sydie

To suggest that the venerable sociological fathers were especially interested in sexuality seems almost lesé-majesty. Sociology, as a product of the nineteenth century, was, however, a part of that discursive explosion about sexuality that Foucault (1980: 17) suggested characterized Western societies from the eighteenth century. Far from neglecting the question of sexuality, classical sociological theory is constructed on the need to 'place' sexuality *in* society. Sexuality was thought to represent the border between nature and society, so that in the debates on sexuality the 'real subject' was political and social power (Coward 1983: 12). Sociologists were especially interested in sexuality in relation to the political and social position of women. Some of the immediate antecedents to the sociological debates around sexuality can be found in the claims advanced by increasing numbers of women for equality with men. An important basis for these claims lay in the seventeenth-century Cartesian divorce of mind and body which allowed women to claim that if they were educated like men they could be as rational and reasonable as men. As Browne (1987: 82) points out, the 'Cartesian emphasis on the mind's independence of the body weakened arguments from physiology against women's rationality'. Weakened perhaps but did not entirely eliminate such arguments.[1] There may be 'no sex in souls', or minds, but the soul and the mind are situated in the body and the body of the female provided a particularly heavy, material anchor on the rational abstractions of the mind in the view of many social theorists.

In the aftermath of the French Revolution many women, such as Wollstonecraft, assumed that the transformation of political relationships from the traditional, divinely ordered authority of king and court to democratic authority elected by rational, equal and autonomous citizens would provide for women's equality with men. In theory all were potentially free, autonomous citizens and, as citizens, unconstrained by arbitrary or traditional ties, all had the potential for the development of rational understanding. But, for many eighteenth-century political writers and legislators the idea of women as citizens like men was problematic, not the least because they posited 'a strong symbolic link between female rebellion and political upheaval' (Browne 1987: 19).[2] Politically, at the end of the eighteenth century the mind/ body split, rather than neutralizing sex difference, had the opposite effect. There was a tendency to focus on the female, reproductive body in contrast to the masculine, rational mind, especially in relation to the 'body' of the citizen.

In nineteenth-century sociological discourse, the 'body' of the citizen was clearly a masculine body that required, for the health of society, the domestic body of the female. The competitive, individualistic world of contracts inhabited by rational, enlightened males necessarily rested upon the separate, sentimental world of women's domesticity. It is this formulation that provides the framework for the sociological fathers' accounts about gender relations and sexual desire and practice. These accounts are interesting because they arise during the first organized protest movements by women for the sort of rights claimed by Wollstonecraft in her *A Vindication of the Rights of Woman* ([1792] 1967). Generally the sociological fathers reacted to the 'woman question' by viewing it as an aberrant form of protest that confirmed their view that society was in trouble and therefore needed the scientific ministrations of the sociologist. Many agreed with Durkheim ([1933], 1964a: 247) that 'Woman has had less part than man in the movement of civilization. She participates less and derives less profit. She recalls, moreover, certain characteristics of primitive nature'.

With remarks such as the above it is almost too easy to simply point the finger at their misogyny and leave it at that. But their misogyny was not without purpose and it is important to understand what prompted the positions they took on gender relations, especially in regard to sexual desire and practice. In the twentieth century the Western world 'eroticized sex' and made its practice a form of 'personal salvation and self-fulfillment' (Seidman 1992: 9), at the same time making it a site for conflict (as the debates over pornography, sexually transmitted diseases, abortion, reproductive technologies, prostitution and homosexuality illustrate). Although the specifics may be different, the general issues with respect to gender relations seem to persist. Consequently, we need an historical perspective if we are to understand the subterranean agendas in current discourses surrounding gender and sexuality.

The following discussion focuses on the work of only three of the sociological fathers, Auguste Comte, Emile Durkheim and Max Weber. Durkheim and Weber may seem to be more relevant theoretical touchstones for current, Western sociological debates, but Comte's outline of the 'scientific' basis for enlightened and reformed gender relations and sexual desire and practice provide the basic themes by which Durkheim and Weber framed their reflections on these issues. The key themes informing the work of the sociological fathers, as well as current debates, are citizenship, family, heterosexual desire and practice.

The Comtean family

In his discussion of the origins of society, Comte stated that it was the 'pre-ponderance of the affective over the intellectual faculties' that was the most important. All animals, including 'man', seek continuous and varied action in their lives and, as intellectual activity is the 'least energetic' activity, it is the one that occasions 'in most men a fatigue that soon becomes utterly insup-portable' (Comte 1975: 264). The improvement of society only occurs when the affective faculties predominate. The affective faculties give reason a 'per-manent aim and direction' and rescue it from being 'forever lost in vague abstract speculation' (Comte 1975: 265). Thus it is 'normal' that personal 'instincts' predominate over social 'instincts' because if it 'were possible to repress our personal instincts' then 'our social affections, deprived of the necessary direction, would degenerate into vague and useless charity, destitute of all practical efficacy'. Generally, 'personal instinct is the guide and measure of the social' because 'how could anyone love another who did not love him-self' (Comte 1975: 265–6).

Personal propensities and affective faculties provide the 'natural' founda-tion for the social instinct and intellectual activity, and the interrelationship of these four human features provides social individuals who will advance the 'general development of humanity' (Comte 1975: 266). The primary location in which the four features combine to produce the social is the 'true social unit' – the family – 'reduced, if necessary, to the elementary couple that forms its basis'. The family is the necessary intermediary between the individual and society as the 'avenue that man comes forth from his mere personality and learns to live in another, while obeying his most powerful instincts' (Comte 1975: 267). The object is therefore to isolate the 'elementary scientific aspect of the family; that aspect that is . . . common to all social cases' in order to estab-lish the correct, positivist form of future families (Comte 1975: 267–8). What Comte discovers as common are 'two orders of relations – namely, the sub-ordination of the sexes, which institutes the family, and that of ages which maintains it'. Positive sociology proves then that the 'equality of the sexes, of which so much is said, is incompatible with all social existence' (Comte 1975: 268) because 'women's life is essentially domestic, public life being confined to men' (1975: 374).

Comte's certainty about dichotomized gender roles relates to the four fea-tures of individual and social life – the affective and personal instincts and the intellectual and social capacities. Intellectual capacities differentiate men from animals and are more highly developed in men than women. Consequently, women are 'unfit . . . for the requisite continuousness and intensity of mental labor, either from an intrinsic weakness of her reason or from her more lively moral and physical sensibility, which are hostile to scientific abstraction and concentration' (1975: 269). However, this gender difference is positive because women's more highly developed affective and personal instincts provide for 'more spontaneous expansion of sympathy and sociality' and this modifies or curbs the 'excitement of the social instinct' and the extremes that might result from the 'cold and rough reason' so characteristic of men (Comte 1975: 269).

Positivism dictates that women's 'social mission' is to ensure that men's activities are always guided by 'universal love', defined as the 'subjection of self-interest to social feeling' (Comte 1975: 377). Because women take on this task they always merit the 'loving veneration' of men who recognize that women embody the 'purest and simplest impersonation of humanity' (1975: 373). The subordination of the wife to the husband is not onerous because the 'most respectful spontaneous obedience, on the part of the inferior' is without 'degradation' as the absolute authority of the 'superior party' is 'united to entire devotedness, too natural and too genial to be regarded as a duty' (Comte 1975: 269). The ties that bind are silken, but unbreakable.

As for feminism, Comte states that the claim by 'some visionaries' that women should exercise political power on the same terms as men is the result of an inaccurate understanding of men's and women's fundamentally different biological constitutions.[3] Women are superior in personal feelings and thus sociality, but in the means to attain social ends they are inferior. 'In all kinds of force, whether physical, intellectual, or practical, it is certain that man surpasses woman in accordance with the general law prevailing throughout the animal kingdom' (Comte 1975: 374). This is an important point for Comte because it is force rather than affection that governs the 'unremitting and laborious activity' of practical and political life.

Woman's mission is to humanize modern men. Women, as wives and mothers, provide the essential basis for the rejuvenation of a society plagued with alienated, morally and sexually unstable men. Sexual passion might, according to Comte, provide the first impetus for the marital union, but it was its least important aspect. It is 'not necessary in all cases to gratify the instinct' and abstinence may well 'serve to strengthen mutual affection' (Comte 1975: 377). Sexual desire was only a stage in an individual's progress towards the 'final object of moral education – namely, universal love' (Comte 1975: 377). Consequently, 'sexual love' might become a 'powerful engine for good, but only on condition of placing it under rigorous and permanent discipline' (1975: 377). That positivist discipline was marriage. Thus it was critical that marriage be 'both exclusive and indissoluble' if the 'high purposes' for which it was designed were to be achieved. Divorce was out of the question and the 'perpetuity of widowhood' was a 'moral duty' (Comte 1975: 378).

In the positivist system women were moral anchors for the potentially troublesome physical and intellectual qualities of men. In fact, in marriage a man enters a 'voluntary engagement of subordination to woman for the rest of his life' and in so doing 'completes his moral education' (Comte 1975: 379).

Lest the term 'subordination' be misinterpreted, it should be noted that this is submission to the 'ennobling influence' of affection but by no means an alteration of the patriarchal power of the husband/father.

For Comte, and later Durkheim, it was the character of modern society and the demands it made on men that made the patriarchal family so important. Industrial, capitalist society requires the individualistic, autonomous worker, but one who is also a stable, conscientious, dutiful worker. The most irrational desire – sexual passion – must be controlled and contained in modern society. Social identities in modern society are 'fragmentary and contradictory' and the social relations of 'isolated, abstract, *individuals*' are only apparent to them 'in alienated and mystified forms' and are produced and reproduced endlessly (Sayer 1991: 71–2). The panacea for the 'lonely crowd' was to be found in the loving embrace of the family. The 'haven in a heartless world' was produced by women for men and in the interests of the political and economic structures of the modern world. Despite Wollstonecraft's protest and those of others who followed in her footsteps, the modern citizen and worker was male and his female counterpart existed as his dependant who provided the loving comfort the public realm denied him – a situation that was, in Comte's view, a 'consolidation and improvement of the natural order' (1975: 380).

The Durkheimian industrious citizen

Comte's neat gendered divisions re-appear in Durkheim's work, but the comfortable predictions of harmony are upset by the empirical evidence. Durkheim finds in his study of suicide that the 'moral equilibrium' that marriage provided for men appeared to have quite the opposite effect on women (Durkheim 1951: 270). The finding was troublesome because Durkheim also saw modern individualism as a challenge to the authority of the social and he, like Comte, suggested that part of the solution lay in making marriage indissoluble. The 'cult of the individual' undermined society's control over man's natural passions. Because 'society surpasses us, it obliges us to surpass ourselves; and to surpass itself, a being must, to some degree depart from its nature ... We must, in a word, do violence to certain of our strongest inclinations' (Durkheim 1964b: 338–9). The 'strongest inclinations' are the egoistic 'sensory appetites'. These appetites represent and are the object of individuality but they stand in contradiction to the universalized, impersonal dictates of morality (Durkheim 1964b: 327). Like Comte, Durkheim suggests that the modern, nucleated family is the means by which the selfish, personal interests and desires of the solitary male citizen could be persuaded/coerced into collective or social actions and interests.

Women are best located in the family but it is precisely this realm that

Durkheim discovered encouraged female suicides, in contrast to men who are physically and psychologically healthier when married. Durkheim asked, 'must one of the sexes necessarily be sacrificed, and is the solution only to choose the lesser of two evils?' (1951: 384). His answer was in the affirmative, with the proviso that maybe in the future woman may be rescued when provided with greater social involvement 'peculiarly her own' (Durkheim 1951: 385). This is not to imply that woman would ever become equal to or 'more similar to the male', on the contrary she will become quite different (1951: 385).

Durkheim finds that there are physical and mental differences between men and women as a result of the evolution of civilization. In *The Division of Labor in Society* ([1933] 1964a) he suggests that in the past women were little different from men, either physically or psychologically, but as social and individual differentiation and specialization progressively occurs women, 'among cultivated people . . . lead a completely different existence from that of the man' (Durkheim [1933] 1964a: 60). Women are gradually differentiated from men in the morphological characteristics of height, weight and even brain size – women's are smaller than men's – so that the 'two great functions of psychic life' are separated, one taking care of the 'affective functions and the other of intellectual functions' ([1933] 1964a: 60). This progressive differentiation of the sexes is part of the 'conquest of society over nature' (Durkheim [1933] 1964a: 386).

The conquest of nature involved the 'subordination of external forces to social forces' so that freedom and autonomy, at least for men, are the product of the regulation of 'the state of nature' (Durkheim [1933] 1964a: 387). Man becomes a social being to the extent that he 'raises himself above things and makes a law for them, thus depriving them of their fortuitous, absurd, amoral character' ([1933] 1964a: 387). As women represent those who are most closely identified with the state of nature and are 'By constitution . . . predisposed to lead a life different from man', then women clearly require the control and regulation of men ([1933] 1964a: 264). Indeed, man is 'more highly socialized than woman' because 'his tastes, aspirations and humor have in large part a collective origin, while his companion's are more directly influenced by her organism' (Durkheim 1951: 385). Because women are thus less social, more 'natural', than men, then the health and welfare of the modern, specialized male is potentially jeopardized unless women are firmly located in the confines of domesticity.

The control of the natural is imperative because the body and soul, the animal and the social, representing the dualism of human nature and the 'two states of consciousness', are antagonistic (Durkheim 1964b: 327). The sensory, animalistic body is 'egoistic' whereas the soul is the site of morality that is disinterested and based on 'attachment to something other than ourselves'. Antagonism arises because 'We cannot pursue moral ends without causing a split within ourselves, without offending the instincts and penchants that are most deeply rooted in our bodies' (1964b: 328). The sensory body is the source of passion and opposition to reason. Women represent sensory nature through their bodily specialization, or reproductive capacity, thus the maintenance of civilization makes it imperative that women be controlled by rational, moral men.[4] In particular, women's 'sexual needs have less of a mental character' than those of men and, being a 'more instinctual creature' she requires men's regulation. For Durkheim, just as for Comte, the modern, conjugal family in which there is the 'legal subordination' of the wife to the husband as a 'necessary condition of family unity' was an absolute necessity for the moral health of a society and, more specifically, to combat the potential anomie of the modern, individualistic male (1980: 209).[5]

More than Comte, Durkheim was concerned with the potential social problem that individualistic desires, especially sexual desires, represented to the stability of the modern, industrial state. The progressive rationalization of life that produced the modern 'individual' required the 'subjection of the animal *in* man' (Bauman 1991a: 111). Consequently, control over instinctual sexual passion was imperative and that control was masculine because women's bodily specificity meant that they were locked into the instinctual in a way different from men. The dichotomy of animal–human is associated with other relations of inferiority–superiority, and attached to various groups and collectivities on the order of: women–men, children–adults, barbarians–civilized, the masses–gentlemen, and, most importantly, the body–mind/passion–reason split (Bauman 1991a: 111). In the last dichotomy, reason is identified with 'objectivity' understood as the 'monopoly of argumentative consensus in the grounding of legitimate beliefs' (Bauman 1991a: 117). Therefore, it is adult, civilized, gentlemen who are the appropriate, 'objective' observers of the social world and, by extension, the appropriate authorities to regulate and control society. For Durkheim, the sociologist is the one individual 'uniquely able to provide the rational basis for a common morality' because only 'rational opinion could be allowed in moral argument' and such opinion depended on 'expert knowledge' of which the sociologist was possessed (Hawthorne 1987: 119). In gender terms, Durkheim would take it for granted that sociologists were generally civilized, rational males.

Durkheim regarded the individualism of modern societies as having the potential to undermine the progress of modernity. This made the need to 'place' men and women in relation to their 'natural', biological, political positions imperative. The key was to find the moral restraint over individualistic passion and desire to produce the industrious, male citizens and promote social solidarity.

Durkheim's answer was that the state had to be the source of moral regulation and control, 'calling the individual to a moral way of life' (1992b: 69). The state was the only possible source of control and regulation because only the state had sufficient authority to both advance and protect individual rights. As he pointed out, 'our moral individuality, far from being antagonistic to the State, has . . . been a product of it. It is the State that sets it free . . . Its tendency is to ensure the most complete individuation that the state of society will allow' (1992b: 69).

The role played by the state in the advancement and protection of individuality was, however, gendered in respect to public economic and political life. The future relationship of individual citizens to the state was to be mediated through professional associations because these were the groups 'to which the individual devotes his whole life, those for which he has the strongest attachment' (Durkheim 1992b: 96). Professional groups were to become the 'basis of our political representation as well as of the social structure of the future' (1992b: 97). As women were not, ideally, a part of the public world of politics and work, it is clear that they would be somewhat marginal citizens in the future society. It was the industrious male citizen who is the focus of Durkheim's concern. For women, the state's role was to preserve marriage and family life for which their 'natural' specialization fitted them. In a critical review of Marianne Weber's work, *Ehefrau und Mutter in der Rechtsentwicklung: Eine Einfuhrung* (1907), Durkheim maintained that her call for equality before the law of husbands and wives failed to 'see the complexity of the problem' (1980: 288).

> Her whole theory rests on the premise that the patriarchal family has brought about the woman's complete subservience . . . the assertion is wide open to question. To be sure, such a domestic regime has given rise to women's legal status as a minor in civil life. But on the other hand, in this patriarchal family type, family life is much more intense and more important than in previous types; the woman's role, which is precisely to preside over life indoors, has also assumed more importance, and the moral scope of the wife and mother has increased . . . for the same reason, husband and wife have become closer, more directly and more constantly in touch, because the centre of gravity in the life of the male has ceased to be sidetracked away from the home as much as in the past. The more family matters intervene to occupy a man's mind, the more he falls out of the habit of regarding his wife as an inferior. This result is all the more notable as the patriarchal family becomes more powerfully and more solidly organized.
>
> (Durkheim 1980: 288)

Durkheim concluded that feminism 'deceives itself' with its demands for equality with men. Women should seek for change in domestic life in respect to the 'functions commensurate with her nature' (1980: 296). Any 'weakening of the organic unity of the family and of marriage must inevitably dry up the source of women's rise to a higher status' because the 'feelings of respect that have been directed her way and have become more pronounced with the further progress of history originate, in large part, in the religious respect inspired by hearth and home' (Durkheim 1980: 288).

The problem both Comte and Durkheim confront is the problem of *masculine* individuality. The demands of modern society produce the alienated worker who is the antithesis of the autonomous individual of philosophical and political theory. The alienating world of rational calculation, competition and specialization could, however, be mitigated through the affectionate realm of the family where the 'real' self could emerge. The authentic self that emerges is the masculine self as the authentic feminine self is almost a contradiction in terms. The authentic feminine is only evident when the self is submerged in and subordinated to the family collectivity. The concern with the alienation and anomie of modern life is directed at potentially unstable males in the public realm. The alienation of women in the domestic realm is less problematic despite the fact that such alienation seems to suggest that the domestic comfort offered to men was highly questionable.

For the sociological fathers the stakes were high – no less than the reformulation of society in terms of empirically grounded, objectively determined 'truths' of social behaviour. And in this regard, although their specific positions on the question of method might vary, the sociological fathers were agreed that sociology was the key 'science' for modern society. Sociology might be a 'young' science, but Durkheim insisted on its ability to make a substantial contribution to the amelioration of social problems. As he remarked, 'nothing is so vain and sterile as that scientific puritanism which, under the pretext that science is not fully established, counsels abstention and recommends to men that they stand by as indifferent witnesses, or at least resigned ones, at the march of events' (Durkheim 1956: 104). Although Max Weber counselled neutrality for the sociologist in political matters, nevertheless it was a neutrality only in terms of the practice of politics, not in the knowledge contributions sociology might make to the 'heroic leader' (Weber 1964: 128). Science uncovers the 'facts' and thus provides the basis for social action, and the facts uncovered by sociology were critical to reform or change in society. For Weber (1964: 155), the 'fate' of the twentieth century was 'characterized by rationalization and intellectualization' and, above all, by the 'disenchantment of the world', as the 'ultimate and most sublime values have retreated from public life either into the transcendental realm of mystic life or into the brotherliness of direct and personal human relations'. A part of the disenchantment lay in the transformation of erotic desire and its consequences for gender relations.

Weber and erotic desire

In the accounts offered by Comte and Durkheim there is an obvious contradiction in the equations linking gender difference, sexuality, individualism and alienation. First, the major source of irrationality – sexual passion – that could jeopardize society was to be enclosed in the home to run rampart in the very individual – woman – who was 'naturally problematic' in this respect. Although women were more natural and thus more attuned to their 'animality', they nevertheless must be the providers of moral discipline in the home because of men's sensual instability and irrationality brought on by the demands of the rational, specialized world of work. Modern men overcome their disenchantment with the world in the home and family, but this can only be accomplished by women contradicting their own 'nature'. Max Weber's position also endorses marriage as a refuge from the world and sexual passion. As he pointed out, for the 'vocational specialist type of man' the marital relationship should 'reject every sophistication of the sexual into eroticism' in order to promote an 'ethical responsibility for one another' (Weber 1964: 349–50). It was this ethical responsibility that ensured that 'something unique and supreme might be embodied in marriage' (1964: 350).

Max Weber's views on the issue of gender relations are, however, somewhat less straightforward than those of Comte or Durkheim. Weber recognized that modern monogamous marriages were a social and historical product and represented the necessary routinization of sexuality in a capitalist society. 'Innerworldly and rational asceticism . . . can only accept the rationally regulated marriage' which is the means to control man who, according to salvation religion, 'is hopelessly wretched by virtue of his "concupisence " ' (Weber 1964: 349).

This religiously based regulation of the body and sexual desire is critical to the production of modern, rational, self-disciplined, moral individuals who will labour diligently in a calling. The asceticism of modern life 'gathers the primal, naturalist and *un*sublimated sexuality of the peasant into a rational order of man as creature' and harnesses the 'diabolical power' of sexuality that can threaten 'salvation and civilization' (Weber 1964: 349–50). All 'rational regulation of life' therefore involves the regulation of 'sexual intercourse in favor of *marriage*' (1964: 344). Although the emphasis is on heterosexual relations the reason for the regulation is about the relationship between men. Weber remarks that 'The brotherly ethic of salvation religion is in profound tension with the greatest irrational force of life: sexual love' (1964: 343). The regulation of sexuality, especially orgiastic sexuality and eroticism, in marriage meant that 'civilized' relations among men could be consolidated. But the routinization of sex in marriage stands in contrast to, at the same time that it encourages, eroticism.

Eroticism, understood as the 'joyous triumph over rationality' could only have a place, in modern rational society, in extra-marital affairs.[6] Erotic love, removed from 'everyday affairs', was the 'only tie which linked man with the natural fountain of life' (Weber 1964: 346). But, the 'natural fountain' was woman, made into an erotic sexual object. Under modern 'intellectualist cultures', man is emancipated from the 'naïve naturalism of sex' practised in the 'old, simple, and organic existence of the peasant', with the result that eroticism assumes a special position (Weber 1964: 344). Woman comes to embody the more primitive 'natural fountain' and as the object of man's erotic desire, represents 'a gate into the most irrational and thereby the real kernel of life' (Weber 1964: 345).

Erotic love offers the 'unsurpassable peak of fulfillment' in the 'direct fusion of the souls of one to another' but it is dangerous, especially for women (1964: 347). Weber points out that, 'To the unrestrained feeling of warriordom, the possession and the fight over women has ranked about equally with the fight for treasure and the conquest of power' (1964: 347). While the sanctioned forms of erotic relations progress from the outright brutality of the warrior to the more civilized relations of 'salon culture', nevertheless eroticism must remain attached 'in a certain sophisticated measure, to brutality' (Weber 1964: 348). In fact the more sublimated, the more brutal such relations were likely to be. The brutality lies not simply in 'jealousy and the will to possession' but also in the 'most intimate coercion of the soul of the less brutal partner' (Weber 1964: 348). That is, brutality is not simply physical but can take the form of spiritual or psychological brutality which masquerades as 'the most humane devotion' but which is the means for the enjoyment of the self 'in the other'. The 'other', who is the means for the pleasure of the more powerful partner, undergoes a coercion that is, in Weber's view, 'never noticed by the partners themselves' (1964: 348). To the extent that the normative gender assumption in heterosexual relations is that women 'surrender' to men, and men 'conquer' women, it would seem that women are the most likely recipients of the brutality of erotic love. Indeed, to the extent that 'heroic ecstasy and heroic regeneration' is, for the warrior or the knight, an erotic experience, and, in Max Weber's account, the first indications of the sublimation of sexuality, then the brutality of erotic relations must be masculine, at least in its origins.[7] For Weber, in world politics as in domestic politics, and 'even in the most intimate relations of personal life and the deepest recesses of the human soul, conflict and struggle are endemic' (Bologh 1990: 205).

In the domestic sphere, conflict arises when gender roles are undifferentiated. An interesting illustration of this point is found in Marianne Weber's biography of her husband. She indicates that her husband desired her 'individuality, her inner freedom, and her independence' so that she might 'stand beside him tall and proud' (Marianne Weber [1926] 1975: 186). But for Max Weber, the best way to assure her equality was to 'provide her with a domain in the household that he could not reach'. Consequently, he counselled her to have a focus that was not in 'the purely intellectual-philosophical realm' but to have some 'domain of practical activity that is out of bounds to me' and thus he suggested that she should not disdain the 'housewifely sphere of duty and work' (Marianne Weber [1926] 1975: 187–8). The practical, domestic sphere was, in his view, the complement to his teaching and one that would provide a 'definite sphere of activity that is *valuable* to you as such, so that you will not be dependent upon the fluctuations of my temperament' (Marianne Weber [1926] 1975: 188). These comments are somewhat ironic given that the very sphere Max Weber recommends to his bride as her own was one to which she did not give much credit. Max Weber had admonished Marianne that she should not 'think with such contempt of those who are "only housewives". I mean this in your own interest' (Marianne Weber [1926] 1975: 187).

There is a sense that the discussion of 'other-worldly rational asceticism' applied to marriage reflected the Webers' own marriage. Max Weber saw the 'linkage of marriage with the thought of ethical responsibility for one another' as embodying something 'unique and supreme' in marriage which could transform the 'feelings of love which is conscious of responsibility throughout the nuances of the organic process, "up to the pianissimo of old age", and the mutual granting of oneself to another and becoming indebted to each other (in Goethe's sense)' (Max Weber 1964: 350). Such a relationship was, however, antithetical to erotic love.

Erotic love is irrational and problematic because it competes with brotherly love. Erotic love is regarded as a 'pathological obsession' by salvation religions because the 'euphoria of the happy lover is felt to be a "goodness"; it has a friendly urge to poeticize all the world with happy features' but this always 'meets the cool mockery of the genuinely religiously founded and radical ethic of brotherhood' (Max Weber 1964: 348). Brotherly love is impersonal and represents service to others; erotic love, in contrast, is the pleasurable satisfaction of one's own desires. But brotherly love is almost impossible to practice in the modern world. The 'ethic of brotherliness' stands in tension not only with erotic love but also with 'purposive-rational conduct' (Max Weber 1964: 339). The tension is connected with the problem of worldly means and ends of rational action.

> The question is whether and to what extent the responsibility of the actor for the results sanctifies the means, or whether the value of the actor's intention justifies him in rejecting the responsibility for the outcome, whether to pass on the results as an act to God or to the wickedness and foolishness of the world which are permitted by God.
> (Max Weber 1964: 339)

Whatever the resolution of the tension, it is clear that it is the 'brotherhood' who decides the issue. Women, as the representative of 'these worldly life forces' that are 'essentially non-rational or basically anti-rational' are unlikely to make any contribution to the resolution of the tensions of religiously dictated rational action in the world.

The world of the modern brotherhood is ultimately an alienating world of calculation and conflict that means there is 'hardly any room for the cultivation of acosmic brotherliness, unless it is among the strata who are economically carefree' (Max Weber 1964: 357). Cultural progress is marked by man's 'emancipation from the organically prescribed cycle of natural life' but that progress leads to 'an ever more devastating senselessness' (1964: 357). The irrational is increasingly sublimated by both 'theoretical thought, disenchanting the world' and the attempt of 'religious ethics . . . to rationalize the world' (Max Weber 1964: 357). Sublimation of the irrational finds one outlet in erotic relations in which women represent the 'natural' and necessary, although submerged, counterpart to modern rationalization and men's 'disenchantment' with the world. Erotic, heterosexual relations are one of the means by which men may achieve re-enchantment.[8]

The subtext of the rational, autonomous citizen is desire, body and passion. Women are the means for both the satisfaction of masculine erotic desire and the control of unruly passions that might threaten the political and economic world of the brotherhood. But these loving, maternal saviours are themselves sexually problematic because of their closer connection to the 'natural'. While the sexual passions of men are ideally solved with the domestic/work split, for women there was no similar compartmentalization, all was confined in the home and family. This was largely because women's sexual desire and thus their irrationality is conflated with the reproductive capacity and it is when this capacity is incorporated into modern, rational, social goals that the domestication of women becomes imperative.[9] Both sexually and reproductively the sensory, desiring female body as the problematic half of the constitutional duality of man provided the 'natural', logical explanation of women's subordination to men. Ultimately, women's erotic gratification cannot be a part of a rational world just as her status as a citizen is always compromised by her sexual and maternal family function.

Sociological theorists and citizens

In the twentieth century, women's 'civil, political and social rights' were assured (Evans 1993: 249–50), but although women have entered state and market relations they have not been either 'structurally or ideologically' allowed to leave the family and they are therefore 'not sexually responsible citizens as men are'.[10] Institutional roles may have changed but status structures, such as male/female, that provide 'personal identities' have been most resistant to change (Curtis and MacCorquodale 1990: 137). Curtis and MacCorquodale (1990: 150) believe that 'Suffrage appears to be a relatively permanent gain because it affords women a public status – that of citizen'. However, it is clear that the public status of citizen – the change that Wollstonecraft and others hoped would be the basis for gender equality – remains compromised by the familial and sexual role and status structures that perpetuate patriarchal power. It is not surprising, then, that critical issues for twenty-first century female citizens continue to revolve around women's sexual and reproductive rights and capacities, that is, around issues of abortion, reproduction, pornography, sexual preference and desire.

In the classic sociological texts women are 'outside the frame' (Smith 1987b). This is strange given the ferment of various women's movements in the nineteenth and early twentieth centuries. Although sociology was the newest and most radical intellectual endeavour, it remained blinkered with respect to women. The description of the modern world offered by the sociological fathers was compromised by their inability to recognize that sexual desire and expression was as much a cultural construction for women as for men.

The analysis of sexuality and gender in the work of Durkheim, Weber and Comte[11] is contradictory. The connection of women with 'nature' and men with 'culture' is both explanation and justification for the subordination of women to men. By theorizing women as more 'natural' and thus more sexually unstable than men, the regulation of women to a private, enclosed household sphere could be justified. But these same unstable creatures are also the means for the regulation of men in their public persona. Industrial capitalism requires disciplined, punctual, focused workers, able to resist, or at least suppress for the required working hours, any sexual impulse or desire. By physically segregating women from men in the productive sphere and designating the private sphere of home and family as the place for normative sexual and affectual relations, the modern gender division of labour was produced. It was also assumed that the health and welfare of the state was dependent on these divisions, especially on the ability of the 'angels' in the home to ensure the daily reproduction of docile, willing male producers. Max Weber (1958: 167) pointed out that an important part of the Protestant legacy was the condemnation of any 'spontaneous expression of undisciplined impulses' because they led away from 'work in a calling and religion'. The result was a 'powerful tendency toward uniformity of life' that, in turn, aided the 'capitalistic interest in the standardization of production', all having their basis in 'the repudiation of all idolatry of the flesh' (Max Weber 1958: 169).[12] In this complex equation it is not surprising that the ideal worker for industrial capitalism was the disciplined, compliant, adult male.[13]

The male worker remained sexually problematic because his desire was only contained by the promise of satisfaction within the confines of normative, heterosexual marital relations. The unmarried man could suffer sexual anomy because he 'aspires to everything and is satisfied with nothing' (Durkheim 1951: 271). But as long as he was attached 'forever to the same woman', the 'salutary discipline to which he is subjected makes it his duty to find his happiness in his lot', and if his 'passion is forbidden to stray, its fixed object is forbidden to fail him: the obligation is reciprocal' (Durkheim 1951: 270). The routinization of sexual desire in marriage is, however, uncertain because such routinization is accompanied in modern society by the contradictory celebration of erotic love.[14] The eroticism of modern life, centred in the body, is a central problem for the sociological fathers because it represents the contradiction to, or antithesis to, the abstract, rational explication of social processes and institutions. Frank (1991: 92) points out that 'If the body is the subject of sociology, theory becomes possible insofar as the theorists share that embodiment'. For the embodied sociological fathers, the erotic possibilities of modern existence seem to have represented a threat to (their) male autonomy and sexual desire and thus to the social order, most especially to the precarious harmony in public relations among men.

For most of the sociological fathers, sexuality was the terror that could undermine the painfully constructed world of rational, autonomous citizens. Redfield (1975: 101) remarked that culture represented the 'translucent screen against the terror of nature'. Women are the representation of nature that terrifies as well as the objects through which men might conquer this unruly, threatening force. But the terror of nature is precisely because it is shut out of the world of calculation, exchange and power.

The terrors of the natural, the emotional, the sensual and the erotic remain significant, as the reluctance, until recently, to admit the body into sociological accounts and the resistance to the work of feminist sociologists attest. Max Weber's ([1919] 1946) 'polar night of icy darkness and hardness' confronting the rational, vocational man left him with no choice but to meet the 'demands of the day in human relations as well as in . . . vocation' in a stoic manner. Perhaps meeting the demands as a sociologist in a disenchanted world of gender problems would be easier if Jaggar's (1990: 165) point is accepted that 'Emotions are neither more basic than observation, reason, or action in building theory, nor are they secondary to them. Each of these human faculties reflects an aspect of human knowledge inseparable from the other aspects'. As feminists point out, the detached, omnipotent observer of social life is a myth and one that produced, in the past, a less than adequate description of the world of differences, whether of gender, sexual preference, race, class or ethnicity, that cannot be ignored or safely relegated to some presumed 'private' place any longer.

Notes

1 Mary Wollstonecraft in 1792 claimed that if women were not educated like men they would 'stop the progress of knowledge and virtue; for truth must be common to all, or it will be efficacious with respect to its influence on general practice' ([1792] 1967: 24). Wollstonecraft herself came to find that her emotional life was not easily divorced from her intellectual life, and the birth of her first daughter taught her that the body could not easily be ignored. Wollstonecraft's attempt to reconcile what the Cartesian formula separated is apparent from her published correspondence. See Wollstonecraft (1987).

2 When the Jacobins declared the Republic of Virtue in 1792, women were called upon to be 'the divinity of the domestic sanctuary' (Pope 1987: 141).

3 Comte observes that equality claims have been made without the consent of women despite the fact that he must have been aware that women had advanced such claims, at least during the Revolutionary years.

4 Durkheim pointed out that the difference between the sexes was confirmed by the fact that with the dissolution of marriage, women tended towards crime and misdemeanours more readily than men. This tendency was explicable because 'woman's moral sense is less deeply rooted than man's' or, 'Put another way, woman's nature is less strongly socialized than man's, a truth which we have backed up with further proofs in our *Suicide*' (Durkheim 1980: 414).

5 If Coser's (1977a: 146) remarks are to be credited, Durkheim's own domestic situation was the epitome of rational, bourgeois respectability. Coser indicates that Durkheim's wife 'seems to have devoted herself fully to his work. She followed the traditional Jewish family pattern of taking care of family affairs, as well as assisting him in proof-reading, secretarial duties and the like. Thus, the scholar-husband could devote all his energies to his scholarly pursuits'.

6 Weber's reflections on the extramarital place of erotic love were not entirely theoretical. Mitzman (1970: 304) suggests that around 1910 'Weber personally participated in this liberation of Eros' and it would seem to have staved off another relapse into the sort of psychic despair that had afflicted him earlier. Mitzman (1970: 277) continues with the observation that, 'between 1911 and 1914, Weber did have an extramarital relationship with a young woman in Heidelberg . . .' Green (1974: 165) is clearer, and identifies Else Jaffe, later to be married to Max's brother Alfred, as the woman in question, and indicates that on his deathbed Max Weber 'would call for Else' and that he 'died in the presence of his wife and Frau Jaffe, both of whom had joined in caring for him in the end, and it seemed to those intimate with the whole situation, that his divided love for the two was tearing him apart'.

7 If the connections between the brotherhood of warriors and erotic love discussed by Weber are credited, then any assumption that current fascinations

with the masculine transformations of 'Iron Johns' and their variants as benign extensions of feminism, is highly questionable. Weber (1978: 489) points out that with the 'routinization and regimentation of community relationships' that occurs with political and military types of prophecy 'directed exclusively by men' the 'cult of the warlike spirit is frequently put into the direct service of controlling and lawfully plundering the households of women by the male inhabitants of the warrior house, who are organized into a sort of club'. More specifically, where the 'rebirth of the hero is or had been dominant, woman is regarded as lacking a higher heroic soul and is consequently assigned a secondary religious status'.

8   Weber (1964: 343, 345) does not discuss erotic relations among men, other than as a feature of the 'classic Hellenic period when the "comrade", the boy, was the object demanded with all the ceremony of love', and in a brief mention of 'profane heterosexual, as well as homosexual, prostitution' as a 'survival of magical orgiasticism'. In the subsequent discussion of eroticism in the Western world, it is clearly heterosexual relations that are meant and this makes sense in that the irrationalities of heterosexual desire can be regarded as inevitable given women's nature, but homosexual desire calls into question in a direct and unambiguous way the idea of innate, masculine reason and control over the instinctual/natural for modern males.

9   Jordanova (1986: 98) indicates that in the eighteenth century sexuality had two, contradictory, meanings. It was positive if understood as the 'impulse to procreate responsibly', but it was negative if its expression was 'premature, illicit, excessive, or simply for carnal gratification', and although this applied to both men and women in theory, in fact a 'surfeit of passion or voluptuousness was stereotypically associated with feminine weakness'. By the nineteenth century, however, women were thought, ideally, to be devoid of sexual passion and thus the perfect partners for the control of unruly masculine desire. The 'angel in the home' was an asexual, nurturant, sentimental, natural being. But as the prostitute demonstrated, the pure angel was always somewhat suspect; there was always the possibility that sexual relations might awaken the 'natural' untamed instincts and produce the erotic, desiring woman.

10   Evans (1993: 250) points out that in the 'fetishisation of the family' and 'state practice in "liberalising" family law and statutes dealing with sex crime, essential gender sexual differences have been reconstituted rather than questioned'.

11   Other sociological fathers could have been included, for example Herbert Spencer, Ferdinand Tönnies, Vilfred Pareto and Georg Simmel. The concentration on Comte, Durkheim and Weber is a selective, first foray into the issues raised in this account.

12   In Weberian style, no causality is implied here, rather a more complex relationship is involved. As Weeks points out, since Rousseau, sex has been regarded as the 'assertion of self against the preternaturally distorting effects of

modern, and later industrial civilization'. Industrial capitalism requires the asexual, disciplined, working body which, paradoxically, finds the essence of being in sexual desire and practice *as opposed* to productive activity (Weeks 1985: 12).

13 In the various surveys of early industrial work one of the frequently recommended reforms was the separation of women from men in the new factories because of possible sexual impropriety, with the ideal being, of course, the elimination of women and children from any wage work.

14 For a more extensive discussion of the sociological treatment of love in various guises, see Bertilsson (1991: 297–324).

3   Elective affinities: Georg Simmel and Marianne Weber on gender and modernity

Theresa Wobbe

'I would appreciate sitting at the tea-table in your living room and reviving the memory of so many shared pleasant hours. If only we could expand those hours!' In July 1918, as World War I drew to an end, this letter travelled from Strasbourg to Heidelberg, from Georg Simmel (1858–1918) to Marianne Weber (1870–1954). By then, they had been exchanging letters for about two decades. Simmel addressed his letters to his 'dear friend' Marianne, who in turn enjoyed the thoughtful conversations with Simmel (Weber 1948: 382).

Only once in the course of their friendship did Marianne Weber discuss Simmel's work in public. Referring to his essay 'The relative and the absolute in the problem of the sexes' (Simmel [1911] 1994), she disputed the sociologist's concept of gender relations. However, although Simmel warmly thanked Marianne Weber for passing him her critical essay, he downplayed the contested points: 'Some questions seem to be different only because we are observing the phenomena from distinct distances' (Weber 1948: 382). Marianne Weber, in turn, reduced these distances when noting in her autobiography: 'It was easy to go forward there where the master had finished' (Weber 1948: 382).

Philosopher Gertrud Simmel, who had been Marianne's friend for over 25 years, flatly refused the gender metaphysics of her husband:

> I don't know if it is permitted, but I feel great impatience about all that men state about us, including Georg ... I wish that we would become again human beings, female human beings instead of exaggerated femininity, over-determined by an orientation to men, that we have practised already about a thousand years and which I refuse to consider our female nature.
>
> (Simmel cited in Weber 1948: 383)

It was precisely this distinction between woman as an essentialist category and women as a social one that Marianne Weber stressed in her discussion of Simmel's essay. Around 1900, both the founders of sociology as well as feminists in Germany debated this distinction, which was, at least among those involved in feminist politics, the focal point far beyond German borders (Cott 1987; Allen 1991). Within this constellation Georg Simmel and Marianne Weber provide a nice example of the affinities between sociological classics and feminist politics. Sociological knowledge and feminist politics were alert to the many faces of the 'social question'. By developing new social knowledge (academic and non-academic) they added to the discursive dynamics of both the social and the woman question.

The sociological classics of the formative decades (1880–1930) witnessed the first wave of the international women's movements and most of these scholars referred in some way to the 'woman question' (Kandal 1988). Within Simmel's sociology, this issue gained a prominent analytical status. By systematically including gender relations within his framework of modernity, Simmel recognized the feminist movement as a signifier of the shifting relations between the sexes. With his concepts of social differentiation and gender differentiation, he was claiming a sociological concept of men and women that differed from the biological one. Similarly, Marianne Weber's ideas on the cultural patterns of women's sociation provided a specific link between sociology and feminist practice. Referring to both fields of knowledge, she developed visions of female solidarity and social reform. Put in sociological terms, Simmel's and Weber's communication addressed the interrelation between gendered modes of individuation, social differentiation and gender difference.

It has been argued that Simmel's concept of culture contains essentialist or even 'Wilhelminian' dimensions with respect to women (Coser 1977b). Suzanne Vromen has focused on Simmel's concept of gender difference, which according to her 'is based mostly on a biological model' (Vromen 1991: 336). She stressed Simmel's 'inability to transcend a biological model of womanhood and to accept fully the influence of socialisation' (Vromen 1991: 337). In addition, Lieteke van Vucht Tijssen offered the following synopsis of Marianne Weber's ideas on gender relations: 'In the end, women will catch up with men and will be able to meet the same standards' (van Vucht Tijssen 1991: 214). These interpretations fail to convey both the scope and the limits of Simmel's and Weber's analyses of gender. On the one hand, Coser and Vromen emphasize Simmel's essentialist ideas without moving beyond the narrow biology–culture scheme themselves. Van Vucht Tijssen, on the other hand, downplays Marianne Weber's highly ambivalent diagnosis of gender relations in modern society. Such perceptions lead to the conclusion that the disagreement between Simmel and Weber was based on a misunderstanding due to ideological differences, but they obscure the complexity of the problem under discussion. In this chapter, I suggest a different line of reading, one which reveals the differences between Simmel and

Weber, while also uncovering the familiar patterns in their arguments that are embedded in broader cultural schemes of their time. Linking these fields of knowledge, the chapter benefits from an emerging body of literature concerning the intellectual history of sociology, gender history and gender sociology (Deegan 1991; Felski 1995; Honegger and Wobbe 1998; Silverberg 1998; Chafetz 1999; Witz 2001).

Simmel and Weber shared an interest in questions that were at the very centre of sociological thinking on modernity at the turn of the century. As Shmuel Eisenstadt and Miriam Curelaru have underscored, the uniquely sociological problematic (*Problemstellung*) focused on the conditions and possibility of social order (Eisenstadt and Curelaru 1976: 58; see also Luhmann 1981). Hence, the social order of modernity represents a crucial point of focus within the classics. My discussion of Simmel's and Weber's perspectives on gendered individuation will show that for both gender is highly relevant for social integration, hence for the possibility of the social order. This chapter, then, focuses on an examination of Simmel's and Weber's understanding of the social and of modern gender relations.

In the first section, Simmel and Weber are located within the broader context of both the new discipline of sociology and the feminist movement in Germany. The next two sections deal with Weber's and Simmel's concepts of gendered individuation. Weber's notion of the *new woman* will take centre stage, followed by a discussion of Simmel's approach to social and gender differentiation. I shall argue that, although both Simmel and Weber offered a gendered view on individuation, their interpretations are quite different. One way of understanding the differences between their two interpretations is in relation to the extent to which their approaches were infused by masculinist or feminist perspectives on the social.

Simmel and Weber's exchange in the broader context

According to Guenther Roth (1988), Marianne Weber, with her career as both Max Weber's editor and as a feminist writer in her own right, was part of the educated classes of the German Empire. Marianne Weber received her fundamental political inspiration from the feminist movement of her time. She was part of an emerging professional generation within an expanding women's movement that linked social reform and social research. Thanks to the growth of an intellectual history of sociology, social history and gender history, the sociological potential of Marianne Weber's writings has recently been recognized (Wobbe 1997, 1998a, b; Meurer 2003).

Elsewhere I have argued that Simmel's and Weber's exchange may serve as an example of the elective affinities which arose between the emerging discipline of sociology around 1900 and early women sociologists, many of whom were involved in social reform (Wobbe 1997).[1] In social terms, both women and the discipline of sociology entered the academic system as newcomers. In cultural terms, both were strangers in the social system of academia. Eventually, in cognitive terms, they shared a distinct perspective on social order and a specific affinity with social problems. The elective affinities thus provide different dimensions of social distance and modes of incorporation. In Simmel's writings the sociological position of the stranger (Simmel [1908b] 1971) represents both closeness and remoteness and allows for innovative perspectives. According to Donald N. Levine's analysis of the sociology of the stranger, we can identify the heterogeneity of inclusion as a variation of stranger statuses (Levine 1971: x). According to Merton (1968: 320, 344), the marginalized identify with the group and seek incorporation. The case of sociology and early women scholars covers both dimensions: as newcomers they sought to become part of the scientific community; as strangers they developed distinct perspectives on social order.

In the introduction to his *Sociology* (1908a), Simmel described the new discipline – still in the process of carving out its territory alongside the other disciplines – as the El Dorado of the homeless and uprooted. Simmel was aware that as a new field of knowledge, sociology opened up new possibilities for Jews and women to participate in intellectual experiments and professional training. In fact, the first women sociologists entered German academia at the same time as the new discipline of sociology itself.

Almost 40 years later, Viola Klein, born in Vienna in 1908, echoed Simmel's perspective by employing the tools of Mannheim's sociology of knowledge.[2] In her study of *The Feminine Character* ([1946] 1971), Klein developed her argument about the affinities between the social sciences and the women's movement. During the nineteenth century it was virtually impossible for women, Jews and immigrants to enter the established professions. Instead, the emergence of innovative fields provided these groups with the opportunity to obtain professional positions. Klein argued that the two newcomers, namely social reform and the women's movement, shared important similarities through their break with traditional ideas of social order:

> There is a peculiar affinity between the fate of women and the origin of social science, and it is no mere coincidence that the emancipation of women should have started at the same time as the birth of sociology ... But the relation of women's emancipation to social science does not only spring from a common origin; it is more direct: the humanitarian interests which formed the starting point of social research, and practical social work itself, actually provided the backdoor through which women slipped into public life
>
> (Klein [1946] 1971: 17)[3]

Klein pointed out that the phenomenon of the newcomer is grounded in the changing social structure of modern society itself. She described the inclusion of new groups in the professions as the outcome of social differentiation and social mobility, 'which enables outsiders to force their way, or to slip, into the established system' (Klein [1946] 1971: 19).

In the historical context of the German Empire, both sociology and women scholars formed a part of the new professionals in the educated classes. They could only enrol as students and become members of the academic community through roundabout ways. From 1902 onwards they could enrol at universities in Bavaria, and from 1908 to 1909 onwards they could enrol in Prussia, the German Empire's largest state. Only after 1920 could women pursue a university career in Germany (Albisetti 1986; Wobbe 1996).

In view of the German tradition of the educated classes (*Bildungsbürgertum*) we know that the status of university graduates was more than just one of possessing professional skills or particular knowledge. The academics were at the core of the social strata forming the specific cultural milieu that Lepsius, drawing on Max Weber, identified as the 'corporate sociation of the advanced classes' (Lepsius 1992; see also Clark 1987). The social closure of the academic elite – or the German mandarins (Ringer 1969) – was powerful concerning the male structuration of the academic community. Against this background, the exclusive structure of the German academic elite formed a distinct obstacle for newcomers (Frevert 1989; Wobbe 1997).

Klein opened our perspective on the structural sensibility that did exist between the social sciences and the women's movement. Both emerged in the course of modernization and secularization and both were collective actors in the process of social differentiation. In this respect, the social sciences and the women's movement transformed questions about the natural conditions of social order into those of the nature of the social.

But there is more to be mined from Klein's analysis. While elaborating on the close ties between the newcomers, she also illuminates the different paths they took. The great transformation from the *ancien régime* to modern society, from domestic to market production carried a distinct dilemma for women because divergent expectations and standards persisted with respect to men and women (Klein [1946] 1971: 33, 43). Klein pointed to the fact 'that women gradually gained access into a ready-made culture which by its origin and peculiar character is masculine' (Klein [1946] 1971: 34). Regarding the current concept of equality she concluded: 'In a society whose standards are predominantly masculine, women form an "out-group", distinguished from the dominant strata by physical characteristics, historical tradition, social role and a different process of socialisation' (Klein [1946] 1971: 4). The point I wish to make here, then, is that Klein's analysis echoed those of Georg Simmel and Marianne Weber. That is to say that Viola Klein, like Georg Simmel and

Marianne Weber before her, was centrally concerned with the problematic status of women in what they all recognized as man-made modernity.

Weber's concept of the modern woman

Weber's main scholarly work is represented in her study *Wife and Mother in the Course of Changing Codification* (Marianne Weber 1907), in which she examined the changing legal status of women and mothers by employing an approach drawing from legal studies and sociology. Her monograph contains a comparative analysis of how maternity laws and legal norms underwent changes with respect to the women and children. The study covers a broad range of historical periods and empirical sources. As current evaluations of her writings indicate (Roth 1988; Lichtblau 1996), this study should be read in close connection with Max Weber's *Protestant Ethic* (Max Weber [1920] 1956a). One main section of her study deals with the transition from the Catholic universalism of a religious pre-modern order to the secular modern society in Europe (Marianne Weber 1907: chap. 4).

Weber was interested in determining to what extent the transformation from tradition to modernity shaped the legal position of women. She concentrated on the Reformation as the decisive turning point, when the institution of marriage became secularized. Although the position of the wife became more important within the realm of the household, it turned out that within Protestantism marriage was the only domain to offer role models to women (Roper 1990). In contrast to Protestantism, the *sponsa christi*, the Catholic institution of convents, provided women with different role models which allowed a status of the *religiosos* and thus spiritual recognition to both men and women.

The abolition of spiritual institutions in the course of the Reformation brought about dramatic changes for women in general and for unmarried women in particular. According to Marianne Weber, the Reformation narrowed female role models to marriage and as a result 'the problem of the unmarried woman' arose. The existing institutions and the cultural recognition of unmarried women within the Catholic tradition had been eroded. Within this context, Weber examined emerging modern institutions that transformed man's position into that of a sovereign subject, while subordinating women under this dominant position. Yet she also pointed to the egalitarian dimensions of the Calvinist and Puritan (Marianne Weber 1907: 288, 290), which came to serve as a point of reference for her normative programme of ethical values (see Roth 1988; Lichtblau 1989/90).

Weber's reflection on the highly ambivalent individualization of women refers to this broader historical range of social and cultural change in Europe (Bock 1998). Against this background she discussed the different types of codification in Europe regarding the unequal legal status of women. The Code

Napoléon, she argued, contained 'the worst kind of medieval patriarchalism' (Marianne Weber 1907: 318; see Gerhard 1997). In her section on the German civil code she offered a legal-political critique of the Wilhelminian patriarchal society that did not confer married women with the authority of individuals in the sphere of family law (Weber 1907: 407ff; see Gerhard 1978; Gerhard Chapter 6, this volume).

Marianne Weber's analysis of gender relations in modern society centred on the concept of female role differentiation. In her essay 'The new woman' (1914a) she discussed the relevance of social change with regard to cultural orientations, arguing that the erosion of the former hierarchical sexual division of labour in which women occupied a particular social position brought about a loss of social function for women. Weber described the key problem of women in modernity as that of uncovering functional alternatives to the former social position of women without forcing them into the same process of rationalization that men are subjected to. In other words, she focused on the problems women faced as they achieved cultural recognition in the process of modernization. According to her, the 'new woman' represented the cultural potential to demand and realize recognition for women under the condition of modernity.

The modern woman, dedicated to the cultural and social self-determination of her own sex, forms 'a first movement'. In contrast to 'the typical woman of the past', who was fixated on the home and not active on behalf of her own sex, the new woman's intention is the 'shaping of her self and the world'. According to Weber, her goal is 'the organized community' with other women. Within the traditional division of labour, women were competitors. Conditions for female solidarity emerged only thanks to the expansion of the domestic sphere (Marianne Weber 1914a: 135f.), where the new woman embodies a cultural type, a new mode of female sociation and individualization. In contrast with the traditional type, the new woman is orientated towards self-determination. Her essay 'Woman and objective culture' (Marianne Weber 1913), which engaged directly with Simmel's writing on the relativity of gender relations (Simmel [1911] 1985b), was centred around this notion of the new woman. Weber used the term 'new woman' and 'modern woman' synonymously.

In her dispute with Simmel, Weber outlined her view of the condition of women in modern society as follows. The 'splitting of the species in two', as a social fact, made room for two interpretations. On the one hand, the fact that woman represented a different sex meant that she could not be compared with the other sex, and thus woman could not be equal with man. On the other hand, the fact that woman, like man, was a human being implied that she was comparable with man, and thus could be equal with the other sex.

According to the first notion, woman could not embody a person, in other words, an individual in her own right, and so would lack a transcendent potential in the objective world. According to the second notion, she would be unable to compete with male norms of cultural achievement, and so remain 'a second-class *human being*' (Marianne Weber 1913: 95, 97). Moreover, within this matrix, women would be considered hybrid 'mixed beings', that is, 'female human beings with male characteristics' (Marianne Weber 1913: 104f.). Weber touched on a phenomenon identified in contemporary gender sociology as a cultural, highly complex social interconnection of difference and inequality, difference and sameness.[4] Weber was struggling against the deep ontology of difference that underpinned prevailing conceptualizations of 'human being' through her analysis of the fundamentally social position of woman. By doing so she was trying to think women into the social order of modernity, effecting a parallel move to masculinist discourses that arrogate the qualities of sociality and humanity exclusively to men (see Chapter 1, this volume). According to Weber, the professional achievements of women in society provide the same distinct emotionalism and 'salvation through work' (*Werkseligkeit*) (Weber 1913) as they do in the case of men. She thereby maintained that the modern woman embodies the capacity of transcending the male world of norms and rules.

However, due to the domestic sphere, women's role differentiation is not like that of men's. Since women perform both familial and professional roles, the distinct cultural formation of the new woman gives women the exclusive potential to mediate between the personal and the public sphere.[5] Within Weber's framework, the prospect of female individuation did not imply fewer opportunities than male individuation. Rather, in relating female social existence to human existence, the modern woman would gain 'a new extended idea of female determination' (Weber 1914a: 140). Equally important to Weber, the feminist movement offered the cultural and political context in which the concept of female solidarity (*Gemeinschaftshandeln*) could be realized. It served as a generator of feminist politics as well as a cultural network for women. With respect to the association of women, Weber was in agreement with Simmel's differentiation theory as presented in his formal sociology (Simmel 1908c).

Simmel's approach to gender differentiation and individuation in modernity

Between 1890 and 1911 Simmel published about 15 essays on the topic of women and gender relations. From his earliest writings until his late remarks on the sexes he emphasized both the distinct dynamics and the asymmetric dimensions of the process of gender differentiation (Levine 1971; Kandal 1988; Wobbe 1997). Moreover, Simmel's work on culture and aesthetics, and on social interaction and individuality, is deeply permeated by his gender sociology. Differing from his contemporaries,[6] Simmel's sociology provides close ties with gender issues. Whereas his specific ideas changed over various fields, from psychology to sociology and philosophy, the *leitmotif* of his reflections on the path of the sexes in modern society did not. Rather, as I have argued elsewhere (Wobbe 1997: 48), the relation between the sexes represented to him a prototypical case of the reciprocal structure of sociation itself.

As early as the 1890s, Simmel was already concerned with the link between social differentiation and differentiation between the sexes (Simmel [1890] 1985c). At this point, differentiation denotes a formal structure signifying both a social-cultural process and the relation between men and women. Social differentiation, in particular, points to the emergence of a multisphered structure on the macro level and of different roles on the micro level designating the functional and rationalized dynamics of modern society (Simmel 1895; Simmel 1908c; Simmel 1978).

According to Simmel, the intersection and multiplication of *social circles* becomes an indicator of individuality and culture. Increasing membership in modernity correlates with the expansion of individual agency. It is within this process of differentiation that the dissolving of smaller circles and local bonds enables social mobility. But although the emergence of a multisphered society serves as a crucial force of modernity, this process applies to men only (Simmel [1890] 1985c: 293). Women are still focused on the social system of the family (Simmel 1908c: 335).

In his essay on the 'Psychology of women' ([1890] 1985c) Simmel introduced his concept of gender differentiation. Drawing on Herbert Spencer's theory on the transition from the undifferentiated, homogenous to the differentiated, heterogeneous unity, Simmel applied this evolutionary scheme to gender relations. Men developed into the differentiated and specialized sex, whereas women became the unified and undifferentiated one (Simmel [1890] 1985c: 28, 36, 39, 40, 43, 44). Simmel considered this distinction rooted in the division of labour, in other words, as a result of the dissociation between the household and the market economy (Simmel [1890] 1985c: 46). Since men had earlier participated in the expanding division of labour whereas women remained within the household, it was only man who was involved in the process of rationalization and functional differentiation.

In his early writings Simmel even regards differentiation itself as a fundamentally relational term, emphasizing that the poor differentiation of women must always be conceptualized as a gradual one compared with that of men. Simmel did not conclude by stating that women's non-differentiation may be thought of as a deficit but by stating that it should be regarded in the context of women's cultural potential regarding their relevance for the home as a locus of intimacy and harmony (Simmel 1997, [1911] 1985b, [1890] 1985c). Keeping in mind Gertrud Simmel's remark on her impatience with men's scholarly observations on women, the interesting question here is the extent to which her husband came to terms with women's individuality and individuation.

In his *Sociology* (1908a), Simmel discussed the shift of women from dissociation to association or, using Weber's notion, the phenomenon of the new woman. He described this development as a 'sociological evolution which the term woman had recently undergone, and which provides a set of formal complications which cannot be observed as clearly in other cases' (Simmel 1908c: 313). Simmel noted a paradox. Until then, he stated, all women had shared a common social condition insofar as their domestic function did not allow solidarity among them. 'The parallelism of women' hence prevented 'the associational use of equality' (Simmel 1908c: 315). Instead of group solidarity, their occupation with the domestic sphere only provided association between unequals, namely, between men and women.

In the course of the nineteenth century, gender relations were affected by modernization and functional differentiation. The 'sociological singularity of the woman' underwent a fragmentation, and as a result, women as a social group also became caught up in the process of social differentiation. According to Simmel, the women's movement was a crucial factor in this. By establishing a 'partisan difference' (Simmel 1908c: 336) against men, it created exchange and solidarity among women. In building up a new political difference, the function of the women's movement was to offer an alternative to traditional models of gender distinction. Hence, according to Simmel, the former concept of woman was transformed into that of 'a group which belongs together' (Simmel 1908c: 336): a social movement. But the question is whether or not this entailed women's individuation and, if so, what this would mean for modern culture.

The transition described by Simmel regarding gender relations revealed a specific tendency in modern culture, which he characterized as a 'dual nexus of generality and individuality' (Frisby 1992: 19). The *Philosophy of Money* (1978) provides the *locus classicus* for Simmel's discussion of the increasing domination of rationality and formal exchange on the one hand, and growing fluidity of distinctions and boundaries on the other. Much of Simmel's writings explore 'these simultaneously liberating and depersonalizing aspects of modern life, as exemplified both in the institutions of money as a general principle of exchange and in the new and distinctive modes of experience engendered by the modern city' (Felski 1995: 42). From this perspective, Simmel framed the transformation in gender relations as part of the broader changes between objective and personal culture (Simmel 1978: chap. 6).

By referring to the cultivation of the individual through the agency of external forms, culture has two aspects for Simmel. Whereas objective culture denotes the complex of ideal and actualized products, subjective culture designates the extent to which individuals can integrate this objectification into their personal orbit (Levine 1971: xix). Objective culture encompasses the creation of the objective and normative world, that is law, science and norms, whereas subjective culture denotes the extent and intensity of the individual's participation in culture. Simmel's central argument states that the dilemma of modernity is the lag of subjective culture behind objective culture (Simmel 1978: chap. 6). Whereas objective culture would increase faster, subjective culture could not grow proportionately. The latter came under the attack of the unlimited growth of the former (Simmel 1908a). Particularly in periods of transition and new complexity, this dynamics of *dissonance in modern life* (Simmel 1908a: 234) develops.

It is against this background that Simmel discussed female individuation and the women's movement. He discussed the 'two value questions' (1997: 46) raised by the modern women's movement. Besides the aspect of increasing female participation in modern culture, he examined the question of whether the feminist movement would add new elements to objective culture (Simmel 1997: 47).

Simmel's disapproving discussion of this question is rooted in his masculine notion of culture and following from this, in his concern with the rationalized and fragmented male individual. In the first place, a culture that is irrelevant to the sexes does not exist, rather, such a claim would be naive: 'Our objective culture is thoroughly male. It is men who have created art and industry, science and commerce, the state and religion' (1997: 47). In the second place, Simmel identifies the fragmented male individual, who is caught in a dense web of interests and expectations, while rarely experiencing personal unity, as the other dimension of modern culture, contrasting the differentiated and specialized, but personally fragmented, male subject with the undifferentiated woman. The latter represented 'a more integral nature' (Simmel 1997: 50) which is linked to the realm of subjective culture. In other words, according to Simmel the undifferentiated woman was experiencing a personal unity in contrast to the specialized man who represented the social (Witz 2001; Chapter 1, this volume).

Ultimately, Simmel's ambivalence towards the women's movement as well as his sceptical view of women's individuation must be understood in the light of this concept of culture. Through his lens, women's individuation would serve to enlarge the complexity of objective culture, thus exacerbating man's fragmentation rather than correcting it. Since Simmel's concern with the endangered male individual and his path of personal evolution was his central one, his concern with the nature and direction of gender differentiation receded into the background.

Now Simmel expanded his view on the 'radical dualism' of modern society increasingly to the sexes, which he identified as 'two existential totalities' (1997: 51). With his theories on the process of social and gender differentiation, Simmel offered a sociological route to explaining the individuation of women. But now, by focusing on the polarities of the sexes, the former concept vanished out of sight. This change highlights the contradictory and problematic legacy of Simmel's analysis of gender and modernity. As Felski (1995) and Witz (2001) have argued, Simmel ultimately succumbs to a metaphysically grounded notion of men and women as 'two existential totalities'.

Various faces of the social

Early in the twentieth century Simmel and Weber had been discussing the transformation of gender relations in modern society. They observed the break-up of the Wilhelminian gender order and witnessed the rise of new gender roles that had not yet replaced, but co-existed with, the old ones. Unsurprisingly for Weber, Simmel observed this transformation from a distance (Simmel, cited in Marianne Weber 1948: 382).

Simmel discussed the transformation in gender relations in terms of the erosion of the boundaries between the sexes and the cultural implications of this. From this perspective, the cultural power of Woman was the possibility to represent the Other, in other words, the undifferentiated and synthesized female principle that sustained Man and enabled him to come to terms with his own identity. Hence, women's social function was to reduce the complexity of the highly fragmented male individual caught in the web of different roles and interests. According to Simmel, sexual difference embodied a unique boundary experience that is beyond functional differentiation. As Witz (2001) shows, Simmel's thinking becomes ontologically driven. Despite his insightful analysis of the relation between gender differentation and social differentiation he retreats into a metaphysical ontology (see Chapter 1).

Following this metaphysical line of thought, women's function is to reduce complexity, and in this way to sustain the male individual in his disconcerting and potentially debilitating experience of both specialization and wholeness. However, if they are to perform this cultural function, women themselves cannot distort their own essential nature by similarly embarking on the path to individuation. Hence women must necessarily only occupy restricted spaces, restricted that is to the personal domain, within the social and cultural institutions of modernity. This is in order to alleviate the existential anxiety inherent in the complexity of the male individual, one which is exacerbated by the escalating threat to the male psyche of 'subjectification' posed by the increasing complexity of objective culture, a culture of man's own making. It is against this background that Simmel ultimately interprets the break-up of the traditional gender model as an indication of the erosion of differences and a destabilization of the social. It becomes clear that for Simmel the male individual and a masculine culture must necessarily take centre stage.

Weber, on the other hand, worked with an entirely different scenario. Unlike Simmel, her engagement and sympathies with the aims of the women's movement translated into a sociological analysis that understood the position of women in modernity to be more powerful than Simmel did. Her evaluation of the cultural relevance of the women's movement differed from Simmel's. According to her, the feminist movement generates female solidarity, encompassing different role models and maintaining a plurality of female *life concepts* both within and outside the family. Weber focused on the distinct communicative function that women require for social integration. The feminist movement generated new role models for the sexes, with the politics of *organized motherhood* serving as a cultural marker, that is, as the politics of women's social integration (Cott 1987; Allen 1991; Bock and Thane 1991).

Whereas Weber considered women's individuation a potentially powerful political force for change, Simmel was unable to push his analysis of women's individuation in this direction because, ultimately, he valorized and prioritized the masculine experience of individuation. From Simmel's point of view, then, women's individuation enforces the dynamics of assimilation, thus destabilizing the boundaries of the difference between the sexes. As a result, both Weber and Simmel focused on different faces of the social as they referred to different fields of knowledge. Simmel elaborated on a masculine-marked concept of the social that was centred around the growth of male personality that depended on the Other. By performing the role of the undifferentiated Other, women were reducing complexity. But they had to pay a price for it. Their path to individuation was blocked. Weber managed far more successfully to translate her feminist politics into a sociological analysis where she worked with a concept of culture that allowed for both men's and women's individuation. Contrary to Simmel she refused to consider women a group that had not been either infected or affected by the destructive features of modern culture. Rather, she pointed to the other faces of the social, arguing that women's life within the family and the household was already indelibly marked by processes of rationalization and differentiation in that family life in modernity was by no means beyond the social, but a part of it (Weber 1913).

In addition, she claimed that the significant social function of women was to bridge objective and subjective culture. By doing so, women could perform a new roles in personal and social contexts. Through Weber's lens, modern culture depended on, and would be enriched by, the participation of women in public institutions such as in the fields of social work and politics. As a result, society's need for women's social competence served as a legitimate reason to claim women's increased participation in public institutions.

Despite their differences, Simmel and Weber also converged on some significant points. In the first place, both worked with a concept of difference that was deeply encoded by a masculine dimension of the social. The division of labour and the notion of work itself were infused with male connotations associating work with men and male activity. Weber and Simmel contrasted the traditional woman in the domestic realm with the modern woman leaving the household for work. While the sphere of social action for the traditional woman was restricted to the family, the modern one was also engaged in work activities beyond the sphere of the household.

Weber's and Simmel's attempts in the nineteenth and early twentieth centuries to grapple with the implications of modernity for women's spheres of social action nonetheless slipped off the agenda of social theory. In reminding us of an 'old', yet neglected, problem, Viola Klein ([1946] 1971) was later to point out that:

> Another error into which we easily fall through the shortness of our memories and the influence of an ill-conceived feminist propaganda, is the idea that women were, of old, excluded from the economic life of society, and are only now reluctantly and gradually being admitted into the masculine sphere of work. This is a misinterpretation of facts. Before the agricultural and industrial revolution there was hardly any job which was not also performed by women. No work was too hard, no labour too strenuous, to exclude them.
>
> (Klein [1946] 1971: 9)

We have learnt from recent literature in gender history that the male concept of labour has to be considered a social construction that was established during the nineteenth century only (Scott 1993; Silverberg 1998). In contrast, the female worker was created as a particular group of the labour force that had to be protected against the threats of the market. In the half century since Klein's publication, there has been a wealth of feminist literature that has challenged, and finally toppled, the tacit assumption that the modern worker is by definition male. Yet, a clear recognition of this point informed the work of both Simmel and Weber over a century ago, and led them to critically interrogate distinctions between the domestic and the public spheres of social action, particularly the ways in which sociological analyses of modernity failed to confront the ways in which such distinctions overstated male roles while obscuring those of women. The fact that the delineation between private and public spheres of social action was encoded by notions of male and female difference was a point acutely recognized by both Simmel and Weber and subjected to rigorous analysis. Effectively, Weber and Simmel placed the question of gender and modernity firmly on the sociological agenda.

Notes

1   With respect to the United States the affinity has been explored regarding the new empiricism and nineteenth-century feminism in Leach (1980) and Chicago sociology and Hull House during the Progressive Era in Fitzpatrick (1990). The contributions in Silverberg (1998) elaborate on the systematic

argument regarding American social science and gender in the formative years. The affinity has been explored regarding the social reform–social research nexus in Bulmer *et al.* (1991).

2   Klein, who received her first PhD in literature from the University of Prague, emigrated to Great Britain in 1938. It was there that she wrote her second dissertation in sociology, together with Karl Mannheim (Kettler and Meja 1993).

3   With respect to the roots of social survey, social research and women's participation, see Bulmer *et al.* (1991); with respect to the first generation of women sociologists in Chicago, see Fitzpatrick (1990).

4   Regarding organization theory, R.M. Kanter (1977) has conceptualized this dilemma in terms of the token woman who is in conflict with her professional role and her gender role. L.C. Ridgeway has examined this dilemma with respect to the impact that gender status beliefs have on social interaction in the workplace (Ridgeway 1997). Regarding the politics of history and paradoxes of feminist movements, see Scott (1998).

5   Weber's ideas were closely linked to the concept of a particular female mission that was generated as the politics of organized motherhood (see Cott 1987; Bock 1998: chap. IV, V).

6   Regarding Tönnies and Weber, see Lichtblau (1989/90, 1996); regarding the masculine thinking in Weber, see Bologh (1990); regarding Durkheim, see Lehmann (1991, 1994) and Roth (1989/90).

PART II

Contesting the canon: founders, feminists and excluded voices

The Englishwoman Harriet Martineau (1802–76) might be seen as the 'first sociologist' (Rossi 1973) given that she not only astutely analysed modern society as it was developing, but was also a successfully published, feminist social scientist. Martineau, who from the 1830s was able to live on the royalties from her publications, was an extremely versatile and productive author who worked in diverse fields and formed opinions in disparate disciplines: of particular note here are her religious papers and papers which criticize religion (for example, Martineau 1822; 1830), her educational advice (for example, Martineau 1849), her historical writings (for example, Martineau 1849–50), her political statements and comments (for example her contributions in the *London Daily News* between 1852 and 1866) or her literary essays aimed at both adults (for example, 1839) and children (for example, 1841). But it is her extensive sociological works that allow us to distinguish her from other successful nineteenth-century female authors, for it is here that she produced writings that pose genuine sociological questions and spark empirical research. Posing the question of how societies can be analysed and understood ([1838] 1989) led her to develop an original method and set up methodological principles to govern research into social reality. She did not stop at simply reflecting on research strategies, however, but applied these empirically to actual societies asking, for example, what is the relationship between theory – the promises of equality – and practice in American society (1837)? Elsewhere – in a cross-cultural comparative study – she looked at socio-historical and religious lines of societal development (Martineau 1848). In these works she always connected micro and macro sociological perspectives. For example, while micro sociological field studies shed light on the reality of life for women servants (Martineau 1838–9), Martineau recognized the ubiquity of unequal social relationships such as those of class, sex and race which framed them. Thus, contrary to the position taken by those recognized in the mainstream as the 'founding fathers' of sociology, inequality is not principally or solely the expression of class relationships, to which further inequalities, such as the relationship between the sexes, is subordinate or even naturalized. For Martineau, social antinomies are grounded in the relational 'circumstances' of individuals, and not in their psycho-physical, biologically determined dispositions. She explicitly criticized the insistence of her contemporaries on the 'all-pervading power of natural predispositions' as speculative, going against the ideas of the Enlightenment and progress and, due to its typifying effect, as an ideological instrument to ensure patriarchal hegemony. In her sociological writings she investigated the background to these 'circumstances', the consequences of different socialization processes and a politics of inequality derived from self-interest. As we will show, Martineau developed a consistently sociological approach in her writings, and even in the early stages of the discipline of sociology as we now know it, she generated central sociological concepts which remain valid today.

Biography and publication

> Authorship has never been with me a matter of choice. I have not
> done it for amusement, or for money, or for fame, or for any reason
> but because I could not help it. Things were pressing to be said; and
> there was more or less evidence that I was the person to say them.
>
> (Martineau 1877: vol. I, p. 188)

Harriet Martineau, born 1802 in Norwich, is a 'typical daughter' of the Age of
Enlightenment which, in England, was predominantly characterized by the
concepts of utilitarianism and deism. Belonging to a quite liberal and tolerant
middle-class English family, brought up as a Unitarian, she received a remarkable education even in subjects that were not typically taught to women.[1] A
sickly child, she was mainly taught at home by her elder brothers and sisters.
Supplementing this 'unformalized formal' education with an intense self-
study of several economic, political and theological theories, she was able to
acquire a relatively diverse and extensive knowledge. Her father's occupation
as a manufacturer meant that Martineau had a fairly comfortable childhood.
After his death in the 1820s the family became impoverished and Harriet
Martineau was left to rely on her own resources. At this time she started writing and publishing: first novels and stories.

Her transformation into an author who was respected in broad circles
came with the publication of her popular writings on economics: *Illustrations
of Political Economy* (1832–4), and subsequent works, prompted by politi-
cians, on the revision of the poor law (1833–4) and the revision of taxation
law (1834). Her decision to make the 'laws' of political economy, which
formed the theoretical frame of reference for her middle-class lifestyle (at
least until her father was ruined as a manufacturer), accessible to the
uneducated classes was rooted in the direct observation of social tensions in
the wake of crude, boom and bust Manchester capitalism, as well as in her
own understanding of the writings of Jane Marcet (Martineau 1877: vol. I,
p. 138) who, in the early years of the nineteenth century, produced a much
respected essay in the form of a mother–daughter dialogue which addressed
questions of political economy (Marcet 1816). In her *Illustrations*, Martineau
gives us well-founded, didactically constructed short stories. The plot around
which she wove her historical and internationally based stories was taken
directly from the works of the political economists – Smith, Bentham,
Ricardo, Malthus and John Stuart Mill. She packaged their central ideas (the
utilitarian principle of the maximum benefit or the 'holy dogma' of the
'greatest amount of happiness for the greatest number of people') in short
stories on subjects such as the principles of political economy, capital and
labour, population growth, finance and free trade, as well as addressing the
poor laws and taxation law (Escher 1925; Orazem 1999). Her interest as a

didact and communicator was at the forefront, as a broadening rather than a (critical) deepening of an enlightened education. Despite a negative prognosis for the success of her plans (Martineau 1877: vol. I, p. 169), Martineau made a commercial breakthrough with her *Illustrations* (Hoecker-Drysdale 1992: 33f). Her uncritical attitude to the core tenets of political economy brought her lasting recognition among broad sections of the population, including the political classes and contemporary authors in political economy. The acid-tongued critic of political economy, Karl Marx, clearly preferred to ignore her contributions by pouring his biting scorn on her in a brief aside (Marx 1975: 664).

After completion of *Illustrations*, Harriet Martineau decided to take an enjoyable and relaxing journey to America. En route she started to pull together methodically reflected ideas about 'how to observe' any society. She spent two years in America, where she tested her empirically orientated ideas. On her return from the United States she reported her observations in *Society in America* (1837) and in a shortened, more popular version in *Retrospect of Western Travel* (1838). In the same year, she published her principles and methods of empirical social research in *How to Observe Morals and Manners* ([1838] 1989).

In 1851 she began a translation of Auguste Comte's *Cours de philosophie positive*, aiming to win recognition for Comte's ideas. Following on from her earlier project, of popularizing the theories of the political economists and thereby enlightening broad sweeps of English society on the conditions and laws of societal development, the systematic grounding of science in the *Cours de philosophie positive* appeared to her to be the appropriate, and ultimately unique, correct answer to the increasing differentiation of sciences, which ought to be made accessible to an interested public – in the service of enlightenment:

> We are living in a remarkable time, when the conflict of opinions renders a firm foundation of knowledge indispensable, not only to our intellectual, moral, and social progress, but to our holding such ground as we have gained from former ages. While our science is split up into arbitrary divisions; while abstract and concrete science are confounded together, and even mixed up with their application to the arts, and with natural history; and while the researchers of the scientific world are presented as mere accretions to a heterogeneous mass of facts, there can be no hope of a scientific progress which shall satisfy and benefit those large classes of students whose business it is, not to explore, but to receive. The growth of a scientific taste among the working classes of this country is one of the most striking of the signs of the times. I believe no one can inquire into the mode of life of young men of the middle and operative classes without being struck

with the desire that is shown, and the sacrifices that are made, to obtain the means of scientific study.

(Martineau 1853: VII)

Comte's work seemed to her to be too long-winded in its exposition and too heavy duty in its language and 'overloaded with words' (Martineau 1853: VI). To achieve a broader acceptance of the work, she decided to condense the original into two volumes. This interpretive achievement was such a success that Comte preferred the English edition to his own French version, and used it as the basis for a revised edition (von Petzold 1941: 43). Above all, Comte himself praised her abridgement and assured her that he felt 'sure that your name will be linked with mine, for you have executed the only one of those works that will survive among all those which my fundamental treatise has called forth' (Comte, cited in Hill 1989: xlvii). Nevertheless, this achievement, which was expressly acknowledged by the 'founding father' of sociology, was not enough to secure her a place in this developing discipline.

Martineau died in 1876. In her home town of Norwich, a place where history and tradition are otherwise very important and where other significant people lived, there is no longer anything to remind us of her. On the house in which she spent her childhood there is, however, a small plaque which reads: 'James Martineau (1805–1900), Unitarian philosopher and teacher was born in this house and spent his boyhood here'. James was Harriet Martineau's younger brother, her self-confessed favourite.

'Though the facts sought by travellers relate to Persons, they may most readily be learned from Things' – moral and methodical conditions in observing a society

Until now, sociologists have been little concerned with characterising and defining the methods they use to examine social phenomena . . . A chapter of *Cours de philosophie positive* is almost the only original and important treatise there is.

(Emile Durkheim 1895: 103)

If Monsieur Durkheim views the chapter of Comte's *Cours de philosophie positive* as being '*almost*' the only original and important treatise on methodical questions, of whom else was he thinking when he said 'almost'? It was certainly not Harriet Martineau, although he could (and surely should) have known her. Her 'freely translated and condensed' edition of *The Positive Philosophy of Auguste Comte* (1853) gained some recognition at least, even in France. However, the promised 'link', of which Comte had spoken, was not strong enough. In his considerations on how to observe social phenomena, Durkheim wrote much about Comte and Spencer but not a word about

Martineau. To him she obviously didn't exist. Certainly he could have learned a lot from the methodical reflections she developed in about 250 pages of her book *How to Observe Morals and Manners* ([1838] 1989). Durkheim's *Règles de la méthode sociologique* (trans. [1895] 1982), which is still regarded by the discipline as the first fully elaborated and therefore significant sociological work of methodical consideration, would probably have been to some extent unnecessary.

There are some assumptions and notions about 'how to observe' any society which are shared by Martineau and Durkheim. Let us examine an example of this 'intellectual affinity' between Martineau and Durkheim here. For instance, Martineau wrote:

> There is no department of inquiry in which it is not full as easy to miss truth as to find it, even when the materials from which truth is to be drawn are actually present to our senses. A child does not catch a gold fish in water at the first trial, however good his eyes may be, and however clear the water; knowledge and method are necessary to enable him to take what is actually before his eyes and under his hand. So is it with all who fish in a strange element for the truth which is living and moving there: the powers of observation must be trained, and habits of method in arranging the materials presented to the eye must be acquired before the student possesses the requisites for understanding what he contemplates.
>
> (Martineau [1838] 1989: 13)

And 60 years later, we find in Durkheim:

> Thus our rule implies no metaphysical conception, no speculation about the innermost depth of being. What it demands is that the sociologist should assume the state of mind of physicists, chemists and physiologists when they venture into an as yet unexplored area of their scientific field. As the sociologist penetrates into the social world he should be conscious that he is penetrating into the unknown. He must feel himself in the presence of facts governed by laws as yet unsuspected as those of life before the science of biology was evolved. He must hold himself ready to make discoveries which will surprise and disconcert him.
>
> (Durkheim [1895] 1982: 37–8)

It may be that the spirit of the time led both to form similar or associated ideas. It is fact, however, that Martineau developed and published her thesis a considerable time before Durkheim.

Martineau's considerations start with the problem of how the evident differences in social life within one society and in different societies can be recorded, interpreted and transferred into what we would call today an ethnographically sound description. In her writing, Martineau develops quasi ideal/typical assumptions of a 'good' society, which are used as the benchmarks for assessing the level of development of the society being analysed. In this way, historical process can be understood as an ascending and, when all is said and done, goal-orientated development process: societies pass through various stages of civilization, from a 'barbarous state' to an 'enlightened state'. The criterion for achievement of this final stage is the extent and distribution of 'happiness'. For Martineau, the measure of this 'happiness' is the freedom within which man can act in a morally responsible manner. Hallmarks of the 'ideal' society are the fair distribution of material wealth, comprehensive public education, the realization of sexual equality, effective and ordered self-government and a progressive cultural and scientific development. With these criteria upon which to measure itself, no society could conceive of reaching the end of its developmental life. She therefore questions the consequences of the dominant morals and manners in relation to different social practices. If there is still inequality despite increasing civilization, through which moral ideas and social practice is such inequality legitimized?

Consequently, she enquires into the nature of social experience. At first glance the relationships between people – between men and women, between individuals of different social positions or of race – appear to define such experience. The way in which these relationships are concretely shaped, however, is dependent on the prevailing ethical/moral principles and the resultant actions and behaviour (manners). This difference between the appearance of a social phenomenon and its nature makes it imperative that a well-founded research methodology and a method be drawn up; a method which deciphers the meaning of a 'social fact' using interpretative processes.

And how can the 'morals and manners' of any civilization be established? This is precisely the question that Martineau aims to explore in her reflections on 'how to observe morals and manners'. First, an independent method of research and logical enquiry are required. The would-be social researcher must undergo three-fold training: intellectual, ethical and practical.

On the intellectual level, the researcher must acquire an appropriate competence that enables critical reflection on personal impressions and prejudices. He or she must be careful to not create prejudice. Martineau sees the main obstacle for social progress and human development in the production and reproduction of narrow-mindedness regarding foreigners and unknown social and cultural habits. Therefore she insists on creating specifically responsible ethics, to leave the restrictions of unreflected observations behind. This specific research ethic – which is also the second stage of training – includes three indispensable 'requisites': first, the observer should define the aim of his or her observation. She or he must be certain what she or he actually wants to know.

Just collecting information by observing the people of a foreign country does not really help our understanding of the distinct habits of individuals or the cultural and social differences between the nation visited and the traveller's country of origin. Coming to the second requisite – finding out the common denominator of observations – Martineau is looking for the opportunity to obtain some useful results. What can be concluded from discovering the various ways in which people live together? What judgements can be drawn from observation of the divergent circumstances existing in different societies? The following quotation illustrates how Martineau examines social practices by taking gender and cultural differences as categories for analysis:

> In the extreme North, there is the snow-hut of the Esquimaux, shining with the fire within, like an alabaster lamp left burning in a wide waste; within the beardless father is mending his weapons made of fishbones, while the dwarfed mother swathes her infant in skins, and feeds it with oil and fat. In the extreme East, there is the Chinese family in their garden, treading its paved walks, or seated under the shade of its artificial rocks; the master displaying the claws of his left hand as he smokes his pipe, and his wife tottering on her deformed feet as she follows her child – exulting over it if it be a boy; grave and full of sighs if heaven has sent her none but girls. In the extreme South, there is the Colonist of the Cape, lazily basking before his door, while he sends his labourer abroad with his bullock-wagon, devolves the business of the farm upon the women, and scares from his door any poor Hottentot who may have wandered hither over the plain. In the extreme West, there is the gathering together on the shores of the Pacific of the hunters laden with furs. The men are trading, or cleaning their arms, or sleeping; the squaws are cooking, or dyeing with vegetable juices the quills of the porcupine or the hair of the moose-deer. In the intervals between these extremities, there is a world of morals and manners, as diverse as the surface of the lands on which they are exhibited.
>
> (Martineau [1838] 1989: 30f)

The duty of the responsible traveller now consists of working out the common denominator of all observations. What connects and underlies all observable manners? Only if he or she figures out this, can he or she be certain of having a useful criterion and test for all his or her observations. It is the pursuit of happiness that connects all manners. Furthermore, sensitive research requires 'a philosophical and definite . . . notion about the origin of human feelings of right and wrong' (Martineau [1838] 1989: 51). Contradicting the popular notion that the 'human feelings of right and wrong' belong to the natural make-up of human beings, Martineau insists that these feelings are formed by circumstances. Here she argues with a historical and a cross-cultural perspective:

> Now, mankind are, and always have been, so far from agreeing as to right and wrong, that it is necessary to account in some manner for the wide differences in various ages, and among various nations . . . A person who takes for granted that there is an universal Moral Sense among men . . . cannot reasonably explain how it was that those men were once esteemed the most virtuous who killed the most enemies in battle, while now it is considered far more noble to save life than to destroy. They cannot but wonder how it was that it was once thought a great shame to live in misery, and an honour to commit suicide; while now the wisest and best men think exactly reverse. And, with regard to the present age, it must puzzle men who suppose that all ought to think alike on moral subjects, that there are parts of the world where mothers believe it a duty to drown their children, and that eastern potentates openly deride the king of England for having only one wife instead of hundred . . . We see that in other cases – with regard to science, to art, and to the appearances of nature – feelings grow out of knowledge and experience; and there is every evidence that it is so with regard to morals.
>
> (Martineau [1838] 1989: 33ff)

The third requisite relates to the problem of acknowledgement. Although Martineau disputes that there is such a thing as an innate 'human feeling of right and wrong', the question of pinpointing the origin of human morals remains. Or to put it another way: is there a universal moral value that is also central to the idea of justice? And who guarantees this universal moral value? In her view it results from a 'gigantic general influence' (Martineau [1838] 1989: 51) that is to be understood as an external, divine-like system or metaphysical value. The social observer is obliged to acknowledge this universal principle. Even if the fundamental principle is a universal principle, ideas of how to achieve it depend on the different social and cultural practices of the various societies. All behaviour must be interpreted on the basis of this generally applicable moral principle. Martineau warns inexperienced researchers about the 'observation trap', whereby an action may be considered moral in one society but have negative connotations in another. Recognized behaviour from one's own society must not be used as a key to the moral basis of behaviour in another. All forms of ethnocentrism represent a serious risk for those who wish to understand other cultures by observing them.

On the practical level of research (Martineau [1838] 1989: 232ff), Martineau suggests the use of diverse, carefully implemented investigative techniques such as making a field diary, recording conversations or copying registers. Having established the conditions necessary for observing in a 'good order', Martineau glances at the object of observation: what must be observed to gain true ideas about the state of morals and manners in any society? Is it necessary to interview men and women? Martineau doesn't think so. Instead, she advocates careful collection of social facts:

> The grand secret of wise inquiry into Morals and Manners is to begin with the study of *things*, using the *discourse of persons* as a commentary upon them. Though the facts sought by travellers relate to Persons, they may most readily be learned from Things. The eloquence of Institutions and Records, in which the action of the nation is embodied and perpetuated, is more comprehensive and more faithful than that of any variety of individual voices. The voice of a whole people goes up in the silent workings of an institution; the condition of the masses is reflected from the surface of a record.
>
> (Martineau 1838a: 73f)[2]

Since Martineau sets herself the task of assessing the moral status of societies as a whole, and since this assessment depends largely on the empirically gathered facts (although interpreted in the light of universal principles), the quality of the observation data is of vital importance. Martineau repeatedly and emphatically makes the point that observations must be representative. Bias is to be avoided. All institutionalized specimens must be observed in all locations, within all classes, in all areas. Observers must not be influenced by the ruling classes and must, at the same time, remain open to opinions and insights – a difficult task even for experienced researchers.

Within this part of her reflections Martineau presents an abundance of examples and evidence of how the 'institutions' and 'records' of any nation can tell a story about the specific morals and manners. She explores in fields that include culture ('religion', 'general moral notions'), economy ('domestic state') and politics ('idea of liberty', 'progress'), themes like national identity, domestic relations and their consequences for the situation of women, social classes, types of religion, normality and deviance, types of suicide and the meaning of repressive social institutions. The recording of micro sociological phenomena – for example, the differences in the lives of those who live in the town and those who live in the country, different eating and drinking cultures, cultural habits and tendencies both at home and outside the home, the provision of commodities, family life, the significance of the dead for the living and so on – provides us with information about the macro sociological status of a society, that is the ethical constitution of a society. To give an example:

> The traveller everywhere finds woman treated as the inferior party in a compact in which both parties have an equal interest. Any

agreement thus formed is imperfect, and is liable to disturbance. The degree of the degradation of woman is as good a test as the moralist can adopt for ascertaining the state of domestic morals in any country. The Indian squaw carries the household burdens, trudging in the dust, while her husband on horseback paces before her, unencumbered but by his own gay trappings. She carries the wallet with food, the matting for the lodge, the merchandise (if they possess any) and her infant. There is no exemption from labour for the squaw of the most vaunted chief. In other countries the wife may be found drawing the plough, hewing wood and carrying water; the men of the family standing idle to witness her toils. Here the observer may feel pretty sure of his case. From a condition of slavery like this, women are found rising to the highest condition in which they are at present seen in France, England and the United States – where they are less than half-educated, precluded from earning a subsistence, except in a very few ill-paid employments, and prohibited from giving or withholding their assent to laws which they are yet bound by penalties to obey.

(Martineau [1838] 1989: 178f)

Martineau's methodological proposals are those of a sophisticated social theorist who keenly understands two critical and fundamental principles: first, that all observers, irrespective of how carefully they work, make mistakes, can read too much into something and can become the victims of their own assumptions, and second, that it is in our nature that human beings are selective and make interpretations in their intervention in the social world.

'While woman's intellect is confined . . .' – on the position of women in the US

Men are ungentle, tyrannical. They abuse the right of the strongest, however they may veil the abuse with indulgence. They want the magnanimity to discern woman's human rights; and they crush her morals rather than allow them. Women are, as might be anticipated, weak, ignorant and subservient, in as far as they exchange self-reliance for reliance on anything out of themselves.

(Martineau 1837: 162)

In *Society in America* (1837), in which she compared life in North America with the theoretical claims of a democratic system, Martineau describes the political and legislative institutions in the US, its economy, social norms and cultural life. She stresses the differences between agricultural practices in Great Britain and those in the US, concerns herself with the effects of the slave trade on the economic system and analyses the position of women.

In the section on women, Martineau argues that a democracy in which the power of the ruling class depends on the consent of those being governed, yet one that simultaneously excludes women completely, is absurd. She found that although the legal status of women in the US was better than that in Europe, their position was basically the same as that of slaves in that they had no political voice, their life was heteronomous and they were invisible in public life. This exclusion from political reality was camouflaged as gallantry, which resulted in destruction of women's individuality. Martineau was a harsh judge of 'pro-women' campaigners such as Jefferson in America or John Stuart Mill in England. She strongly rejected the view that it would be best if women were represented by their protective husbands or fathers. She argued that the interests of women and men are not the same and thus could neither be 'delegated' to men nor withheld from women. When comparing the education of women in both England and America, she found similarities in that in both countries women were only given a smattering of knowledge and hence remained excluded from the professions. The greatest disadvantage to women in America was their systematic exclusion from gainful employment.

Martineau also addressed, in her conclusion, the issue of how such an asymmetrical social relationship was established and maintained. She discovered that, essentially, women in America were subjected to a hegemonic relationship which, whether they knew it or not, left them scarred. This hegemonic relationship is characterized by the dominance of the 'masters' – legitimized as chivalry – over women. So what happens to women during this process? They are swindled out of their individuality and are subject to the illusion that they can realize themselves in their exile to the familial and private spheres. How did this prevailing ideology of gender become ingrained in the minds of women?

Martineau concludes from her observations that this situation is the outcome not of an individual, but a structural power/dominance relationship where the conditions of socialization seem to be responsible for the subordinate role played by women in gender relationships. In marked contrast to predominant scientific ideas of the time, Martineau did not see nature as the cause of the apparent difference between the sexes. So what were the methods of education? Martineau makes a distinction between two forms that are causally related. There was an official and a sinister syllabus for the education of the sexes. The official syllabus, which is addressed relatively early in life, determined what boys should learn and what girls should learn, and which abilities and skills they should develop. This, in turn, was determined by the content of the 'sinister' syllabus for the education of the sexes resulting from the 'discipline of circumstance' (Martineau 1837: 157). The content of this 'sinister syllabus' for women suggested that, as there were no concrete roles for women in public life, women did not need comprehensive education or training. Martineau draws a direct parallel here between (backward-thinking) English education and (supposedly democratic, egalitarian) American education. There were abilities and skills that everyone learnt in both countries, the essential outcome of which was to maintain women in an inferior position:

> The intellect of woman is confined by an unjustifiable restriction of both methods of education – by express teaching, and by the discipline of circumstance . . . There is a profession of some things being taught which are supposed necessary because everybody learns them. They serve to fill up time, to occupy attention harmlessly, to improve conversation, and to make women something like companions to their husbands, and able to teach their children somewhat. But what is given is, for the most part, passively received; and what is obtained is, chiefly, by means of the memory. There is rarely or never a careful ordering of influences for the promotion of clear intellectual activity.
> (Martineau 1837: 157)

How could women develop as individuals under these circumstances? What opportunities and perspectives did they have? Martineau makes the point that in the US they could hope for nothing but marriage. An alternative to this would be another genuinely female area of work: religion. Martineau exposes this apparent option as pure ideology, for in contemplating religious questions, women find, at best, a way of passing time and gaining a moral education. For Martineau, the 'true' domain of intellectual discussion is not religion itself, but the science of religion, or theology. Yet here, as with other areas of scientific endeavour, women were denied entry. In this respect, women in America (just like their European sisters) were forced back to the institution of marriage, for which they were exclusively and systematically prepared, and at the same time learnt to act as though they wanted nothing more.

Martineau concluded that female morals and consciousness, in American society too, are suppressed and corrupted. The 'discovery' made during the Enlightenment, that all people have the gifts of reason and understanding and must *responsibly* take their place in society, now evidently applies to only part of humanity. If gender-specific education fails, in the sense that women are no longer content simply to adopt their allocated place in the 'house and home', there is a more polished instrument available which is to send them back behind their barriers. The public opinion machine pounces on those who express subversive political opinions. This repressive ruling apparatus functions superbly. Martineau describes the repressive strategies used on many women in her writings on slavery. She concludes that women are 'permitted' to act charitably and compassionately, but not politically.

Martineau asserts that the division of the relationship between the sexes, the allocation of the 'public' sphere to men and 'private' sphere to women, is the result of a repressive process of assertion of ownership and dominance. This superordinate/subordinate relationship between the sexes is established using the vehicles of education and gender politics. What began as a socially mediated socialization process has been de-socialized and quasi-naturalized. Martineau disputes the prevailing view that there are typically male and typically female virtues. She does not deny that there are specifically male/female capacities for labour, something that cannot be addressed by any researcher since people are already social beings. However, it is not scientifically sound to conclude from this, anecdotally, that virtues generally considered 'robust' can be attributed to men, and that the more gentle virtues can be attributed to women. This kind of model does not explain the difference between the sexes, but legitimizes what is ultimately a patriarchal relationship.

When 'founding fathers' were adversaries. Jenny P. d'Héricourt and the critique of emerging sociological discourse

> Each [political writer] gives himself his own theme; each takes off from his own ideas, his own system, and his own theory, and often his ideas are prejudices, his system is a novel and his theory a chimera.
>
> (Comte 1816–28)

When the French social philosopher Jenny P. d'Héricourt was criticizing contemporary social thinkers in journal articles and open letters in the 1850s, it was not just her severe comments and her provocative opinions that caused a sensation. Just as scandalous was the fact that a woman was meddling in the discussion of modern society. Pierre-Joseph Proudhon, a writer on political economy in whose work both the emergence of a theory of anarchy and theorems of early sociology were worked out (Ansart 1967), was one of those who picked up the debate with d'Héricourt, only to abruptly break it off again. In December 1856, d'Héricourt had published an open letter entitled 'Mister Proudhon and the women's question', which contained a severe critique of his repeated derogatory remarks regarding the 'natural' lesser value of women and the impossibility of an egalitarian societal arrangement between women and men. In January 1857, Proudhon informed his critic, also in the form of an open letter, that he might well enter into an intellectual debate with her, but that she ought to allow herself to be represented by a male 'guardian' (*parrain*) who would sign her articles and take responsibility for everything she said. He declared his intention to perform an 'intellectual and moral autopsy' on her. In this endeavour he would necessarily have to infringe all the 'rules of propriety' that men are expected to observe for women – and to which he personally felt obliged – as Jenny P. d'Héricourt had herself asked him not to sacrifice his powers of argument to gallantry. Admittedly she would not like this – Proudhon knew his opponent – but this, he wrote, was a disadvantage of her position as a woman that she would have to bear bravely. And another reason listed by Proudhon that had little to do with propriety yet went to the core of the dispute was the fact that by addressing his views to a woman, he would be acknowledging her. It would be inconsistent and indeed paradoxical to argue for the predominance of the man by entering into debate with a woman, Proudhon wrote, anticipating his opponent's comment. D'Héricourt could not possibly have imagined, he concluded, that he would fall into this trap (Proudhon 1857: 166f).

Indeed, to have recognized a woman as a partner in debate would have meant granting her authority as a speaking subject in a discussion of the social. This was precisely what Proudhon was so fervently rejecting. In this sense, this dispute should not be treated as an isolated incident. Instead, this episode can be seen as a paradigmatic expression of what is at stake here: the contested foundations of the masculinization of the subject ('the sociologist') and the object ('the social') in the debate about modern society at a time at which the 'incubation period' of sociology was drawing to a close and the actual 'foundation period' of the discipline was about to come into being (Lepenies 1981a: IX). Our intention is to show that although this masculinization was asserted as self-evident, it was at the same time contested and fragile. Pierre-Joseph Proudhon's refusal to respond to a woman addressing him demonstrates the efforts to impose the social and cognitive identity of a discourse in which the literal masculinity of the speaker and the metaphorical masculinity of the social are mutually reinforcing.[3] It is significant that the literal woman, Jenny P. d'Héricourt, need not be silenced, but must be made to vanish behind a literally masculine guardian. This not only illustrates the dependence of the metaphorical masculinity of the discourse on the literal masculinity of its speaker, but also the dependence of the literal masculinity of the speaker on the metaphorical masculinity of the discourse – hence the emotional undercurrent of Proudhon's reaction to his opponent. More well-disposed, but just as irritated as Proudhon, the literary critic Jules de Goncourt declared that d'Héricourt had 'in her style the omnipotence of the beard' (quoted by Adam 1904: 55), while others, somewhat less amicably, maintained that she was a 'reasoning machine' (quoted by d'Héricourt [1864] 1981: XI). Quite clearly, the irritation caused by a woman arrogating to herself authorship in the discourse on the social can only be nullified by a metaphorical 'defeminization' or even 'dehumanization' of the author or by the literal 'masculinization' of her words by a 'guardian'.

D'Héricourt was, of course, less than impressed by Proudhon's demand and steadfastly pursued her critique publicly and under her own name. Her

point was precisely to assert *as a woman* the right to shape the discourse: 'Now
. . . it belongs to me, a woman, to speak myself on behalf of my rights, without
leaning on anything but Justice and Reason' (d'Héricourt [1864] 1981: 208).
This is how she introduces her deliberations on social theory in her book,
Women Affranchized (1800). The declared aim of this book was not to explain
society, but 'to prove that woman has the same rights as man' (d'Héricourt
[1864] 1981: IX). However it was her analysis of the conditions of female existence in society, as well as her critique of contemporary theories on femininity
and masculinity, that steered her thinking in genuinely sociological directions, despite the fact that there were as yet no clear lines of demarcation
between discussions of 'the social' and those of philosophy, literature or the
natural sciences. This discourse on 'the social', however, already had a
'founding father' in the person of Auguste Comte, and it was with Comte that
d'Héricourt engaged critically. As a preface to d'Héricourt's critique of Comte
we first recapitulate the author's biography in brief.

Biography

Jenny P. d'Héricourt was born in Besançon in 1809 as Jeanne-Marie-Fabienne
Poinsard, daughter of a Protestant and republican couple (see Offen (1987)
for more on d'Héricourt's biography). The pseudonym 'd'Héricourt' was
taken for the Lutheran village of the Franche-Comté her father came from
and stresses her attachment to her religious and political origins. After her
father's death in 1817, the family moved to Paris. In 1827 d'Héricourt finished training to be teacher; in 1832 she married the civil servant Michel-
Gabriel-Joseph Marie whom she left four years later. From 1836 on she took
private lessons in anatomy, physiology and history of nature. In 1852 she did
a course in midwifery at the Maternité in Paris and subsequently opened a
consulting room for women and children. Already having placed 'herself on
the ground which men preserve for themselves' (d'Héricourt quoted in Offen
1987: 156) by studying natural sciences and practising medicine, she
encroached further on masculine terrain by intervening in the theoretical
debate about modern society and the question of women. This wasn't, however, her first engagement in post-revolutionary social theory and politics.
Jenny P. d'Héricourt had already some experience as an adherent of the early
communist movement in the 1840s, having worked with the communist
Etienne Cabet, writing articles and short stories for his newspaper as well as a
novel, at the heart of which was an intense social critique. By 1848 she had
abandoned her commitment to communism, criticizing the lack of consideration of the status of women in the communist movement. She had participated in the early feminist movement whose demands were ignored by the
Seconde République in 1848 and which was totally repressed by the regime
of Napoleon III in the 1850s. In these years d'Héricourt became a collabor-

ator in the Parisian *Revue philosophique et religieuse*, a liberal and Protestant review concerned with social philosophy and politics. In this review she wrote critiques of Christianity, several articles on homeopathic medicine, as well as critiques of Auguste Comte, Pierre-Joseph Proudhon and the historian Jules Michelet. In 1860 her main work, *La femme affranchie. Réponse à MM. Michelet, Proudhon, E. de Girardin, A. Comte et aux autres novateurs modernes* (1860) was published and four years later an abridged version was translated into English.[4] In this book she re-published her articles from the *Revue philosophique et religieuse* and added further critiques of political and social movements and theorists. Furthermore, she developed her own social theory, wrote about the social and legal position of women in France and provided a programme for a feminist movement as well as an educational programme. In 1863 Jenny P. d'Héricourt moved to Chicago, where she worked with the American feminist movement until her return to France roughly ten years later. She died in 1875 and left some manuscripts that were probably burnt after her death.

Auguste Comte and the female brain: the scientific critique

Jenny P. d'Héricourt would probably have disagreed with a history of sociology that declares Auguste Comte as a 'founding father' of the discipline. Admittedly, she engaged with the 'late' Comte, the Comte who in the last decade of his life declared positivism to be a 'religion' and who had, in 1852, written a *Catéchisme positiviste ou Sommaire exposition de la religion universelle de l'humanité* which is not counted as one of the canonical texts, even in the history of sociology, but rather is attributed to a pathological personality development.[5] Yet d'Héricourt, too, distinguishes the Comte of the catechism as the promulgator of a 'socio-religious organization' from the 'rational' Comte of the *Cours de philosophie positive* and the *Système de politique positive* (d'Héricourt [1864] 1981: 119) – whose dissemination a critically informed Martineau had made her own task. D'Héricourt is, however, convinced that, while the former Comte was no more than the vulgarizer of his teacher, Saint-Simon, the latter Comte was the true, original Comte. And the writing of this Comte could not be recommended 'unless in your heart and soul you believe yourself deserving of many years of purgatory, which you prefer to expiate on the earth' (d'Héricourt [1864] 1981: 119f). It was not only Auguste Comte's poor style, which was and continues to be obfuscatory, that caused readers endless suffering. More importantly for Jenny P. d'Héricourt, who had been trained in Enlightenment rationalism and Kantian thinking, were 'the clouds and mists of metaphysics' in which Comte's thinking enveloped itself and threatened to envelop others (d'Héricourt 1855: 47).[6]

With typical irony, d'Héricourt seizes on the 'mission' that Comte places on women and translates it into an authorization of her position as an intellectual opponent:

> Being a woman, I am, in Mister Comte's opinion one of the greatest representations of the Great Being, a piece of the highest social providence, a moral providence. With all these titles, I must be heard respectfully by the grand priest of humanity. He shall listen to me then.
>
> (D'Héricourt 1855: 55)

Auguste Comte was, of course, not thinking of theoretical critique when he spoke of the unique moral mission of woman, as in his eyes it was by affectivity, not intellect, that the female character defined itself. And he saw this exclusive affective competence as being grounded in the female brain that, for its part, did not give women the capacity for intellectual or productive activity. From these anatomical 'facts' Comte derived sex-typed functions: women belong to family and home where they fulfil their mission in making men sociable and moral persons and therefore in providing the necessary condition for society. Influenced by female affectivity, men can learn to temper their natural tendency to individualize, synonymous with egoism, and to develop instead their sociability, synonymous with altruism. Women, while making society possible, do not engage *in* society, defined as it is as the net of inter-relationships of productive and intellectual *men*. Hence, women are the theoretical matter of 'social statics', while men are the theoretical matter of 'social dynamics' which constitutes the proper object of the science of 'sociology'. Women therefore are at once charged with the most fundamental problem of modern society – the guarantee of social integration – and at the same time excluded from society. They were supposedly able to exert an imminent influence on men while at the same time subjected to patriarchal control by men in the family and the state.

There are reasons associated with the history of science for the proto-sociological question of the organization of society overlapping with natural-science argumentation in Comte's anatomical foundation of an order of things in this vein. On the one hand, proto-sociological discourse was heavily associated with the biological sciences.[7] On the other hand, the biological sciences themselves were increasingly important as a reference point for the elaboration of sexual difference and gender relations which was given impetus by the upsurge of the excessively meaningful 'women's special anthropology' in the eighteenth and nineteenth centuries (Honegger 1991b; see also Jordanova 1989; Laqueur 1990). D'Héricourt does not deny that there could be a relationship between the biological and social conditions of women and men. She too has recourse to Comte's expert witnesses on the subject of female affectivity and male intellectualism and productivity that phrenology attributed to differentiated brains. Yet natural science thinking does not mislead her into the determinist reductionism for which she rebukes Comte:

> Since you believe in Gall and Spurzheim, you know that the encephalon of the two sexes is alike, that it is modifiable in both, that all education is founded on this modificability; why has it never occurred to you that if man *en masse* is more rational than woman, it is because education, laws and custom have developed in him the anterior lobes of the brain; while in woman, education, laws, and custom develop especially the posterior lobes of this organ; and why, having established these facts, have you not been led to conclude that, since organs are developed only in consequence of the excitants applied to them, it is probable that man and woman, subjected to the same cerebral excitants, would be developed in the same manner, with the shades of difference peculiar to each individuality; and that for woman to be developed harmoniously under her three aspects, she must manifest herself socially under three aspects? Be sure, sir, your principle is thrice false, thrice in contradiction to science and reason; in the presence of the physiology of the brain, all theories of classification fall to the ground: before the nervous system, women are the equals of men: they can be their inferiors only before muscular supremacy, attacked by the invention of powder, and about to be reduced to dust by the triumph of mechanism.
>
> (D'Héricourt [1864] 1981: 132f)

D'Héricourt first denies any causal-deterministic relation between a fixed brain structure on the one hand and sex-typed functions and a corresponding social structure on the other hand. Against this sort of reductionism, she uses a scientific argument for a sociological consideration of sexual differences and gender relations. She argues that all human organs, including the brain, are modifiable and by that modifiability humans get a 'second nature' by habitualization specific to the social milieu and the educational influence. Hence, d'Héricourt insisted on the social, cultural and historical dimension of differences between women and men: if women were indeed less rational and more affective than men, this was an effect of societal organization and cultural customs and therefore subject to historical change. For d'Héricourt there is a comprehensive potential in all humans, independent of their sex, and unbalanced development of this potential leads to a perversion of human nature:

> But you, who wish to annihilate woman, from what principle do you draw such a consequence? That she is an affective power, you say . . . yes, but, as to that, man is such, likewise; and is not woman, as well

as he, alike intellect and activity? By reason of a purely accidental predominance, can one half of the human species be banished beyond the clouds of sentimentality? And ought not all serious discipline to tend to develop, not one phase of the being, but the ponderation, the harmony of all its phases? Want of harmony is the source of disorder and deformity. The woman who is solely sentimental commits irreparable errors; the man who is solely rational is a species of monster, and the person in whom activity predominates is but a brute.

(D'Héricourt [1864] 1981: 132)

From this perspective, far from proving a natural difference and natural inequality between women and men, phrenology instead reveals a natural equality of all human beings. As in a truly modern society where everyone is equal before the law – the allusion is evident – everyone is 'equal before the nervous system'. To follow d'Héricourt's own reasoning: since everyone is equal before the nervous system, everyone is equal in society and there is no scientific justification possible for the confinement of women to affective functions and their subordination under the political control of men. Comte's scientific reasoning was revealed as nothing other than a political option which d'Héricourt called unmistakably the 'social annihilation' of women (d'Héricourt [1864] 1981: 69, 132).

Theories of classification: the epistemological critique

Since Comte's and others' outlines of a social theory were operating with underlying theories of sexual difference, d'Héricourt added to her scientific critique an epistemological critique which resulted in what may tentatively be called an 'agnosticism' towards every attempt to theorize sexual difference. Her starting point was that all existing definitions of maleness and femaleness didn't match the heterogeneity of social reality: 'Men, and women after them, have deemed it proper hitherto to class man and woman separately; to define each type, and to deduce from this ideal the functions suited to each sex. Neither has chosen to see that numerous facts contradict this classification' (D'Héricourt [1864] 1981: 225). D'Héricourt didn't deny the existence of a presocial sexual difference; she was even convinced that biological differences between the sexes relate to an ontological difference. However, this ontological difference could be neither described nor theorized:

> We do not give a classification, because we neither have nor can have one; the elements for its establishment are lacking. A biological deduction permits us to affirm that such a one exists; but it is impossible to disengage its law in the present surroundings; the veritable

feminine stamp will be known only after one or two centuries of like education and equal rights.

(D'Héricourt [1864] 1981: 243f)

Therefore, a social theory that claims the naturalness of differences result-ing from socialization and prescribed social positions mistakes for pre-social sexual difference what in fact is an effect of power relations and the will to tame heterogeneity:[8] 'Ah no, gentlemen, these are not men and women; they are the deplorable results of your selfishness, of your frightful spirit of domin-ation, of your imbecility . . .' (d'Héricourt [1864] 1981: 245). Since the existing differences between women and men are social and not ontological facts, these differences cannot in any way be a legitimation for sex-typed social functions and political inequality, and neither can they be legitimized by an appeal to ontological difference that must be assumed but at present cannot be known.

If the ontological difference between the sexes could be recognized when – and only when – the social influence is precisely determined, then know-ledge of the difference between the sexes itself remains, at best, doubtful and purely speculative. The essence behind the phenomenon of the difference between the sexes is fundamentally beyond human knowledge and the methods of the scientific view: 'Our reason can only recognise the phenomena and their laws, but not the essence of things or their ultimate causes. These do not belong to the domain of science' (D'Héricourt 1860: vol. II, p. 253). The reality beyond its manifest phenomenon can never be adequately represented by knowledge, because knowledge always organizes itself in categories, which abstract from the variety of social reality. These categories systematize and classify reality, but do not coincide with it. Since objective reality is only mani-fest in the appearance, the abstracts of 'femininity' or 'masculinity' exist only as qualities of a female or male individual. If the category of 'sex' is only conceivable through abstraction from the individuality of all women and men and, at the same time, the quality of 'sex' is only realized in the individual being, then neither does the individuality dissolve in membership of a sex, nor is the sexual identity suspended in individual being: 'There are as many differ-ent men as there are male individuals, as many different women as female individuals' (D'Héricourt 1860: vol. II, p. 114). And this also means that once centuries of non-sex-typed education and social organization have passed, any reason for classification of humanity into women and men will become superfluous: 'then there will be no need of a classification, for the function will fall naturally to the proper functionary under a system of equality in which the social elements classify themselves' (d'Héricourt [1864] 1981: 243f).

D'Héricourt argues from a position between biological determinism and social constructivism and thus within those epistemological parameters in which the modern debate over the difference between the sexes and sexual relations is caught. Given, however, that neither of these two perspectives admit a primacy of knowledge of the difference between the sexes, she argues against reductionisms of any kind and opts for an ontologically agnostic attitude. Thus she wrenches the phenomenon of the differences between the sexes from the grip of the biologists, and opens it up to a genuinely sociological analysis. In this way she extends the reach of sociological consideration of society and the modern. She asserts, again in opposition to Comte and the contemporary hegemonic thinking regarding the difference between the sexes, the possibility and facticity of female individuality that in the context of modern social theories also means the possibility and facticity of female capacities to associate in modern society.[9]

Beyond masculinity: the empirical critique and fragments of a theory of modern society

If Auguste Comte positioned his desk vis-à-vis a mirror and 'was always looking at himself' when he wrote (Lepenies 1988: 46), then d'Héricourt must have worked at an open window. Her thinking was shot through with a clear and unwavering sense of social reality, which anchored her theoretical activity. She criticized Comte's theory precisely because it ignored the reach of empirically observable social change. 'They say, gentleman, that you don't read anymore, and I could convince myself of that fact, since it seems that you don't know a word about the mental and material state of the different elements of our French society, especially in what concerns my sex' (d'Héricourt 1855: 59). For woman, d'Héricourt claimed, 'is no longer confined to the care of children and household, but instead she is engaged more and more in the production of national and individual welfare' (d'Héricourt 1860: vol. II, p. 273).

Yet this factual 'integration' of women into the labour market was paralleled by her exclusion of civil and political rights, by her subordination under patriarchal control in the state and in marriage, and this, d'Héricourt was convinced, revealed an imminent social pathology. Woman must be man's equal in every aspect of social life, 'because the progress of Enlightenment, in which woman participates, has transformed her in social power, and because this new power produces evil in default of the good which it is not permitted to do' (d'Héricourt [1864] 1981: X). Therefore the emancipation of woman is not only the political imperative of an enlightened society that claims to constitute itself as a just one, but also a social necessity.

Implicitly, d'Héricourt's reasoning relates to the problem which was of most intense concern to pre-sociological discourse and through which this discourse gained its specificity that should lead to the emergence of the sociological discipline: the question of how social order is possible (Luhmann 1996: 21). It was her claim for female individuality which led d'Héricourt to face this problem more radically than Comte did, while her critique revealed that her adversary's theorizing of female and male functions was far more than an ephemeral issue of his sociology. Auguste Comte saw a modern society that was founded on the division of labour, as constantly menaced by an excess of (male) individualization through specialization that would inescapably lead to disintegration. His theoretical construction of egoistic, individualized man tending to disintegration, and altruistic, non-individualized woman as the bulwark against such disintegration was therefore intricately woven into his answer to the question of social order in a modern society. This radical and essential dualism of women's and men's functional positions in society was, for Comte, nothing less than an indispensable condition of social integration.

For d'Héricourt, what was fundamentally wrong in this theory – besides the mistaken ontology of sexual difference – was Comte's idea of (male) individualism leading genuinely to disintegration if it was not tamed by (female) altruism:

> To live for others, this is the basis of your moral. My answer to you is: this moral is false and unjust; false because it does not take account of the two elements of any moral code: the individual and society; unjust because if it is bad for the collective to be absorbed by the individual it is no less so for the individual to be absorbed by the collective.
>
> (D'Héricourt 1855: 57)

Comte's reduction of the individual to social benefit seemed to d'Héricourt to be just as incorrect as the utilitarian reduction of society to its benefit for the individual against which Comte argued. In trying to overcome both these errors, d'Héricourt confronted a problem that would become, some decades later, the main concern of Emile Durkheim, disciple of d'Héricourt's close friend Charles Renouvier. This is the problem of the compatibility of a 'regulated social order with individual freedom and personal autonomy' (Müller and Schmid 1996: 481) and is at the root of attempts to theorize the relationship between the individual and society in a non-reductive way (Luhmann 1996: 31).[10] In grappling with this problematic, d'Héricourt was developing the outlines of a concept of integration in modern society that Durkheim was to make a milestone of sociological theorizing through his elaboration of the concept of 'organic solidarity'. For Durkheim, the division of labour is the source of organic solidarity that, in contrast to mechanical solidarity, integrates not the equal but the unequal into a social body. Organic solidarity presupposes that individuals differ from one another and only becomes possible 'when each has his completely autonomous field of activity, when he thus has a personality' (Durkheim [1893] 1996: 183). The more divided the labour and the more personal the activities are, according to

Durkheim's thesis, the stronger the social coherence. D'Héricourt had used a similar formulation around 30 years earlier:

> You should not forget that reason and science prove to you that every-thing is *composed*, consequently has an *extent*, is *divisible, limited* and *relational*, that *diversity is the condition of unity* and that *a being is the more perfect the more it is composed of diversity*
>
> (D'Héricourt 1860: vol. II, p. 253)

Applied to society, this means that social cohesion grows proportionally with the degree of social differentiation – social order demands a 'variety of capabil-ities that are too diverse for any single one of us to be able to combine them within ourselves' (d'Héricourt 1860: vol. II, p. 14). D'Héricourt sees the condi-tions of this development in industrial and scientific progress which increas-ingly differentiates all productive activities and in which women participate.

Since she did not make a distinction between the female and the male potential for individualization and the corresponding right to specialized activity and an individualized existence, d'Héricourt was compelled to think through the problematic of social order in a modern society more radically and the question of the relationship of individual and society more fundamentally than was Comte, precisely because she included women. And unlike d'Héricourt, Durkheim would not derive the concept of organic solidarity from personal potential and the right of each individual to develop his indi-viduality, but from the sexual division of labour as the first and original form of social differentiation. Durkheim also believed – and in this he was not too far away from Comte – that he could get around the risk of social disintegra-tion with a progressive differentiation of the sexes (Durkheim [1933] 1964; Lehmann 1991; Roth 1992; Chapter 1, this volume). And in an unbroken tradition, he was to draw on Gustave le Bon's phrenology to support this line of reasoning. D'Héricourt, meanwhile, relied in a theoretically more rigorous fashion on the integrative effects of an individualization that also breaks through the difference between the sexes. When solidarity comes about as a result of people being reliant on each other because of their differing capabil-ities, only the free development of all individuals, including women, can create social cohesion. Here she was not only adding a social-theoretical argu-ment to the philosophical reasoning within feminist discourse, but also liber-ating proto-sociological discourse from the restrictions of a speculative and hierarchical ontology of sexual difference.

While modernity for us may be marked by masculine individualism, gen-der dualism and the exclusion of women, for d'Héricourt it was a still unfulfilled promise of a non-gender-divided society. Being confronted with social theories that deprived women of equality by denying their individuality in the putative interest of social integration, she opted for individualization as at once a liberating and integrating force. Aware of the possible disintegrating effects of individualization, she conceived the relationship between individual and society as a non-reductive one. This was her alternative to Comte's system where women provided the moral 'sealing agent' of society and it led her to formulate what has since become the core problematic of modern sociology: the necessarily complex relation between the individual and society, or between agency and structure.

Since the French Revolution, the question of the social position of woman was integral to the question of interpreting and organizing the post-revolutionary social (Fraisse 1992: 49). That women appear in the 'classical' canon of sociology as the 'other' of the social is not to be ascribed to the forgetfulness of the classics, but has a systematic reason behind it. D'Héricourt's critique demonstrates that it is not the much cited 'blind spots' that caused the 'disappearance' of women from the discourse of sociology so bitterly resented by feminist scholars in the twentieth century. Instead the disappearance of women from the social is revealed by d'Héricourt as a delib-erate 'social annihilation' of women. And this annihilation was constitutive of a sociological discourse that conceptualized society as a 'code word for the interests and needs of men' (Sydie 1987: 46; see also Marshall 1994). It was d'Héricourt's critique of precisely this masculinist coding of society and social theory which led her for her part to pose the question of the possibility of social order in a society of individuals in a manner that opens this question up as a distinctly sociological problematic. This gains her a place between Comte and Durkheim in terms of the history of sociological theory.

Annihilated: the contested foundations of a discipline

A theory can be considered as a classical one when, as Luhmann argues, it poses a problem that continues as an open but essential question while the form in which this problem is expressed varies with the historical context (Luhmann 1996: 19f). As we have demonstrated in this chapter, both Martineau and d'Héricourt must surely qualify as sociological classics from this perspective – Martineau in respect of her methodological ideas, d'Héricourt in respect of her social-theoretical thinking, and both together in respect of their genuinely sociological thinking about the social construction of the differences between the sexes and the relationships between the sexes.[11]

The fact that they do not occupy a canonical position is a demonstration of the stubborn inertia of the masculinity of both the subject and the theor-etical object of sociology. The 'social annihilation' of women was not only successfully secured within the now canonized classics of sociological dis-course, which knows no female sociologists and codes the social as masculine, but has also made its indelible mark on the historical identity of the discipline, which does not include feminist critique of early theories of society in its tradition. Hence it is not only the 'social annihilation' of women as possible subjects and objects of the discourse on the social, but also the 'historical annihilation' of the contested foundations of a masculinized sociology, that belongs to the history of the 'disciplining' of sociology.

Acknowledgements

Translated by Gerald Dennett and Kirstie Tyler.

We should like to thank Judith Janoska and Claudia Honegger for encouraging us to study Harriet Martineau and Jenny P. d'Héricourt and having repeatedly given us their helpful support in uncovering the traces of these two pioneering women sociologists. We should also like to thank the participants in the Feminism and Social Theory Network meeting held in Ross Priory, 2002, who engaged us in deep and thoughtful discussions of this material.

Notes

1 The following biographical details are mainly taken from Harriet Martineau's three-volume autobiography (1877), as well as from other sources (Clarke 1877; Katscher 1884; Bosanquet 1927; Pichanick 1980; Hill 1989; Hoecker-Drysdale 1992).

2 Durkheim follows Martineau in his *Rules of Sociological Method* ([1895] 1982) – sure enough without referring to her – in observing social facts as things. Yet Martineau went further than Durkheim, considering also the discourse of persons as an empirical data of social facts, while Durkheim used mainly statistical data to figure out social facts. Her suggestion leads to an empirical method that – as we would say today – could collect, measure and interpret the social world combining quantitative and qualitative research.

3 On the difference between virtual configurations of masculine/feminine and institutional configurations of men and women, see Chapter 1 (this volume).

4 Quotations from *La femme affranchie* by Jenny d'Héricourt (1860) are generally taken from the English translation dated [1864] 1981. Some of the citations used, however, are not to be found in the heavily abridged English version, and these parts are taken from the French original.

5 For a general review of Comte, see Pickering (1993); with regard to the interrelationship between Comte's biography and his work from the perspective of constructing male/female identity, see Kofman (1978).

6 Hence it is not just contemporary feminists who deplore the metaphysical saturation of the meaning of woman in the sociological tradition (see Witz

2001; Chapter 1, this volume), but also feminist intellectuals of the period (see also Chapter 3, this volume).

7 See also Lepenies (1981b, 1988); on Comte's reception of biology, see Canguilhem (1981), McLaren (1981) and Vernon (1986).

8 And this, d'Héricourt states, is the case whenever social or cultural differences are reified by theory, 'whether in castes, in classes, or in sexes' (d'Héricourt [1864] 1981: 244).

9 For an analysis of French feminist discourse in the nineteenth century with relation to the discourse of individuality, see Scott (1996).

10 Practically nothing is known of the line from d'Héricourt through Renouvier to Durkheim. The possibility that Durkheim was aware of d'Héricourt's writing cannot, in any event, be excluded.

11 For a collection of portraits of 'female sociological classics' from a perspective of deconstructing and reconstructing the sociological tradition, see Honegger and Wobbe (1998).

5　Feminizing the citizen: British sociology's sleight of hand?

Eileen Janes Yeo

British sociology took a different turning from some of its continental counter-parts. Several chapters in this book will argue that sociological theory con-structed women in such a way as to root their essential nature in nature and the family and thus to exclude them from the sphere of the social and the realm of the citizen. In the British tradition of social science, the social domain was created precisely as a counterpoint to the economic and the political spheres of modernity (Riley 1988: chap. 3; Yeo 1996: 24–5). From the early nineteenth century, the social realm made room for supposedly feminine qualities such as love, compassion, caring and service, and for womanly objects of concern such as the family, the elderly and the young. By contrast, the emerging sciences of political economy and government erected egotistical males at their centre, rational calculators who lusted after wealth and power.

By the opening decades of the twentieth century, these male models had been demoted, even discredited as 'degenerate specimens' (Bosanquet 1902: 183). Instead, in the strands of sociology that loomed large in the Sociological Society (founded in 1903), the fully developed human being was conceived as a citizen capable of conscious altruistic purpose and of rendering personal and community service, traits previously largely associated with women. This chapter will explore how the definition of the citizen was remade, not least by feminist efforts to enter social science in the mid-nineteenth century using a sexual communion of labour strategy which asserted the necessity of women working alongside men in all public as well as private activity. The paradoxical legacy of this communion of labour formula for early twentieth-century soci-ology will then be considered, not only for sociological theory but for women, not least the social science professionals who married the pioneer male sociologists.

Masculine and feminine sciences, 1820–80

To begin at the beginning, when the Enlightenment enquiry of moral philosophy fractured and some of the fragments re-appeared as the first specialized social sciences, gender impregnated the divisions. The new Ricardian political economy and the utilitarian science of government were essentially bourgeois sciences of the public sphere. The practitioners of this new philosophical radicalism did not set out to create knowledge which mirrored hardening gender divisions: indeed some, like John Stuart Mill, had a deep commitment to extending women's public role. Nonetheless in the early period, political economy and the science of politics were pre-eminently the sciences of the male elements of human nature and of male activity in the public sphere. The early utilitarians worked with an abstract deductive method and erected at the centre of their science a psychological model of an egotistical individual whose happiness consisted in rational pursuit of 'the leading objects of human desire; Wealth, Power, Dignity, Ease: including escape from the contrary; Poverty, Impotence, Degradation, Toil' (Mill 1835: 278).

It is striking how limited James Mill's roll-call of desire was. The pleasures and pains itemized here were very much the glittering prizes and murky pitfalls of the public world of politics and commerce. Some leading objects of bourgeois desire at the time were clearly missing from the list: salvation, morality, benevolence, love and family, to name but a few. These qualities fell outside the scope of the sciences of public life, and were increasingly consigned to a separate science of morals, to the feminine part of human nature and to the private sphere which was of interest only at the margins to the public sciences. That the rational public actor was a man was usually an unquestioned assumption. However, in James Mill's influential *An Essay on Government* ([1819] 1978: 79), middle-class men were scientifically discovered to be the most capable of acting in the interest of the whole community and the most fit to be the virtual representatives of their dependants, including workers and women.

Social science was created precisely to challenge some aspects of the partition of human nature and the sciences. From the 1820s, the largely working-class Owenite socialist movement monopolized the term social science, by which they meant the science of the happiness of the greatest number including working-class people, and which they used to attack the political economists and the utilitarians (Yeo 1996: 34–8). They not only lambasted the economists' reductive model of human motivation. They also insisted that character was socially conditioned, that men and women shared mental and moral capacities and that both had a right to develop their potential within optimal social relations, which were envisioned as communities of mutual support.

The early socialists operated with the idea of a 'social system' that involved the interplay between social values and social relations of power (Yeo 1996: 46). They made a pioneering analysis of capitalism as a system, which was riddled with contradictions and prone to crisis, and which Friedrich Engels, who frequented their Manchester Hall of Science, relayed to Karl Marx. They also made a devastating analysis of the bourgeois family as a key site for the creation of competitive values and habits of gender domination and subordination, both serviceable to the ethos and inequalities of capitalism. Like their St Simonian counterparts in France (Moses 1993: 44–65), socialist feminists punctured the bourgeois family romance soon to be installed at the centre of continental sociology. Far from being a haven of harmony and stability, the conjugal nuclear family contained inequalities and conflicts as sharp as any in the public sphere. In William Thompson's blunt words, 'a domestic, a civil, a political slave, in the plain unsophisticated sense of the word – in no metaphorical sense – is every married woman' ([1825], 1983: 67). The socialists proposed easier divorce in their communities where childcare would be collectivized. These proposals drew the greatest venom from powerful religious voices that condemned community as 'one vast brothel'.

The acrimony surrounding the socialists was yet another factor, along with the masculine focus of emerging political economy and political science, that complicated the entry of women, as thinkers or objects of scrutiny, into the public sciences. Aspiring women writers, as well as the emergent intellectual community receiving them, were highly sensitive to the issue of gender division in intellectual work. The experience of Harriet Martineau (1802–76), one of the few successful 'lady economists', whose sociological work is explored in Chapter 4 of this volume, makes this clear. She negotiated the division between public and private spheres with immense care. She used a secularized version of a religious calling to justify her public work, arguing that she had an imperative duty to bring out her *Illustrations of Political Economy* (1832–34) because the book was wanted by the People, in the double sense of needed and desired. And she 'thought of the multitudes who needed it – and especially of the poor – to assist them in managing their own welfare' (1877: vol. 1, p. 171).

She recounted the saga of finding a publisher as a melodramatic wrestling with obstacles and despondency, not as a smooth path to success. Published in 1833, her work received mixed reviews, all putting gender to the forefront. The responses ranged from the conservative *Quarterly Review*, damning her as a 'She Politician' and a '*female Malthusian*' (1833: vol. 49, p. 151), to the more appreciative *Edinburgh Review* which nonetheless warned against creating 'a millennium of her own, in which our ladies will have taken out of our monopolising hands the cares of Parliament and public life' (Empson 1833: 3). The doughty Martineau persevered with her political economy tales, insulated to some extent from conventional femininity by her deafness, her unmarried state and by her dream life in which her masculine side found robust expression.[1]

It was during the mid-nineteenth century that middle- and upper-class women made their entry into social science, but often in a paradoxical way which both extended and restricted their possibilities. The easiest way to force entry was to preserve but at the same time to modify ideas of gender division. Thus, the mid-century feminists who became active in the National Association for the Promotion of Social Science often placed themselves in a communion of labour framework to legitimize their place in modernity alongside men. The feminist version of the sexual communion of labour was expounded most clearly by Frances Power Cobbe.[2] She argued that although God was androgynous, human men and women had different, equivalent and complementary natures. Both natures were needed to make a full humanity and produce what she called 'a stereoscopic view'. This unity could come about only when men and women worked together, on divided tasks, in every area of public and private life. 'Surely, surely', Cobbe exclaimed,

> It is time we gain something from woman of her religious nature! And we want her moral intuition also. We want her sense of the law of love to complete man's sense of the law of justice. We want her influence inspiring virtue by gentle prompting from within to complete man's external legislation of morality. And, then, we want woman's practical service. We want her genius for detail, her tenderness for age and suffering, her comprehension of the wants of childhood to complete man's gigantic charities and nobly planned hospitals and orphanages
>
> (1861: 92)

Love was to complete justice; inner spirit to complement external law. Intuition was to supplement abstract intelligence; attention to individuals and to the particular (particularly among the young, the old and the poor) was to enhance the capacity to plan large-scale institutions.

This communion of labour formula was also attractive to some emerging male professionals, keen to establish their status on a basis of science and service. And what better way to enhance their service credentials than to ally with the most servicing section of humanity, women. A kind of collusion of labour resulted. Women created what are now known as the caring professions in complementary relation to male occupations. Thus hospital and visiting nursing on the Nightingale principle was conceived as spiritual and sanitary caring, taking place alongside the doctor's physical ministering (Rafferty 1996: 31, 40). Medical men were perhaps even more sympathetic to sanitary visiting in the dwellings of the poor, later to develop into health visiting, which could give public health doctors and their inspections a more humane face: the medical journal the *Lancet* praised the effectiveness of women who 'proselytise in quarters where masculine and rougher apostles would scarcely gain a hearing' (19 April 1862). Work with juvenile delinquents was women's special contribution to reformatory science dominated by lawyers, chaplains and prison inspectors. Anglican religious sisterhoods, revived for the first time since the Reformation, and parish-based deaconesses, working under the authority of a male minister, featured in moral science. In all of these caring occupations, unmarried women especially could transpose their maternal instincts into public social work with needy women and children from a different social class.

Another factor creating space in science for so-called feminine qualities was a growing consensus, among some political economists too, that old-style political economy and political science were unacceptably narrow. John Stuart Mill set the ball rolling with his *Principles of Political Economy* ([1848] 1891), which displayed his new Comtist convictions that the 'laws' of political economy belonged to a critical stage of history to be superseded by a more progressive organic period. Indeed, in the book's most popular chapter, 'On the probable futurity of the labouring classes', women were coupled with the working class as both moving from a period of dependence under patriarchal protectors to one of independence characterized not by competition but by mutual support ([1848] 1891: 501–3). Later, in his *Autobiography* ([1873] 1989), Mill heaped fulsome praise on Harriet Taylor, his long-time friend who finally became his wife, for having revolutionized his economic analysis.

> What was abstract and purely scientific was generally mine; the properly human element came from her: in all that concerned the application of philosophy of the exigencies of human society and progress, I was her pupil, alike in boldness of speculation and cautiousness of practical judgement.
>
> (Mill [1873] 1989: 210)

Other political economists jumped on the bandwagon. Dr W.B. Hodgson (1815–80), soon to be appointed Professor at the University of Edinburgh, admitted that 'it was commonly assumed that political economy was a selfish science' but insisted that 'every man who promoted his own interests to the injury of the community, or even without benefit to the community . . . was a traitor to political economy' (NAPSS 1868a: 429–30). Henry Fawcett, MP and Cambridge professor, also felt obliged to redeem the political economist from his popular image as 'a selfish hardhearted being' and urged the study of the distribution and exchange of wealth 'so as to confer the greatest amount of happiness on mankind' (NAPSS 1868b: 114–15). Fawcett's wife, Millicent, later to lead the National Union of Women's Suffrage Societies, shared these views when she taught political economy in the Ladies Department of King's College and wrote in the approved womanly style, producing a textbook for school children in 1870 and *Tales in Political Economy* in 1874. She was the first woman to be nominated for membership in the Political Economy Club, but she was not elected.

Women clearly understood that the communion of labour position, which accepted but subverted sexual difference, was the most acceptable variety of feminism and the most likely to survive and grow. Even before the women's movement became more organized and lively from 1858 onward, Harriet Taylor Mill's *Enfranchisement of Women* ([1851] 1983) had thrown down a more egalitarian gauntlet. Arguing that women had the same rationality as men, she declared her solidarity with the American suffragist demand for women's 'admission, in law and in fact, to equality in all rights, political civil, and social, with the male citizens of the community'. She demolished a series of objections against equality, revealing them to be socially constructed ideology, including the argument based on custom 'that women had never had equal rights with men' and thus were 'barred by universal practice' and the argument based on 'nature', about public activity being incompatible 'with maternity, and with the cares of a household', as well as arguments resting on economic fears that women would aggravate 'competition in every professional or lucrative employment' ([1851] 1983: 3, 10, 17). However logical, this was not a popular position among the very male professionals on whom women's entry into the social science world depended.

Feminizing the citizen, 1880–1920

By the turn of the twentieth century, liberal British sociology of all types had de-centred the selfish male egotist and put an altruistic citizen in his place. Women's persistent efforts to enter social science were now paying dividends, since these sociological schools all made room for both genders in their theories of citizenship and modernity. In this way Britain differed from Germany, discussed by Gerhard in Chapter 6, where some classical thinkers did not allow women into dynamic modernity, and from France, where Durkheim laid down his law about women's natural role in the family to stabilize anomic social tendencies (Pedersen 2001: 248; see also Chapter 1, this volume). But even if British sociology was more inclusive of women, the roles that women were assigned in modernity were still circumscribed. This complex process can be explored in the work of several schools of sociology and social science prominent on the nascent professional scene together with the research focus of the Fabian Women's Group, which marked out a more radical pole in the spectrum of sociological positions at the time.

Among the more conservative liberals, Professor Bernard Bosanquet and his wife Helen Dendy were activists in the Charity Organisation Society (COS) and founders of the London School of Sociology and Social Economics, while

Professor E.J. Urwick was the first Director of the Department of Social Science and Social Administration at the London School of Economics (LSE). Both the Bosanquets and Urwick argued that the good state was an ethical society in which a 'citizen–conception' prevailed. Every citizen would perform service in a range of institutions including the family, the neighbourhood, class (or industry) and the nation-state. Citizens would cultivate a sharp awareness of which forms of these collectives would contribute best to the common good, and then work to bring these forms into being (Bosanquet 1899: chap. 11; Urwick 1912: chap. 7). In this ethical transformation of social institutions, women had a role to play. Despite being hostile to the growth of a welfare state, Helen Bosanquet was a staunch advocate of women's suffrage, even for the 'slatterns' on the street corner (1911), and argued for the proper training of women workers so that they could command a skilled position in the labour market.

Helen Bosanquet had pulled off a brilliant performance in the Moral Tripos at Cambridge and went on to do paid work in the COS. In 1902, she wrote a textbook for training programmes, *The Strength of the People: A Study in Social Economics*, which moved not only the so-called feminine qualities but the family into the centre of the analytical stage. Drawing upon new trends in psychology (Stout, James and Lloyd Morgan), she stressed the difference between animals, driven by instinct, and humans, able to build up habits of being guided by rational and ethical purpose. In her analysis, personal service and self-sacrifice in increasingly larger collectives were identified as the rational purpose most distinctive of humanity at its highest level of development.

She insisted that the family provided the first experience of altruistic habit, 'the easiest and most natural means of emancipation from the narrow cycle of the lower life'. For a number of additional reasons the family had to be a focus for all the social sciences, even economics, however distasteful it might seem to connect economics with 'that consecrated corner of disinterested services, of mute affection, of intercourse which brings pleasure and not merely profit' (Bosanquet 1902: 181, 183). Moreover, the family provided the greatest motive to economic activity. The vaunted egotists at the centre of old-style utilitarian science, with their thirst for power and wealth, were dismissed, as already noted, as 'degenerate specimens'. The family was also strategic for political science 'since it is in the Family that the citizen is made' (1923: 336). Moreover the feminine concern for the practical was to be enshrined in a science that was to be immediately relevant to real life, an 'applied science'.

Much of British sociology was locked into a critical dialogue with Charles Darwin and especially with Herbert Spencer. (Darwin loomed over the British intellectual scene as much as Marx did over the German.) New Liberal and Fabian sociologists developed a radical evolutionism which also dethroned the egotistical individualist. L.T. Hobhouse, appointed to the London School of Economics in 1908 as Britain's first Professor of Sociology, and the founders of the LSE, Beatrice and Sidney Webb, insisted that the suppression of struggle and conflict in social evolution was a key test of progress. Hobhouse argued that 'advance in organisation diminishes the opportunities for conflict. In proportion as life is well ordered the struggle for existence is suppressed' ([1904] 1972: 112). The Webbs wrote ' "the survival of the fittest" in an environment unfavourable to progress may – as every biologist knows – mean the survival of the lowest parasite' ([1911] 1920: 48). If Spencer was keen on reproductive femininity, Hobhouse was sympathetic to women's suffrage as a tonic for flagging democracy ([1904] 1972: 268), while Beatrice Webb, origin- ally an opponent of women's suffrage, came round to supporting it as the only way to get key gender issues onto the political agenda.

If the New Liberal and Fabian thinkers were primarily concerned with human evolution, Patrick Geddes and J. Arthur Thomson, who had trained as biologists, continued to search for evolutionary processes which operated both in the organic and the social worlds. But quite unlike Darwin and Spencer, they argued that cooperation and sacrifice characterized the true law of all life:

> Be it mammal or bird, insect or even worm – all these survivals of the truly fittest, through love and sacrifice, sociability and co-operation, simple to complex – need far other prominence than they can pos- sibly receive even by some mildewing attenuation of the classic eco- nomic hypothesis of the progress of the species essentially through the internecine struggle among its individuals at the margin of subsistence
>
> (Geddes and Thomson 1911: 246–7)

Both in the natural and social worlds, they discovered an anabolic tendency towards constructive nurturing which was complemented by a catabolic metabolism that actively consumed energy. By regarding 'woman as the rela- tively more anabolic, man as the relatively more katabolic' (Geddes and Thomson 1914: 208), and by insisting that both were necessary in the public sphere of modern life, the Geddes school gave a biological dimension to the feminist idea of the sexual communion of labour.

By 1914, in the last of their influential books on *Sex*, Geddes and Thomson reversed their notorious earlier verdict that sex differences 'decided among the prehistoric Protozoa cannot be annulled by Act of Parliament' (1889: 267, 1901: 286).[3] Having learned from feminists like Olive Schreiner, whose *Women and Labour* ([1911] 1978) they praised as 'full of power and insight' (Geddes and Thomson 1914: 251), they now argued that the full nature of sexual dif- ference was not yet known. They translated the feminist argument that women's potential was concealed by social constructions of femininity into biological language, and called for a distinction between what was due to nature or to 'nurture (food, atmosphere, surroundings, education, exercise, habits, etc.)' (Geddes and Thomson 1914: 213).[4] They repudiated the argument, developed by sociologists like Simmel (see also Chapters 1, 3 and 6 in this volume), 'that man is more variable than woman, that the raw materials of evolution make their appearance in greatest abundance in man', and insisted that 'there seems to be no secure basis for this generalisation' (Geddes and Thomson 1914: 208).

Spotting unintentional male bias in scientific study, they asserted that women had to take things into their own hands: 'who can tell what men or women can do effectively until a fair trial is made? Social evolution is an experimental art. And one quite unworkable plan is that man should prescribe what the lines of woman's evolution are henceforth to be' (Geddes and Thomson 1914: 239). Nonetheless, they agreed with Karl Pearson (and the influential Swede, Ellen Key) that 'to reconcile maternal activity with the new possibilities of self-development open to women is *par excellence* the woman's problem of the future' – or, put it in their own words – women faced 'the problem of combining maternity and citizenship, production and reproduction' (Geddes and Thomson 1914: 235).

In their sociological civics, the Geddesites reserved an important place for women's influence but largely along extended communion of labour lines. Geddes used an evolutionary historical scheme where the earliest period was a mother age, followed by the patriarchal period, ending with the industrial age which needed to be moved to a higher stage by woman's effort:

> as eupsychic inspirer and eugenic mother, as instinctive synthetist, as educationalist, as orderly home-planner and citizen; and, by her guidance of consumption, directing industry and skill, ennobling utility into art
>
> (Geddes and Thomson 1914: 244)

The flowery language in which women's special contribution was expressed smacked of worship (like Comte's for Clothide de Vaux), and is nearly unreadable today. Nonetheless, unlike Comte, Geddes did not confine feminine qualities to the home. Art, culture, education, libraries, parks, ethical consumption and social surveys were some of the fields of action for the 'civic matriarch', as she was named by Victor Branford, railway financier and financial lynchpin of the Sociological Society (Branford 1914: 114–22). Social surveys were a key feature of Geddes' civic sociology. He tried to stimulate local citizens to do historical and ecological investigations of their area as well as 'a Social Survey proper' of the present condition of the people 'their occupation and real wages, their family budget and culture-level', as the necessary precursor to civic action (Geddes 1904: 116).

How did the Geddesite position compare with the concerns of the Fabian Women's Group that contained pioneer feminist academics, mainly from economics and economic history? Founded in 1908, initially by a small number of women, most of whom had been imprisoned for their suffragette activity, the Group quickly grew to 200 paying members within a year. These women were determined not to let class issues conceal gender oppression and insisted that 'socialists must recognize that women's economic revolt is not merely against the enslaving economic control of the capitalist state, but against the enslaving economic control of the husband' (Fabian Women's Group 1911: 9). They were more committed to economic independence for women than most of the sociologists already mentioned and, as a result, focused more sharply upon women's position in the public labour market, without the soft soap focus on her moral influence.

The Fabian women declared that 'the greatest stumbling block we found in our way was that women themselves have not studied the question scientifically in their own interests. The available material is presented by the male investigator with his own unavoidable sex bias' (Fabian Women's Group 1911: 12). So they set about creating a research agenda which would be more useful to women, and explored issues like the supposed disabilities of women and mothers as workers and tested the validity of the argument that women were dependants and therefore should receive lower wages.[5] Their claim that 'the economic history of this country from the point of view of the workers, to say nothing of the women workers has yet to be written' was ably demonstrated when Mabel Atkinson, who had studied at Glasgow and later became a lecturer in political economy in London University, tried to fill the gap. In a brilliant analysis, she showed how the separation of household and workplace had affected women of different classes in opposite but equally constricting ways: 'parasitism became the fate of middle class women, ruthless exploitation that of the working class women' (Atkinson 1914: 7). This divergence had created major but not insurmountable difficulties about creating a united women's movement. Although the Fabian women toppled some key pillars of conventional wisdom, they embraced some other sacred cows, especially motherhood. Like Geddes, although without idealizing women, they considered that the great issue of the day was how to combine economic independence with motherhood (Atkinson 1914: 16–18; Hutchins [1915] 1978: 206–7).

Ramifications for real women

The feminization of the citizen in Britain took place in a context of intensified women's activity in the public sphere. Opportunities were expanding, especially in higher education and training, women's professions were growing, notably in the health and social service areas, and women's movements in the economic and political field were proliferating. The various wings of the women's suffrage campaign put huge pressure on the political process in the first decade of the twentieth century and clearly had some impact on changing the understanding of the nature of citizenship. However, it remains to consider what kind of impact the feminization of the citizen in progressive social science actually made on the lives at least of middle-class women. One interesting way of probing this is by exploring the lives of the women most intimately connected with the sociologists already mentioned and with other pioneer social science professionals, namely their wives. Most of the first generation of British sociologists and economists were married, although most histories of theory take little notice of this fact.

Some of the wives were highly educated women. Distinguished Cambridge scholars included Helen Dendy Bosanquet and Mary Paley Marshall, the wife of Alfred Marshall, the creator of the modern discipline of economics. Mary Paley was not only Marshall's student, but then co-authored his first pathbreaking book, *The Economics of Industry* (Marshall and Paley 1879). Oxford students included Sybella Gurney, who had gained a first-class honours in Classics and went on to marry Victor Branford. Of course not all the wives had attended universities. Some, like Beatrice Potter Webb, were home- and self-educated but had tutelage from intellectuals of the calibre of Herbert Spencer.

Nonetheless, gender division was often still a striking feature of most of their marriages and of their social and intellectual work. Indeed the communion of labour pattern in its feminist version seemed to stamp many of the partnerships. Mary Marshall's story is in some ways the most striking. Starting as a full intellectual equal of her husband's, as soon as they married she shifted her position, becoming active in more female-orientated activity. She lectured in economics but only at Newnham, a Cambridge ladies' college. For many years, she chaired the Committee of the Women's University Settlement in Bermondsey, South London, which enabled women university graduates to live in a communal house in a poor neighbourhood and engage in regular but often unpaid social work. In this public capacity, she had a powerful influence on the curriculum of social work training.

John Maynard Keynes, the famous economist, recalled how, at home, Mary Marshall never

> discoursed on an economic topic with a visitor, or even took part in the everlasting economic talks of Balliol Croft. For the serious discussion she would leave the dining-room to the men, or the visitor would go upstairs to the study, and the most ignorant Miss could not have pretended less than she to academic attainment.
>
> (as quoted in Marshall 1947: xi)

Mrs Marshall believed that 'women's successes were to be built on work which complements rather than competes with men', a point her biographer calls 'a Marshallian hobby horse' (Tullborg, n.d.: 23, 37). Supposedly her husband was very supportive of her work in the COS and the University Women's Settlement but resented her success in getting women through the economics tripos. Certainly he became notorious as a gatekeeper excluding women from getting Cambridge degrees or from teaching his subject to men at the university (Berg 1992: 315–16).

A similar pattern can be detected in several social science partnerships. The husband was the publicly eminent intellectual and wrote large books, while the wife, however brilliant, devoted herself to more approved womanly activities, especially social work with the poor and with women and children in particular. Bernard Bosanquet at the time of his death seemed to some the nearest thing 'to the ideal philosopher of the Platonic vision, but along with it the citizen' to others 'a Saint'. But this philosopher king of independent means, who managed to involve himself in the Central Committee of the London COS while holding a chair in philosophy at Aberdeen, found the household visiting of the poor 'uncongenial' as he simply 'did not know what to say' (Bosanquet 1924: 52). He was more comfortable in the schoolroom where he gave evening classes. It was Helen, who became a paid secretary of the Charity Organisation Society after university, who did the face to face visiting as well as writing highly theoretical works on social economics and the treatment of poverty.

It is worth noting that the divisions of labour here were culturally dictated and sometimes bore little relation to the actual personalities or capabilities of the individuals concerned. Some of the men were conspicuously fragile and were shielded from harsh realities by their protective wives. Thus Mary Marshall would actually meet in private with some her husband's intellectual critics to try to persuade them to stop their perceived attacks. One obituary made his dependence even clearer when it described an 'intellectual partnership based on profound dependence on the one side (he could not live a day without her), and, on the other, deep devotion and admiration, which was increased and not impaired by extraordinary discernment . . . She faced everything in order that he, sometimes, need not' (*Newnham College Register* [1871–1971] 1971: 44).

Perhaps the most interesting partnership of the communion of labour kind was that between Victor Branford and Sybella Gurney because he seemed to refashion her both during her lifetime and after her death. While at Oxford, Sybella had taken up the masculine producers' co-operative movement as her cause. A co-operator testified that she would 'throw herself with zest into public speaking, to audiences of workers, in which she took special delight' (Halstead 1926). But after her marriage to Victor, she changed direction and channelled her public energies away from production into co-operative housing and ultimately into the garden city movement. Housing was a more womanly province, as houses contained homes.

Sybella, like Mary Marshall, was the impeccably attentive wife. Lewis Mumford remembered her a bit unkindly as 'an ample, buttery sort of woman, gracious but fuzzy' whose Oxford education irritated her husband. But Mumford added in mitigation that 'Sybella's goodness, her little acts of thoughtfulness and kindness were constant, and . . . she gave Branford exactly the sort of environment that should have met his every need' (Mumford 1982: 261–2). When she died Branford tried to collect her writings together to form what he called her autobiography and which he titled variously 'A woman's way with the world' and then 'The evolution of a modern woman: the tale of Mrs. Victor Branford told from her writings'. This compendium would track the 'progress . . . from economic thought and political endeavours touched vaguely by poetic impulse towards sociology and its applications inspired by religious ideals' (Branford 1927). This is not to suggest that Sybella would have disagreed with his idea of progress. Nonetheless, the docketing of the economic and political as lesser, and sociology, with its concern for moral purpose, as higher, fit comfortably with ideas of the gendered strengths of women.

Postscript: creating the canon

Branford was one of the first to arrange thinkers into a canonical tradition, but like most of the sociologists discussed here, he was not admitted into the sociological hall of fame. In a paper read to the Sociological Society in its inaugural year, Branford paraded Comte, Mill and Spencer and then cited institutional developments in other countries, pointing to Durkheim in France, Simmel and Tönnies in Germany and Lester Ward in the US, among others. He bemoaned the fact that 'in Great Britain, almost alone of leading nations, Sociology is to-day unrepresented by any special institution or periodical of scientific studies and our Universities stand in conspicuous isolation' (Branford 1903: 9). The Sociological Society tried to fill the gap but a number of participants fairly quickly moved out of its orbit, first eugenics in 1908, then in 1912, Hobhouse's brand of social evolutionism, now installed in the LSE, left Geddes and Branford in charge. Then, in 1913 a women's group started, boasting members notable in social research like Mabel Atkinson, Barbara Hutchins, Clementina Black (author of *Married Women's Work*), as well as others like Sybella, who wished to engage in 'serious and dispassionate study of the facts which form the subject matter of what is talked of at the present time as the woman's movement' (Sociological Society Women's Group 1913: 7). In 1914, the group suspended activities for the duration of the war.

Geddes and Branford not only continued the *Sociological Review*, but in 1920 established a freestanding Institute of Sociology in Le Play House as a centre for sociology and civic work with Branford money. The institute was a powerhouse of interwar social survey work, in which women were prominent: Mabel MacKillop, lecturer in economics at London University, became its secretary and both Mrs Branford and then Dorothea Farquarson with her husband were active. Branford was keen on female involvement and appealed to the British Federation of University Women to accelerate 'the long-retarded growth of this culminating science' (Branford 1930: 145). Taken seriously in their day, Geddes' summer schools attracted the luminaries of the period. The LSE sociologists were also involved in the Sociological Institute's activities. But this initiative has dropped without a trace in histories of the discipline. This is no secret history: the institute was well-known in its time, just as the activity of women in the discipline as sociological workers and spouses was well-known.

So the issue is really about how disciplinary canons and histories are made, who crafts them, who is included within them and who excluded and left outside. Increasingly, it would seem that academic status became a necessary ticket for entry. The slow professionalization of British sociology has often been noted and regretted by academic sociologists, rather than seen as a source of strength (Abrams 1968; Goldman 1987). Most early sociology in the British tradition had flourished outside the academy and had been famously linked to social policy and action. This proved impossible for American sociology, which moved very early into universities, and problematic for German intellectuals like Max Weber, who feared threats to free enquiry in the German context (Yeo 1996: 298–300).

Few male British sociologists, with the exception of Herbert Spencer and more recently and rarely Raymond Williams, have made it into the syllabi of academic courses on sociological theory. Both Philip Abrams and Stefan Collini have made attempts to recover the early twentieth-century moment when British sociology crystallized. Collini's *Liberalism and Sociology* (1979) gives careful consideration to the theories of Hobhouse and his concern with social development. Abrams even recuperated Geddes' civics and credited him with a promising vision of urban sociology, but insisted that it remained undeveloped because Geddes 'plunged as an active propagandist into the town planning movement' (Abrams 1968: 116). In both works little was said about women (except for Beatrice Webb).

Women were doubly damned, because they were so linked with 'open-air observation', practical application and social action that their route into the academy was largely via social work and child psychology, and away from the paths that led to being remembered by keepers of the canon. The double amnesia in the canon about both women and British sociologists also resulted from the huge wave of American sociology that washed onto British shores in the 1950s and swamped most of the already existing and sometimes ailing British forms. The insolvent Sociological Institute closed its doors in 1955, two years after the *Sociological Review* had started a new series edited by Keele academics and five years after the *British Journal of Sociology* was started by the LSE figures who would train the generation of sociologists who were to preside over the expansion of the subject in the 1960s and 1970s when academic sociology in Britain was said to have begun.

This chapter has unearthed some curious paradoxes. Sociology and cognate disciplines at the turn of the twentieth century often repudiated the rational choice model of behaviour (which seems to be fashionable again in some versions of social and political theory – see, for example, Chapter 5, this volume), and which assumed a rational actor to be a selfish individual questing after wealth and power. Instead' the altruistic citizen, who was trained to recognize and service the public good in a concentric circle of institutions with the family at its centre and with the world order as its farthest orbit, as the highest human type. But preliminary probing of the marriages of social scientists suggests that the feminization of the construct of the citizen brought about a contradictory situation for actual women. Opportunities expanded in the public sphere in this period, as women fought to open more social space for themselves. But at the same time the communion of labour principle, far from being superseded, was even being fortified in new biological ways. Within evolutionary and social hygiene paradigms, women were seen primarily as race producers, or a softer way of putting it was they were nurturers; their public identity had to embody a recognition of this particularly important role. It was often as worker, mother, citizen or, if single, as social worker, social mother and citizen that respectable radical women constructed themselves. They remained implacably sexed as maternal while men became more caring but still sexless citizens.

Notes

1   Martineau (1877: vol. I, p. 15) recounts a dream which she supposedly had at age four(!) where a stag 'with prodigious antlers', invites her into a public house while later her mother in a bright kitchen breaks sugar and gives her some; pp. 131–3 for reflections on her marital state as 'the happiest single woman in England'.

2   The feminist version of the sexual communion of labour, which gave women a firm place in the public sphere, challenged the Ruskinian notion of complementarity which put women in the home and men in the public world. Emily Davies ([1866] 1973: 16, 178–80) challenged Ruskin's idea in *The Higher Education of Women*.

3   Rita Felski (1995: 156) points to Geddes' and Thomson's 'notorious antifeminist assertion' in 1889, but does not take into account the later development of their views.

4   Geddes and Thomson (1914: 213) urged inquirers to 'discriminate between the innate qualities of maleness and femaleness, masculinity and femininity, all requiring appropriate liberating stimuli, and those which are individually acquired as the direct result of peculiarities of ' "nurture". Along with these must be included the defects that are due to disuse, or to the absence of appropriate stimuli'.

5   See Fabian Women's Group (1909) *A Summary of Six Papers and Discussions upon the Disabilities of Women as Workers*, London: Fabian Women's Group, p. 23, for the agenda; Fabian Women's Group (1910) *A Summary of Eight Papers and Discussion Upon the Disabilities of Mothers as Workers*, London: Fabian Women's Group; and E. Smith (1915) *Wage Earning Women and their Dependents*, London: Fabian Society.

6 'Illegitimate daughters': the relationship between feminism and sociology

Ute Gerhard

The smelting or paralleling of the histories of sociology and feminism raises a series of fascinating questions. In this chapter I argue that both phases of the women's movement in Germany, as in the Western world, correspond not coincidentally to societal developments and, in particular, to a consciousness of crisis which the so-called classical sociologists initiated and which continues to be cast in sociological terms.[1] The first phase of the women's movement had its greatest mobilization around the turn of the twentieth century, while the second emerged in the 1960s. These two phases of the women's movement emerged simultaneously with steps towards modernization that sociologists have identified as the first and second crises of modernity or as 'simple' and 'reflexive' modernities (see Beck 1986; Wagner 1995; Beck *et al.* 1996).

To develop this argument, I first re-read the social theories propounded by the classical writers with the following question in mind: what answers did they give to problems in gender relations arising from the women's movement of their time? Through such a re-reading we can assess Dahme and Rammstedt's (1984: 449) claim about the 'eternal modernity of the sociological classics' such as works by Emile Durkheim, Ferdinand Tönnies, Max Weber and Georg Simmel, because gender difference played a role not only in their diagnoses of the times but also in their theories. However, whereas the woman/gender issue played a central role in classical sociological theories, the new feminism's critique of society, despite a broad-based rhetoric of equality, has not yet exercised a similar systematic influence on contemporary sociological theory.

Feminism and sociology at the turn of the last century

The relationship between the first academic women at the turn of the twentieth century and the new academic discipline of sociology can be described as one of an elective affinity (Wobbe 1995). The metaphor of an elective affinity was used by Viola Klein in her classic study, *The Feminine Character* ([1946] 1971), to develop two arguments. First, she argued that the so-called woman question and the phenomenon of social crisis, which sociology had now started to analyse with reference to 'social facts', had their roots in the same problematic development of modern society. In other words, the gender question was part and parcel of, and indeed lay at the very core of, the social question. Second, Viola Klein had already drawn attention to the fact that the first academic women, who were also members of the women's movement, used their engagement in the field of social reform to promote welfare and social work. They participated as specialists in early sociological investigations and their 'humanitarian interests which formed the starting-point of social research, and practical social work itself, actually provided the back-door through which women slipped into public life' (Klein [1946] 1971: 17).

'The woman question' – precursors in sociological discourse

In the second half of the nineteenth century 'the woman question' emerged. On the one hand, it was dealt with as a series of discrete social 'problems' resulting from economic and social change, such as the need for unmarried bourgeois women to earn a living. On the other hand, sources reveal that contemporaries were also well aware of a far more fundamental social problem posed by the woman question. What would it mean for the bourgeois social order as a whole if women realized their emancipatory aspirations? As a result, in the 1860s, public discussion of the woman question, influenced by the politics of the women's movement, began to frame the issues in terms of a social crisis. Given the model of the bourgeois family, this crisis proved in particular to be 'a problem within the bourgeoisie because it questioned its own norms of behaviour and way of life' (Bussemer 1985: 11).

In the nascent social science literature, the prototype of a 'social movement' was the labour movement (von Stein [1848] 1974, [1850] 1921). In von Stein's definition of modern social movements, what counted as their 'most common cause' was the 'continuing contradiction' occasioned by a 'society of inequality . . . confronted by a concept of human rights' (von Stein 1848: 3). Significantly, he failed to include the contemporary women's movement in his analysis. Nonetheless, as a means of conservative social reform, the woman question played a role in his social theory, since in light of altered means of production and reproduction, it was especially women, and particularly wives, whose consumptive and reproductive activities played an absolutely crucial role in the national economy. Stein was not alone in his view that the family was bourgeois society's fundamental institution, if not the basic pillar of civil society. This assumption was common to political and social studies in the eighteenth and nineteenth centuries more generally.[2]

Others were even more directly and boldly patriarchal. Around the time of the 1848 revolution Wilhelm Heinrich Riehl, a pioneer of empirical social science as well as normative family sociology, denounced the women's movement as a 'notorious emancipation' and as composed of 'feminine demagogues . . . Bluestockings who deny their sex' (Riehl 1855: 10, 18). The women's movement was a danger to bourgeois order and a violation of God-given sexual difference.

At the turn of the nineteenth century we find many outspoken pro-ponents of women's rights,[3] but by mid-century such advocates had become rare indeed. Advocates of equal rights for women, like Flora Tristan or George Sand, whose critique echoed that of the early French socialists such as Fourier (1966) and the St Simonians, were reduced to cliché and the scarecrow figure of a cigar-smoking 'femme libre' (Möhrmann 1977: 45). Fourier's view of women as the 'barometer' of social progress nonetheless continued to influ-ence socialist and Marxist discussion. By the middle of the nineteenth century, however, scholarly writings and attitudes (see especially W.H. Riehl 1855), expounded a specific form of bourgeois patriarchalism. This guided behaviour and legitimated the bourgeois order in marriage, rightly called 'secondary patriarchalism' by René König (1974: 218–19; see also Gerhard 1978: 143). In contrast to the engaged social criticism of other contemporaries such as Hedwig Dohm (for example, 1876) only Mill and Mill's *The Subjection of Woman* ([1869] 1976) gained scientific treatment and evoked numerous reac-tions of German scholars (for instance, Treitschke, quoted in Twellmann 1972: II, p. 190). For Mill and Mill, freedom was liberalism's most important prin-ciple; accordingly, they registered a plea for women's right to develop their individuality. August Bebel's *Women and Socialism* ([1879] 1964) was also a key influence on the ensuing political discussion of the woman question and the relationship between socialism and feminism.

The women's movement as a sign of crisis in modernity

'The crisis we are presently experiencing regarding the "woman question" ' can be explained by 'two tendencies' in social development that appear 'to lay the groundwork for our cultural development' (Lange 1908: 10). One ten-dency is 'women's striving for education', '[their] long-frustrated thirst for knowledge', or 'a spiritual movement of our times' (Bäumer 1904: 11) that propelled women, like men, to demand their share of science and culture, of individualization. Helene Lange, a leader of the liberal women's movement, accounts for this with reference to the liberal doctrine of individual rights. The movement for women's education in the age of rationalism was therefore a forerunner of a 'feminine culture', the Romantic movement providing a 'mal-leable climate for female individuality' (Bäumer 1904: 23). 'Women, too, took part in this process of individualisation, though admittedly far behind men, since women's place and tasks erected greater barriers. But what we recognise today as the heart of the women's movement was the effort to bring this process of individualisation to fruition' (Lange 1908: 19; Gerhard 2001: 74).

The second tendency identified by Lange related to 'economic relations or objective social conditions', which she like others linked to a broad diagnosis and critique of society.[4] Lange's critical ambivalence toward the crisis of modernity is couched in a terminology common to sociological discourse of her time.[5] Conflict typical of modernity arose because the process of 'social differentiation, the increasing division of labour' invaded the:

> circle of women's lives . . . dividing women's energies between home and waged work, between domestic management and production for the market, resulting in a gaping tear in the fabric of individual women's lives, in millions of individual women's lives. Women's destiny now belonged to two systems, each with its own dynamic, following its own goals and mastered by its own laws. In a woman's destiny, the contradiction between family interests and the interests of production are most starkly dissonant; her life a stage where the two tendencies in our cultural development clash most sharply, truly the locus of 'the battle of two eras'.
>
> (Lange 1908: 11)

Heightened consciousness of the contradictions between women's traditional roles and economic, industrial-capitalist development thus formed the background to the rise of the women's movement around 1890. This women's movement also had a new political opportunity structure, relying on a second generation of networks, organizations and media, and had considerable success in communicating an understanding of injustice and social contradiction. Of particular importance were ties to various branches of the international women's movement.[6] In 1894, the Bund Deutscher Frauenvereine (BDF) was born as an umbrella for all 'charitable women's associations' launched to 'promote by their service the well-being of families and the people as a whole, to counteract ignorance and injustice and to strengthen morality' (§2 of the constitution).[7] It mirrored existing political contradictions, especially class conflict, as representatives of the proletarian women's movement, fearing persecution under association legislation, were excluded.[8] Despite differences of opinion between the proletarian and bourgeois women's movements, both tied the concept of emancipation to individual women's rights and transformation of the status quo vis-à-vis gender relations. The increasing numbers of women seeking employment or entering women's professions had new demands and expectations. Wife, homemaker and mother had ceased to be a viable containment of identity, most certainly for the working woman but also by the end of the nineteenth century for the bourgeois woman. As Lily Braun wrote: 'We demand application of the principles of the modern state – basic human rights – including their realization for that half of humanity, women' (Braun 1895: 18).

Women's movement activists did more than simply make demands; they also opened up and occupied brand new fields of work in social reform. For the bourgeois women's movement, social work was more than a programme of self-actualization; it was also the starting point for social reform and a new type of social solidarity between sexes and classes. An excellent example of this was Alice Salomon's pioneering professionalization of social work. Like Jane Addams she envisioned linking 'theoretical instruction in the social sciences' to 'practical social assistance' (Salomon 1913: 64).[9] The first academic women schooled in social work quickly achieved the rank of expert in a field that was either closed to men or to which men found entry difficult (see Milz 1994: 28).

Gender relations in classical sociological theory

At the same time as the 'woman question' was entering the political sphere sociologists were grappling with the contradictions and crises of modernity. Their concern was social cohesion, the social body or *'faits sociaux'*. In contrast to earlier sociological theories, such as those of Auguste Comte or Herbert Spencer who understood the social dynamic as progressive evolutionary development, later writers shared a particular 'scepticism vis-à-vis the self-evidence of progress' and a concern for the consequences of modernization (Rammstedt 1988: 279). What marked their approach as increasingly sociological was the realization that the complicated and increasingly problematic relationship between the individual and society could no longer be explained by means of categories drawn from political economy or political theories of liberalism, nor by appeal to natural laws or individual psychology. Instead, as Durkheim insisted, 'a social fact cannot be explained except by another social fact' (Durkheim [1895] 1982: 162). Thus, the social became the object of its own discipline, sociology.

Ferdinand Tönnies

In *Gemeinschaft und Gesellschaft* ([1887] 1963)[10] Ferdinand Tönnies made a decisive contribution to establishing sociology as an independent discipline (Meurer 1991: 375). Here social development is viewed in terms of the transition from 'community' (*Gemeinschaft*) to 'society' (*Gesellschaft*). Not only are community and society conceived as opposites, but *gender dualism* proved to be constitutive on all levels of Tönnies' analysis, from theoretical conceptualization to empirical illustrations. Gender dualism is expressed through two types of social relationships corresponding to 'two types of individual forms of will' (Tönnies [1887] 1963: XXXV) – 'Essential or natural will and rational will'

'*Wesenwille und Kürwille*' ([1887] 1963: 85). Tönnies is not setting these up as ideal types, but fills them with 'empirical meaning' ([1887] 1963: 146). Tönnies mobilizes gender dualism to distinguish 'the rational will' from 'the natural or essential will':

> It's an old truth – but just for that reason important as the outcome of general experience – that women are usually led by feelings, men more by intellect. Men are cleverer. They alone are capable of calculation, of calm (abstract) thinking, of consideration, combination, and logic. As a rule women follow these pursuits ineffectively. They lack the necessary requirement of rational will [*Kürwille*].
>
> (Tönnies 1955: §33, p. 174)

In contrast to the 'natural condition' of community, whose 'simple expression' is domestic life, to which women provide the anchor, society is 'the public, the world' (Tönnies 1955: 3). The male form of life stands for all that is dynamic and at the same time threatening to modern societies – for individualization, separation, hostility, power and exchange, contracts, abstract reason and, with a gesture toward Marx, for 'work as the source of value' (1955: 79). 'As woman enters into the struggle of earning a living, it is evident . . . the woman becomes enlightened, cold-hearted, conscious. Nothing is more foreign and terrible to her original inborn nature, in spite of all later modifications' (Tönnies 1955: §40, p. 191). As an afterthought to his pessimistic analysis, Tönnies adds a 'hope for the future' (Meurer 1992: 349), with an eye to the women's movement as 'an ally on the road to reform' (Tönnies 1907: 107).

> Possibly nothing is more characteristic and important in the process of formation of the Gesellschaft and destruction of Gemeinschaft. Through this development the 'individualism' which is the prerequisite of Gesellschaft comes to its own. However, the possibility of overcoming this individualism and arriving at a reconstruction of Gemeinschaft exists. The analogy of the fate of women with the fate of the proletariat has been recognised and outlined long ago. Their growing group consciousness, like that of the isolated thinker, can develop and rise to a moral-humane consciousness.
>
> (Tönnies 1955: 191)

Tönnies' typology of community and society had been identified as a 'prototypical' formulation of 'a social model built on gender polarity' (Hausen 1976: 380; see also Greven 1991; Meurer 1991, 1992). The fact that gender is a basic category of social analysis in Tönnies' work is completely overlooked in the reception of and reference to this classical thinker (Greven 1991: 361). This is symptomatic of the way in which sociology regards issues of gender as peripheral to sociological theory-building.

Emile Durkheim

Emile Durkheim's explicit anti-feminism has been thoroughly critiqued elsewhere (see Sydie 1987, Chapter 2, this volume; Kandal 1988: 79; Lehmann 1990 and 1995a, b; Roth 1992; Chapter 1, this volume). Nonetheless, his importance as the founder of modern sociology should not simply be passed over due to his ideas on gender.

What distinguishes Durkheim from earlier social theorists such as Marx, Comte or Spencer is his genuine sociological thesis concerning the relationship between the division of labour and social integration or solidarity. While Comte believed that the increasing division of labour would necessarily lead to social fragmentation, which Marx saw as inevitable in class conflict, Durkheim emphasized that the division of labour was not a purely economic phenomenon. In his view, 'in larger societies, it is only thanks to specialisation in tasks that a [societal] balance can be maintained; that the division of labour is, if not alone, certainly one source of social solidarity' (Durkheim [1933] 1964a: 62). Durkheim distinguishes between 'mechanical' and 'organic' forms of social solidarity. In primitive societies solidarity is derived from similarity (Durkheim [1933] 1964a: 181). Higher societies, in contrast, have more complex divisions of labour. They function like differentiated organisms, leading Durkheim to call the resulting form of solidarity 'organic' (Durkheim [1933] 1964a: 223). Of particular interest here is that Durkheim introduces as a central indicator of organic solidarity the sexual division of labour, examples of which he drew from anthropology and history. A highly differentiated division of labour and distinction between the sexes accompanies a higher level of civilization.

His investigations on 'suicide' illustrate the contradictions in Durkheim's gender theory (Lehmann 1995a; Chapters 1 and 2, this volume). Although Durkheim's women are less socialized creatures than men and should therefore be prone to deviant behaviour, Durkheim is forced to admit that the opposite is true. In comparing their suicide rates, he found that women were less likely to kill themselves than men. However, the danger for married women was slightly higher, while married men apparently benefited from integration and moral leverage in marriage and family. Durkheim is forced to concede that woman clearly 'profits less from family life' than man (1951: 188). He develops as a result a rigid view of morality in marriage, its one-sided benefits in satisfying male interest justified by his assertions that women were 'instinctive creatures' with 'less spiritual character' (1951: 272). Nonetheless, by placing marriage at the centre of his studies of primitive and modern societies, Durkheim greatly influenced the understanding of monogamous marriage as responsible for social and societal cohesion, for which he coined the expression 'conjugal family' (*famille conjugale*). For this reason Durkheim was highly critical of Marianne Weber's self-proclaimed 'modern critique' of the 'contemporary patriarchal legal system of marriage' (Marianne Weber [1907] 1971: 513) and insisted that 'the respect which a woman inspires and which grows with time derives in large measure from the honour demanded by the hearth and home' (Durkheim 1906–09, cited in Roth 1992: 183).

Interim comments on the concept of gender difference in the bourgeois women's movement

In discussions of the gender problematic in classic sociological writings it is argued that it was the women's movement that pioneered a theory of polarized gender roles and a politics of separate spheres (Hausen 1976; Dahme 1986). This is only partially correct. A more nuanced explanation is called for. It is amazing how distinctly and explicitly the earlier thinkers of the women's movement around the turn of the twentieth century referred to sociological theories and diagnoses of the time. One example is Helene Lange's programmatic lecture on 'intellectual boundaries between men and women', which she gave to the Social Science Students' Association in Berlin in 1897 (Lange [1897] 1928: 197–216).

Lange developed a theory of gender difference that was to become the basis of the bourgeois feminist concept of 'feminine distinctiveness' (*weiblicher Eigenart*) or the politics of 'spiritual motherhood'. However, from her critical examination of the latest scientific discoveries concerning the physical and psychological differences between the sexes[11] she draws different conclusions. Women's intellectual abilities are not denigrated but rather her qualities are emphasized and taken into account. Beyond the physical, she recognizes a 'persisting spiritual difference, which does not originate in an anatomical difference in the brain structure, but rather in the differences in their interests and emotional orientations, as determined by different physiological functions'. Nonetheless:

> Instead of regarding motherhood as a quality of the woman that affects her being, colours her particularity, directs her endeavours, and which secures for humanity an irreplaceable aspect of culture, physical motherhood has been regarded as woman's sole purpose of life, which she is eagerly to await, to which she is to devote her life exclusively . . . without realizing that she is thus excluded from the realm of reasonable beings.
>
> (Lange [1897] 1928: 204)

Lange caricatured the 'opinion of the masses' that, on the basis of this difference, would have 'women ceaselessly standing at the hearth busy with the production and utilisation of feelings, while the man commands the world of ideas'. What is common to the 'human being' was, in her opinion, more significant. Nonetheless, she used the argument of difference to show that 'it is also the difference that destines the sexes for mutual complementarity' ([1897] 1928: 207) and hence that women's participation in public life was socially necessary to balance the one-sidedness of (male) culture. As if replying to Durkheim, although without using his name,[12] she draws on his theories of the social division of labour and applies his terminology of mechanical and organic solidarity to analyse the contradictions in modern gender theory. For Lange, the division of labour which places the 'woman in the home but gives the man the world' represents a mechanical and therefore lower level of cultural development, while the present era demands a new configuration, 'corresponding to the spiritual division of labour'. She urges that we 'Give up the mechanical division of labour so that the organic, the more appropriate division of labour may come into being. Give the uniqueness of each gender together a generous space in all areas of the cultural scene' ([1897] 1928: 211).

Max Weber

Max Weber's sociological silence on the woman question and the women's movement is usually explained with reference to the 'unspoken division of labour between himself and his wife Marianne' (Lichtblau 1992: 201). Indeed, Max Weber supported not only the feminist engagement and research of his wife, but also women's studies and women's agitation in general (Marianne Weber 1926: 241). That is, on the woman question he tried to maintain a gender-specific division of labour and, above all, the division between science and politics. However, this doesn't mean that Max Weber's contribution to sociological theory is gender neutral (Mülder-Bach 1987: 115). While a few authors have tried to explain the relationship between 'Max Weber and women' biographically or psychologically,[13] others are more interested in viewing his lack of concern as a systematic vacuum in his theories of modernization and rationalization. Changes and problems in gender relations were not discussed in his analyses of the present. Why, for instance, when he examines the forms of 'legitimate power' (*Herrschaft*), is patriarchal power diagnosed only in the past, despite its relevance to understanding the bourgeois marriage contract in the nineteenth century (Max Weber [1922] 1972: 130–580)?[14] In the legal-sociological investigations conducted by Marianne Weber the same concepts are used to sharply criticize the 'system of patriarchalism' in current law and in its 'daily character' (Marianne Weber [1907] 1971: 495, 500).

Bärbel Meurer has pointed out how Max Weber's principle of scientific objectivity functions in his historical analysis of the family as a 'rational gain' (*Rationalitätsgewinn*) (Meurer 1992: 11) because the historically complex term (family) is not introduced as a 'natural fact'. According to Weber, the term must be historically situated and derives from the nexus of sexual, familial and especially economic motives (Max Weber [1922] 1972: 212–213). Given his value-neutral approach and his conviction that development cannot be reversed, he saw woman's striving for emancipation and individualization[15] as a part of the social process of rationalization and questioned 'the formal closure of the family as a source of certain darkly imagined irrational values' (Max Weber [1922] 1972: 413–14). Nonetheless, Hartmann Tyrell's overall evaluation rings true: that Weber's 'magnum opus' *Economy and Society* was marked by an 'invisible woman' (Tyrell 1992: 399).

Inka Mülder-Bach argues that the 'spirit of ascetic Protestantism' is a 'male spirit', the Puritan 'a professional' whose 'rational style of life' – his control of emotion, suppression of drives and hemming in of spontaneity – can only be imagined as 'forced masculinity' (Mülder-Bach 1987: 125). This form of masculinity formed the basis not only for the modern capitalist economy but also for modern culture as a whole. In contrast, 'the influence of women merely inflated the emotional hysterical aspect of religiosity' (Max Weber [1922] 1972: 298). The 'iron cage' metaphor for the 'inescapable power over people' which imprisons the professional 'under a triumphant capitalism' (Weber [1920] 1956a: 379) is inherently masculine in all of Weber's formulations. As Mülder-Bach argues, 'The feminine . . . remains in Weber's theory of modernity without any place at all' (1987: 125).

Georg Simmel

Georg Simmel not only engages in debates with the women's movement but also considers the contradictions in gender relations as a crisis of modernity in his sociological analyses (see Coser 1984; Dahme and Rammstedt 1984; Wolfer-Melior 1985; Dahme 1986, 1988; Tyrell 1986; Klinger 1988; Cavana 1991; Lichtblau 1992, 1997; Wobbe 1995; see also Chapters 1 and 3, this volume). Here, I will look at three aspects of his gender sociology that indicate a mutual influence between sociology and feminism.

First, gender difference is central to his theory of social differentiation. Women slid into a relationship of inequality and dis-simultaneity by virtue of the social process of evolution as the separation of 'production for the market [from production in] the domestic economy' (Simmel [1898] 1985d: 144) proceeded. In contrast to men, whose work is specialized and segregated, women are the 'undifferentiated' sex, whose 'being' is marked by the 'character of unity' (Simmel [1890] 1985c: 28, 34; compare on this point Tyrell 1986: 450; Dahme and Köhnke 1985: 7). Simmel's theory of gender is not that dissimilar to Spencer's, Tönnies' or Durkheim's. What is distinctive about Simmel's account is the fact that he sees these developments not as problematic but as inevitable.

Second, the women's movement as a social movement serves as a model for his theory of differentiation because 'it emphasizes solidarity of women's interests as against the party of men' (Simmel 1995: 500). The women's movement freed women from their isolation at home and the demands of domesticity which 'impeded going into circles beyond marriage, family, friendship, perhaps charitable associations and religion', hence hindering 'the comradely application of equality' (1995: 499). Here Simmel is addressing the problem of group formation and the question of whether a women's movement beyond class, ethnicity or other forms of social differentiation is possible (see Buechler 1990: 10) or whether it must necessarily be characterized 'by a web of overlapping memberships' (Calhoun 1995: 194–5). For this reason Simmel had no problem with the contradictory aims of the proletarian and bourgeois women's movements, which he explained as resulting from their differing social relationship to the process of 'modern industrialization':

> The industrial mode of production at the present time has, on the one hand, torn domestic activity away from the proletarian woman and, on the other, has atrophied the sphere of activity of the bourgeois woman limited to home. Thus, both events belong equally to the same typical case and are responsible for all the pain of the present, occasioned by the fact that objective relationships have progressed more quickly than individual development and adaptation.
>
> (Simmel [1896] 1985a: 137)[16]

Third, Simmel engaged in a gendered analysis of culture (Wobbe 1995; see also Lichtblau 1997). According to Simmel, tensions in modern gender relations are ascribed to an 'objective', male-influenced, indeed, 'thoroughly masculine culture' which permits only a 'subjective' contribution by women who do not participate in the 'process of perfection of the subject' nor in objectivity or specialization (Simmel 1983: 205).[17] In various works Simmel published after 1890, he sympathetically analysed the problem for women of 'being a stranger' in a male-dominated culture. On the one hand, he saw this conflict between male and female culture as 'an epochal distinction of the present time' (see Lichtblau 1997: 100) – thus granting the women's movement an 'objective meaning for culture' (Simmel [1902] 1985e: 160). On the other hand, he intends his diagnosis to elevate the value of the feminine, so women would not be regarded as 'simply co-relative beings vis-à-vis men' but as 'a unity opposite the man, whose life is splintered to fragments', and as such represent 'perfected or closed being' (*Wesensgeschlossenheit*).[18] This definition of the 'relationship between the sexes, which allows each to maintain its own uniqueness', this 'normative height above all subjectivity and oppositions, the prize of dualism' (Simmel [1911] 1985b: 223) clearly explodes the framework of a sociology of gender and is, in Simmel's words, a 'form of relationship of identity vis-à-vis being itself, whether we want to see it as the basis of nature, or as the mystical, or as the purely metaphysical' (Simmel [1911] 1985b: 222).

Summary

On the whole, placing the sociological and feminist analyses of society at the high point of the first women's movement in Germany around 1900 side by side, we discover an awareness of the gender problematic as central to the crisis in modernity. We can observe a mutual influence between the women's movement and sociology in formulating the problem, and in many cases even a dialogue (for instance between Simmel and Marianne Weber, see Chapter 3, this volume). Women actively critiqued the thoroughly non-objective but clearly partisan boundaries between the masculine and the feminine and the merely functional positioning of the female, whose basic consignment to secondary status seemed to assure social cohesion and was expected to offer compensation for the crisis of modernity (for instance in Tönnies and Durkheim). The early sociologists discussed at length the social problems connected to the woman question and women's emancipatory struggles, but maintained their indifference or resistance to the political aims of the women's movement. Although Simmel in particular approached the women's movement's own concepts in his analysis of the crisis of culture and socially constructed problems of gender, even moderate feminists did not accept his sociological and philosophical solutions to the gender problem, especially not his rigid distinctions between male and female culture. Max Weber's scientific silence on the gender question, despite his engagement with and important critiques of patriarchy, smoothed the way for sociology, and in particular empirical social research, to neglect gender questions under the sign of scientific objectivity and progressive rationalization of relations of power between the sexes in private as well as public realms. 'Homo sociologicus' in all the multiplicity of his roles remained not only grammatically, but theoretically and empirically male (see all examples in Dahrendorf [1965] 1994a).

The new feminism and sociology today[19]

By the end of the 1960s, the renewed women's movement in West Germany was given impetus by a specific 'political opportunity structure' fostered by international encouragement, the civil rights movement in the US and student unrest in France, as well as the student movement in the Federal Republic. Intimate aspects of gender relations were now discussed and social taboos named, and the climate of alleged sexual freedom was recognized as riddled with relations of power and violence (see Millet 1974; Firestone 1975; Schwarzer 1975; Stefan 1975). The realization that even the 'left' failed to question male dominance, or treated the 'woman question' at best again as a 'secondary contradiction' led to a women's movement that was autonomous in two senses, favouring self-determination as well as independence from other political institutions (Knäpper 1984: 120; see also Brand 1982: 40). A 'new political paradigm' (Offe 1985: 817) suggested what was 'new' in these social movements was their targeting of the 'life world' outside institutionalized forms of the political and beyond the so-called productive sphere. This was especially true of the new women's movement that now understood itself to be feminist.[20] Consciousness-raising, practised in numerous groups, embodied a collective learning process through which 'private' problems would be 'politically' diagnosed, such as the gendered division of labour or dominance in sexual relations now understood as structural violence. Not 'only' equal rights but also emancipation; not only participation, but a new concept of the political would be applied to overcome the systematic polarization of the sexes through oppositional concepts of production and reproduction, system and life world. These represented the well-formulated political aims of the movement, poignantly captured in the slogan 'the personal is political' (see Gerhard 1999).

The new 'wave' of feminism emerged along with perceptions of an economic and social crisis whose consequences would be recognized only later and identified according to one's sociological perspective as a new stage of modernization (Zapf 1991), as a 'second' or 'reflexive' modernity (Beck *et al.* 1996) or as the 'postmodern' (Welsch 1988). This was not coincidental, but rather a confirmation of the relevance of gender to contemporary concerns. Central from a gender perspective was the fact that Western democracies had institutionalized a welfare compromise to pacify class antagonisms, which assumed a family with the male as bread-winner and institutionalized the traditional division of labour (Gerhard *et al.* 1988; Lewis 1992).

Modernizing gender relations – that is, including women in the processes of individualization, rationalization and democratization of social relations – thus proved to be not only a practical problem on the level of daily life or a theoretical problem of personal and political emancipation, but also a not so new 'social question' whose answer, according to Max Weber, 'should *also* serve to develop concepts and critiques that will do the work of social science' (Weber [1920] 1956b: 261; see also Nunner-Winkler 1994: 43–6).

Feminism as social theory

Given its interest in social change, women's studies and feminist theory, rooted in the new women's movement, developed first within the social sciences.[21] Yet as a theoretical critique of society, women's and gender research in the social sciences has, since the 1970s, met with a significant amount of scepticism and opposition. Interest in researching the causes and structures of gender inequality as well as a concern to confront epistemological and methodological questions raised by women's experiences and interests was seen as unscientific and partisan, rather than as genuinely sociological. Moreover, women's studies defined itself as an interdisciplinary project setting out to transcend disciplinary boundaries that it saw as excluding women and their research interests (or including them only in so-called hyphenated sociologies – see Pross 1975). Now, after more than 30 years of intensive research and discussion, feminist approaches have become so differentiated that a process of professionalization and specialization now characterizes women's studies. We can no longer talk about a (singular) women's and gender studies or of *one* feminist perspective, and this is not only true in the social sciences. Growing out of the early polemical declarations of war against 'the patriarchy' in the academy itself,[22] many lively debates and a multiplicity of discourses have developed. However, they all challenge the particularity of a male gaze with its false objectivity across a range of subjects and fields.[23] Over time we see a shift in major themes and concerns:

- from focusing on women's status and discrimination against women to analysing gender relations;
- from examining historical and social origins of the structure of gender relations to analysing the meaning, language and interpretation of texts, pictures and cultural representations;
- from dealing with the social problem of inequality to problematizing gender difference and recognizing differences.

Crucially, then, a feminist perspective offers not only a critique of society but also of epistemology. Feminist critique of the validity, objectivity and rationality of social science amounts to a critique of what Simmel would have recognized as masculine, 'objective' culture and epistemology yet, unlike Simmel, goes on to reconsider nearly all concepts and categories in the social sciences, precisely because of their one-sidedness and male bias. Feminist thought, as a radical form of critique and self-reflection, is a genuine sociological way of thinking. It starts by questioning traditional gender roles and societal norms, institutions and practices before going on to analyse the interaction and embeddedness of subject positions and to deconstruct the meaning of social action as well as forms of cultural representation. As Norbert Elias's definition of what sociology is makes clear, 'If you want to understand what sociology is all about, then you must be ready to confront yourself, to step outside yourself and perceive your being one person among others' (Elias 1993: 9).

Nonetheless, danger lurked in the so-called 'linguistic turn', which, given its focus on language, communication and their epistemological premises, risks neglecting an analysis of social conditions and historical context. The radical post-structural or postmodern critique aiming at deconstructing the binary of both sexes as well as 'gender' as a social category (Butler 1991) was criticized by feminist scholars in a number of disciplines, but it has also triggered productive debate (see, for example, Benhabib *et al.* 1993). In particular, it provided a framework for analysing discourses of power which ensured their longevity rather than hastened their demise (see Foucault 1983), interrogating the binary logic behind all gender constructions, including those of feminists, as well as all essentialist visions of femininity or 'woman's being'. It therefore places differences *among* women at the centre of analysis. The specific contribution of this analysis to sociology lies in its 'placing a discursive analysis of the meaning of gender into the historical and social context, with attention paid to specific time and place, and refining this research by applying to it structural analyses of institutions and political economy' (Fraser 1993: 149).

In my opinion, and in the terms of classical sociology, this is a radical rethinking of the relationship between the individual and society in which gender relations, as a property of social structure as well as of symbolic and normative orders, are 'social facts' that are subject to change. This is 'not only something at once realised in history but as something reconstituted by daily activity and in many variations newly anchored' (Dölling and Krais 1997: 8; see also Gildemeister and Wetterer 1992). Because engendering seems to be the special organizing principle of modern society (Marshall 1994), what is needed is a feminist perspective that reconsiders nearly all concepts and categories in social science such as roles, individualization, division of labour, family, politics, the state and modernity.

Sociological diagnoses today: some examples

In contrast to sociology a hundred years ago, neither the theoretical challenges nor the breadth of a feminist perspective seem to be fully appreciated, let alone taken as central, in German sociology today.[24] Most sociological theorists fail to distinguish between feminism as a social and political movement and feminist theory as a critical perspective in the social sciences. For instance, the tardy recognition of the women's movement in social movement studies confirms Friedhelm Neidhardt's thesis that 'the difficulties societies face in dealing with these movements is the same one that sociology has, trying to find suitable concepts for them' (see Neidhardt 1985: 193). The significance of both old and new women's movements compared to other social movements has been underestimated or misinterpreted as 'only' cultural (see, for instance, Raschke 1985; in contrast Rucht 1994).

A prominent example of underestimation, hesitant admissions and paternalism is the career of the woman question in Habermas's social analyses. We can start with his oft-cited simple footnote 15 in 'Keywords to the "Spiritual Situation of the Times" ' where he characterizes the women's movement as having its 'own concretism, clawing on to natural ascriptive categories like . . .

sex' (Habermas 1979: 28). We can then move on to his view of feminism as part of 'the tradition of bourgeois-socialist liberation movements' but in contrast to all other (new) movements, as maintaining a 'particularistic core', despite his admission that it triggers 'an offensive' (1982: II. Bd. 578). Even in his discourse theory of law, he claims that 'aspects' of gender difference and corresponding demands for women's rights 'must first be clarified in public discussion before they can be dealt with' (1992: 513) – and he writes this after 150 years of debate about women's rights!

Compared to other disciplines, sociology's 'particular resistance' and 'ambivalent relationship' to feminist theory has been noted by Stacey and Thorne (1985b: 119), who argue that feminist questions have been both co-opted and ghettoized (in so-called hyphenated sociologies), leaving dominant paradigms largely unaltered. Without doubt, any global critique of sociology stumbles over a division of labour between empirical research and social theory. As a result, the variable 'gender' may indeed be taken into account, but only as one variable among many, as 'always particular' and as 'an ascription of a [person's] belonging to' (see Kreckel 1991: 374), rather than as a structuring category. That means that in mainstream sociology, we have no systematic treatment of gender. At best we have isolated approaches to questions raised by feminists (see, in contrast, Bourdieu 1997: 153), famous footnotes or some references in the field of labour market analysis. We habitually find women in family sociology and related areas, where the female sex itself is the object of research.

Theories of gender difference play no role in critical theory,[25] or in theories of modernization and individualization, and are absent from systems theory. This is particularly so in Ulrich Beck's sociological analysis (Beck 1986, 1993), even though to construct his theory of individualization he identifies, together with Elisabeth Beck-Gernsheim (Beck and Beck-Gernsheim 1990, 1994, 2002), changes in gender relations as significant in numerous publications (see also Chapter 7, this volume). But this does not amount to an analysis of gender *relationships*. Rather, it is simply a matter of noting the devastating consequences, or 'risks', of women's emancipation and their delayed individualization, particularly with regard to men and children. In short, risk for the family is the real issue here. The metaphors of 'decay' and dissolution that run through his analysis of the increasing employment of women, high divorce rates, increasing fragility of marriage and family care, the *childless* society and so on, are remarkable, but they are not new. The crisis scenario following from women's individualization is virtually indistinguishable from Riehl's (1855) fear of the impact of women's emancipation on the family and society.

Contemporary sociological framings of the changing social position of women are not unlike those we encountered in the sociological classics above, where the principal problem of modernity was also represented as the 'tragedy of relationships' – an effect of social differentiation resulting from the processes of individualization and liberation from traditional obligations (see Tönnies, Durkheim and Simmel). What, then, has Ulrich Beck contributed to this discussion? First, he argues that in the second phase of modernity, the individualization process, which now includes women and other under-privileged minorities 'beyond status and class', has induced such a thorough transformation in traditional or reconstructed institutions of society that these are now dramatically eroding. Whereas 'industrial society' – in his termin-ology the first modernity – 'has been dependent upon unequal positions of men and women . . . the entire structure of family ties has (now, in the so-called "second" or "reflexive modernity") come under pressure from individualisation' (Beck 2002: 202–3). This new phase in individualization, dat-ing from the 1970s, serves as the 'motor of social transformation' (Beck 1993: 71) far more than ecological dangers or globalization. It exhibits three dimen-sions: emancipation, loss of stability and reintegration (Beck 1986: 206).[26] While new freedoms and insecurities are dramatized and sensationalized in Beck's analysis by focusing specifically on women in order to post 'warning signs for feminism' (Meurer 1997: 414; see Beck 1986: 200), future scenarios vaguely hint at the need to 'discover the political'. They do not, however, suggest how reintegration in self-constructed networks of acquaintances, partners and working relationships should proceed.

Furthermore, Beck's individualization theory, as a 'product of the labour market', remains captive to criteria derived from a male labour model, and hence the differing behaviour of women in the job market is viewed as an anomaly. Elisabeth Beck-Gernsheim, in her careful analysis of love and con-flict in gender relations and in the tensions between 'living for others' and living 'a life of one's own' (Beck and Beck-Gernsheim 2002: 54–84), discusses the material basis for women's individualization processes. However, even Beck-Gernsheim's rendering of women's individualization as 'tardy indi-vidualisation' tacitly assumes a male model of labour market participation and individualization.[27] The 'double socialisation' (*Vergesellschaftung*) of women (Becker-Schmidt and Knapp 2000) – that is, their involvement in the doubled context of family and market, which potentially offers an alternative form of individualization – is again theoretically erased or rendered a tragedy or dilemma. Market-driven individualization turns out to be social coercion which proceeded behind women's backs, 'unnoticed', 'unwanted', and yet, up to that point 'not reflected upon', that is, 'as a reflex' (Beck 1996: 27–43).

Since *Risk Society* (1986) became a bestseller, was reviewed widely beyond disciplinary boundaries, and was hailed as a 'straightforward diagnosis for our times' (Neckel 1993: 70), Beck's work has often been criticized by sociologists because his theory lacks empirical support and conceptual precision. The prob-lem resides for the most part in that 'causes, descriptions and consequences are squeezed into a single definition', so that it remains unclear at what level the author is arguing (Friedrich 1998: 34; see also Burkart 1995) – on the level of social theory, of social institutions or of micro individual behaviour. Indeed, Beck's social, theoretical and empirical statements are often contradictory in themselves, using the jargon of a journalist's provocative style, consciously unscientific and open-ended – one reason why detailed critique has nothing to latch on to. Interestingly, in the recently published English edition, Beck and Beck-Gernsheim are more careful and defensive in their arguments; especially in their attempt to avoid any misunderstanding of the concept of individualization in the Anglo-American context:

> There is a lot of misunderstanding about this concept of individual-
> isation. It does not mean individualism. It does not mean individu-
> ation – a term used by depth psychologists to describe the process of
> becoming an autonomous individual. And it has nothing to do with
> the market egoism of Thatcherism. That is always a potential mis-
> understanding in Britain. Nor, lastly, does it mean emancipation as
> Jürgen Habermas describes it.
>
> (Beck and Beck-Gernsheim 2002: 202)

To add one concluding example, Niklas Luhmann (1988) gets tangled up in the usual indifference and failure to distinguish between feminism as a social movement and feminism as a theoretical perspective. This is apparent in what Luhmann perceives as a paradox that characterizes feminist thinking and theorizing, as if he had caught women's studies with a deficiency of logic that he must correct, that the code governing the differentiation of woman from man is incompatible with any programme of equal rights. Feminist theory has called this the 'Wollstonecraft dilemma'. Luhmann seems blissfully unaware that, at least since the publication of Wollstonecraft's *Vindication of the Rights of Woman* ([1792] 1967), women have been aware of the paradox of simul-taneously demanding equality as well as a consideration and recognition of difference in relationships between the sexes (see Gerhard 1990b; Pateman 1992: 54f). The ongoing global feminist discussion of equality and/or differ-ence does not – as Luhmann assumes – represent an 'unusual magnitude of self-reference of women's studies' (Luhmann 1988: 48). Rather, it attests to feminism's aptitude for reflection, self-observation and critique, just as sociology itself behaves when diagnosing and interpreting crises in the devel-opment of modernity.

If, despite the tentative nature of my conclusions, I were to summarize the relationship between feminism and sociology today in terms of 'elective affin-ities', I would have to admit that the relationship, far from having become less problematic, is quite the opposite. Even if, in the meantime, the grand-daughters of the founding fathers are ready neither to reject the 'legacy of the mothers' (Chodorow 1985) nor to deny the 'Paternity of the Fathers' (Gouges [1791] 1990), the discipline of sociology treats them like 'illegitimate daughters' – and this, despite the fact that '*la recherche de la paternité n'est plus interdite*'.[28]

Notes

1 A similar parallel between the women's movement and sociology is drawn by Kandal (1988); see also Marshall (1994). On the first female social scientists see Milz (1994); Honegger and Wobbe (1998).

2 There is a wide-ranging feminist literature critiquing key social and political philosophers, from Locke through Kant, Rousseau and Fichte to Hegel and Marx. See, for example, Gerhard (1978, 1990b); Okin (1979); Lloyd (1985); Steinbrügge (1987); Pateman (1988); Honegger (1991b).

3 See von Hippel ([1792] 1977); Condorcet ([1789] 1979); or, the unusually forthright Bavarian defender of public law, Behr (1804).

4 See also Bäumer (1901); Freudenberg (1911); Zahn-Harnack (1928).

5 This is how Simmel's *Philosophie des Geldes* is cited (1900: 18).

6 The bourgeois charitable or 'moderate' branch, from 1894 under the umbrella of the Bund Deutscher Frauenvereine (BDF), was a member of the International Council of Women (ICW). The proletarian women's movement was embedded in the context of the II. Internationale (since 1889), and the bourgeois radicals joined the Americans as the avant garde for suffrage, working together since 1904 in the International Alliance for Women's Suffrage (IAW).

7 See Gertrud Bäumer (1921: 21).

8 See Gerhard (1990a: 170ff).

9 See also Peyser (1958). Incidentally, Max Weber was one of the first professors to teach a course on 'basic characteristics of modern social development' in Berlin in 1893/94.

10 *Community and Society* (first published 1887, 2nd edition 1912; here cited in 1963).

11 Quoted are Havelock Ellis, Herbert Spencer, but also the often cited measurements of various brain sizes in men and women to which Durkheim referred (Lange [1897] 1928: 200).

12 It cannot be confirmed and is probably unlikely that Lange had read Durkheim's 1893 dissertation that had appeared in French; however, she may have seen Gustav Schmoller's review of the work in the *Jahrbuch für Gesetzgebung, Verwaltung und Volkswirtschaft im Deutschen Reich* (1894: 286–9). Regardless, the intelligent reference to the text is remarkable.

13 See Gilcher-Holtey (1988) and Kandal (1988: 126–56). On the consequences of the Webers' relationship with the 'erotic movement', see Lichtblau (1992).

14 See Gerhard (1991, 1990c) on how Weber's analysis of patriarchalism hardly found its way into women's and gender studies.

15 The gender question is approached very indirectly in the chapter on *'Rechtssoziologie'* in the demand for 'freedom of divorce' regarded as a 'return to a sexual freedom of contract' from which one was 'further removed than ever before'. In this context we find the same critical key words concerning patriarchalism in marriage as used by Mariane Weber ([1907] 1971: 412, 500), for instance 'gender vanity' and 'authoritarian instincts' in the male (Weber [1922] 1972: 413).

16 Simmel wrote this in the journal *Zukunft* entitled 'Der Frauenkongreß und die Sozialdemokratie' (The Women's Congress and Social Democracy) ([1896] 1985a) on the occasion of the Internationaler Kongress für Frauenwerke und Frauenbestrebungen (International Congress for Women's Initiatives and Aims), which in 1896 offered the last venue for all branches of the women's movement to participate; it took place in Berlin to great media attention, see Gerhard (1990a: 181).

17 See also Simmel ([1902] 1985e: 159f.). There are two essays entitled 'Weibliche Kultur' (Female culture) (1902) which differ, however, in important nuances that can cause confusion in citation. Unfortunately, the 1983 edition doesn't give the appropriate references.

18 In the essay 'Weibliche Kultur' (1902) he writes:

> The wonderful relationship which the female soul appears to maintain toward the unfractured unity of nature and which distinguishes her entire destiny from the fragmented, differentiated objectivity inhabited by men – this is precisely what keeps her away from our culture's professionally specialized work.
>
> (Simmel [1902] 1985e: 162)

19 In examining the current relationship between feminism and sociology in West Germany, I am necessarily skipping over important mediating steps in both the history of sociology and the development of the women's movement. This is especially true with respect to some of the parallel developments in post-war sociology. For instance, many felt that formal citizenship rights and constitutional equality had answered the woman question, although issues might remain that required incremental redress (Strecker 1965: 67), and bourgeois women's associations were re-established as part of the Allies' political re-education programme (see Rupieper 1991; Both 1993). The renewed launch and consolidation of sociology as a discipline included in its interests women's issues, but largely confined them to family sociology, often legitimating reactionary family policies (for example, Schelsky 1955; for critique see Haensch 1969; Rosenbaum 1973). Material promoting reform, in the sense of catching up with modernity, would not appear until 1966 with the publication of the 'Report of the Government of the Federal Republic on the Situation of Women in Employment, Family and Society'

(Bundestags-Drucksache 1986: 909) to which more than 100 social scientists contributed, including René König and Elisabeth Pfeil. As in other Western nations, factors such as rapidly increased employment rates among mothers, and their dual burden of paid and domestic work, emerged as issues. Women's expectations and demands had grown, as had their awareness of discrimination. The discrepancy between the promise of formal equality and the stubborn persistence of gender inequality was clearly apparent. Betty Friedan's 'problem that had no name', the 'feminine mystique', would label that fact (Friedan 1963).

20 The concept of 'feminism' entered the new German women's movement and marked a radical turning away from establishment women's politics. Instead, it forged a link to the new aims of an international movement. Although in Germany the word 'feminism' was first pronounced in 1896 at the International Congress (Internationaler Kongreß für Frauenwerke und Frauenbestrebungen) in Berlin by a French delegate and thus passed on to a German public, it was then mainly used as a denouncement (see Offen 1993: 106).

21 See the launch of a section on women's research in the German Sociological Association (Deutsche Gesellschaft für Soziologie), 1979, as well as the institution of a women's studies professorship in sociology running since 1987.

22 On patriarchalism see, for instance, Hausen (1986); Scott (1988); Beer (1990); Gerhard (1990, 1991).

23 For an overview of the various discourses and feminist research in Germany, see *Deutsche Forschungsgemeinschaft* (ed. 1994).

24 For exceptions, however, see Tyrell (1986); Treibel (1995).

25 Although Habermas, in response to a broad feminist criticism, conceded in his preface to the revised German edition of *The Structural Transformation of the Public Sphere* (1990) that 'the exclusion of women was constitutive for the political public sphere' and 'had structuring power'. This insight did not change his theoretical approach or conclusions. This was otherwise in the early Frankfurt School, see especially Horkheimer (1988). For feminist commentary on the Frankfurt School, see Benhabib (1982); Benjamin (1982); Fraser (1989); Rumpf (1989).

26 See also Beck *et al.* (1996): 'dis-embedding' and 're-embedding', which also means the liberation of the individual from traditional obligations and renewed anchoring of the individual in self-chosen communities, cited in Schroer (2001: 403).

27 This is all the more astonishing since, from the beginning of women' studies in the Federal Republic of Germany, Beck-Gernsheim has made significant contributions to analysing the contradictions and mutual dependencies in the contexts of women's lives (Beck-Gernsheim 1980, 1983).

28 Paraphrase of Art. 340 of the French Code Civil of 1804 which prevented illegitimate children from making any claims on fathers, valid into the 1930s.

It stands for a fundamental experience of injustice women suffered, already addressed by Olympe de Gouges in 1791 in her *Declaration of the Rights of Women*: she called for freedom of expression (namely the right to reveal paternity) (Gouges [1791] 1990) (see Gerhard 1990b: 49).

PART III
Interrogating modern sociology

7 Gender and the post-structural social

Lisa Adkins

It has been claimed that some forms of recent social theory risk reinstating the privileged masculine subject of classical social theory, thus recuperating the gendered relations of privilege and exclusion which many feminist sociologists have highlighted as being at play in classical narratives of modernity.[1] In particular, those theories outlining the contours and characteristics of a social emerging in the context of a decline or undercutting of the powers of social structure are understood to revisit conceptions of – and indeed normalize – the abstract, disembodied, masculine subject of classical social theory. Moreover (and perhaps rather ironically), this charge is mounted against such theories even though they often proclaim that men and women are being released from the norms, habits and expectations of gender characteristic of modernity, that is, a dissolution of modernity's social arrangements of gender.

What I suggest in this chapter, however, is that in such forms of social theory there is not so much a recuperation of a traditional gendered model of power and privilege but an instatement of a rather more contemporary one. Specifically, I suggest that in recent social theory a hidden gendered narrative is at play, one which associates the object of such analyses – what I term the post-structural social – (more often) with masculinity than with femininity. I thus identify a tendency towards the exclusion of women from post-structural modes of sociality in contemporary social theory, an exclusion that I shall illustrate with reference to reflexive forms of action and processes of individualization. I will suggest further that this exclusion of women from post-structural forms of sociality is not of the same order as that identified by feminist sociologists as operating in accounts of classical modernity. Specifically, while in classical accounts women were excluded from the social, in contemporary social theory women are imagined as overdetermined by societal (and especially socio-structural) forces, an overdetermination that prevents women's participation in post-structural modes of sociality. This chapter therefore highlights not a simple recuperation of the traditions of social theory vis-à-vis gender but an entirely new vision, that is, a new phase in the complex relations between social theorizing and the categories of gender, a phase which may be characterized not by reference to natural women and social men (Sydie 1987), but to social women and post-(structural) social men.

I shall lay out this argument in three stages. First, I shall outline the classical legacy of social theory in regard to gender and especially the privileging of a masculine subject and the various ways in which classical theorizing excluded women from the social. Second, I will consider how this legacy has been understood to shape contemporary forms of social theorizing, that is, how contemporary social theory is understood to recuperate this classical legacy in regard to gender. Third, and with close reference to theories of reflexive modernity, I shall consider exactly how women and gender are understood and imagined in contemporary modes of social theory. This analysis will show not an ongoing exclusion of women from the social but a figure of woman who is now overdetermined by the social – a figure who is stuck in the socio-historical time of first modernity.

The classical tradition: the exclusion of women from the social

In their engagements with and excavations of classical social theory, feminists have pointed to the ways in which the object of sociology and social theory – the social – was imagined and defined in opposition to a pre-social era (variously described as the pre-industrial, the traditional, *gemeinschaft*), and moreover how in such narratives women were overwhelmingly associated with the latter and hence excluded from the modern. For example, and as a range of feminist commentators have noted (see, for example, Sydie 1987; Marshall 1994), in Marx's social and political theory and many Marxist accounts of capitalist society there is a tendency to exclude women from the social. This has been made particularly visible in the case of domestic labour, and especially in the allocation of use and not exchange value to this mode of production. This move excluded domestic labour from what in Marx's view was the key axis of political struggle within industrial capitalism – that between the wage-labourer and the capitalist employer – since in Marx's conception it was only when labour was involved in the creation of surplus value that it could be regarded as production. In so doing Marx stripped women (since 'women' were only ever conceived as family dependants, for example, as wives and daughters of the proletariat) not only of the foundational identity of industrial capitalism, that is, a class identity (since in his view a class position was constituted via a *direct* relationship between wage-labour and capital), but also located domestic production as pre-industrial, that is removed from the very sets of exchanges and relationships which for Marx defined industrial capitalism. Marx therefore located domestic production and hence women as inhabiting the world of tradition – as locked into a pre-industrial mode of production – and hence as not full social and political agents in the new capitalist world. Thus Marx's narrative of modernity was made possible by a dualism of the traditional and the modern, a dualism which rooted women in tradition and excluded them from modern forms of social and political identity and agency.

While feminists have pointed to this exclusion of women from the social in a range of classical accounts of modernity, including those of Durkheim and Weber, they have also noted that this has even been the case when there is a clear recognition of a problematic equation of masculinity with the social (see Chapter 1, this volume). Rita Felski (1995) shows this to be the case for Simmel's social theory, even as his is perhaps the only classical social theory which seriously considered the relationship between gender and modernity and which offered a critique of the equation of masculinity with the modern. Yet while he did so, Simmel simultaneously located femininity as outside of modernity, that is, as outside of the cultural and institutional arrangements his social theory described. Woman is not condemned on these grounds, however, since in Simmel's social theory men are understood to suffer the misfortune of experiencing all of the fragmenting, alienating, individualizing and differentiating forces of modernity (indeed for Simmel this is the tragedy of both modernity and of masculinity) (Felski 1995; Witz 2000, 2001). According to Simmel woman stands outside of these experiences as femininity is understood to be characterized by a wholeness that does not lend itself to such experiences. Effectively, then, feminine identity and woman is understood to stand outside of socio-historical time. The non-differentiated wholeness of femininity ensured that women did not and could not experience or achieve the detachment and critical reflection necessary for participation in the cultural and institutional forms of modernity (Felski 1995). Indeed for Simmel feminine identity and culture occupies the zone of being rather than becoming, of immanence rather than transcendence, a wholeness that could challenge the alienating and contradictory experiences of modernity. Felski argues that what is particularly significant in regard to Simmel's social theory is that it makes explicit what is buried in much sociological and philosophical thought. In particular it makes explicit how in classical social theory women are excluded from the social as there is a yearning for the feminine 'as emblematic of a nonalienated, nonfragmented identity' (Felski 1995: 37) and that this very yearning is at the heart of narratives of the modern. Simmel's social theory, for example, positions woman as the 'overt object of nostalgic desire' (Felski 1995: 37), a desire which locates woman as a symbol of pre-modernity and non-differentiation.[2]

This classical vision of the social has to a large degree shaped the agenda of feminist sociology. In particular, and as Witz (2000) has made clear, this exclusion has led to an overwhelming impulse on the part of feminist sociologists to socialize women. Thus some considerable part of the feminist sociological project may be described as one of placing women within the realm of the social. This latter has taken many forms, including theoretical excursions which have sought to attribute exchange and surplus value to domestic labour; empirical projects seeking to demonstrate that women experience alienation in relation to the labour process; theoretical reconstructions of the public sphere to include the interests of women; revised accounts of modernity which place women and gender not outside of, but at the very heart of, the social; and accounts which have sought to correct dualist understandings of social action. Indeed much feminist sociological work may still be characterized as being defined by this project of socializing women, evidenced, for example, in claims that women too are engaged in the reflexive project of the self; that women are central to postmodern culture; and that women are the subjects and not simply the objects of the male gaze. Indeed, the feminist sociological project has not just simply been one of socializing women in regard to classical social theory (for instance in relation to the social theory of the founding fathers of sociology) but has concerned itself with the *ongoing legacy* of this exclusion within the discipline.

This ongoing legacy of the exclusion of women from the social is particularly evident in regard to recent accounts that have sought to provide embodied accounts of social action (Turner 1984, 1992; Shilling 1993; Williams and Bendelow 1998). Here it is typically pointed out that in attempting to delineate the contours and characteristics of the social, classical sociology overwhelmingly conceived social action as concerning the dominance of the mind over the body, indeed as an issue of the transcendence and transformation of the constraints of corporeality. Thus classical social theory disembodied both human subjects and social action, and constructed a disembodied, abstract, rational subject as the ideal subject of modernity.[3] Contemporary social theorists have pointed to the inadequacies of this conceptualization, outlining and theorizing the embodied character of social action, via, for example, the phenomenology of Merleau-Ponty (Crossley 2001). However, while welcoming such innovations, a number of contemporary feminist sociologists have suggested that this new theoretical agenda tends to overlook a number of issues. First, it overlooks the fact that the mind/body dualism central to classical sociology was a gendered one with women overwhelmingly associated with the body – indeed women were often represented as unable to transcend corporeality and hence participate in various modalities of modern forms of social action. Second, as a consequence, and as Witz (2000) has argued, it therefore fails to register the problematic nature of its own project in regard to feminist sociology. Specifically it fails to register that feminist sociology has an ambivalent relationship towards corporeality since feminist sociological accounts which have attempted to socialize women have done so in an explicit attempt to overcome the association of women with corporeality and hence women's exclusion from the social. Indeed, Witz suggests that the failure of social theorists of the body to register this point means that the forms of embodied sociality which this social theory makes explicit will and can only ever be masculine. And rather ironically this is the case even though contemporary theorists of the body invariably cite the rise of modern feminism as a key impetus behind the project of embodying the social, and ostensibly appear to be challenging the legacies of the classical tradition.

The onward march of the classical legacy?

This charge of privileging the masculine subject and hence of a recuperation of the classical tradition is not, however, limited to recent social theory on the body, for this has been claimed to be the case for a range of forms of contemporary theorizing. And this is so even for recent social theory that claims that the social is being radically re-organized in the contemporary period, that is, for forms of social theory that ostensibly appear to break with many of the assumptions of the classical tradition. For instance a privileging of the disembodied, disembedded masculine subject has been said to be at issue in the emphasis in much recent social theory on increased capacities for the self-fashioning of identity in late modern cultures. Discussing theories of reflexive modernity broadly, but especially the work of Giddens, Lois McNay (1999, 2000) in particular has argued that theories of reflexive identity – especially the notion that identity is an issue of reflexive self-transformation – fail to fully consider issues connected to gender identity. She suggests that an examination of questions related to gender, embodiment and sexuality reveal aspects of identity that are less amenable to processes of re-fashioning. This is not to say that McNay considers identity to be somehow fixed, but she argues that in ignoring more embedded aspects of identity, certain theories of reflexive modernity run the risk of re-instating the disembodied and disembedded subject of masculinist thought.

Indeed it is not just in the cognitive and realist-orientated accounts of reflexivity and reflexive modernity that McNay identifies a tendency towards the reinstatement of a disembodied masculine subject. She also understands this to be the case in accounts that break with the cognitive realism of Beck and Giddens and provide analyses of aesthetic reflexivity (see, for example, Lash 1988, 1990; Featherstone 1992; Maffesoli 1996). What McNay takes issue with here is the understanding of identity transformation provided by such accounts. In such analyses, McNay claims, identity transformations are conceived primarily as an aesthetic process where the possibility for reflexive awareness arises from processes associated with the aestheticization of everyday life. Here McNay is referring broadly to arguments where symbolic change (which McNay understands to be co-determinous with the aesthetic) is understood to open up possibilities for (social) identity transformation and in particular for reflexive awareness towards issues of identity.[4] She has in mind, for example, arguments where an intensification of stylized or aestheticized images of gay, lesbian and queer sexualities are understood to problematize the normative and incite reflexivity in regard to gender and sexuality through intentional forms of experimentation with sexual and gender codes.

What McNay finds particularly problematic about such arguments is the assumption that such images invoke an opening up of social identities to produce a less fixed positioning of subjectivity. Thus she finds in such understandings a problematic conflation of processes of symbolic destabilization with processes of social and political transformation. In other words, symbolic detraditionalization is elided with social detraditionalization (1999: 106). Discussing gender, for example, she suggests that while there may have been a loosening of dominant images of femininity, nevertheless the transformatory impact of these images 'is far from certain' (McNay 1999: 106). Indeed, in eliding the symbolic with the social and hence overestimating the transformatory power of both shifts in visual codes and visual forms of identification, these accounts lead, in McNay's view, to an 'implicit reinstalling of a disembodied, disembedded self who moves freely across the social realm' (McNay 2000: 65–6).

The charge that understandings of the aestheticization of everyday life and of aesthetic reflexivity reinstall a problematic model of selfhood which reinscribe forms of privilege and exclusion historically associated with classical social and political theory is, however, by no means limited to the work of McNay. Rosemary Hennessy (1995, 2000) makes similar claims in her engagement with recent work on aestheticization and sexuality where she argues that such work risks promoting 'an updated, postmodern, reinscription of the bourgeois subject's fetishized identity' (Hennessy 1995: 153). Queer theory (and certain forms of queer activism) is located by Hennessy as particularly culpable in this regard, especially that (following the work of Judith Butler) which stresses the performative aspects of identity. That is, Hennessy locates this tendency in analyses that understand gender and sexuality to be constituted via the linguistic repetition of discursive conventions, and where the reversal of such conventions is made possible via a reappropriation and citation of signifiers of difference.

This is so, Hennessy argues, since analyses that stress this performative constitution of gender and sexuality fail to pay attention to the socio-historical conditions that make such a relation to gender and sexuality possible.[5] She suggests that the option of parodies of gender, including practices such as drag, depend 'on the availability not only of certain discourses of sexuality, aesthetics, style, and glamour but also of a circuit of commodity production, exchange, and consumption specific to industrialized economies' (Hennessy 1995: 153).

Thus for Hennessy a performative relation to sexual identities and hence queer identities and queer visibility are made possible by the socio-historical conditions of consumer capitalism, and especially the 'general aestheticization of everyday life in consumer capitalism' (Hennessy 1995: 164). In particular, Hennessy claims that such a relation to identity is made possible by the emphasis in consumer culture on a self-conscious 'stylized construction of almost every aspect of one's life: one's body, clothes, speech, leisure activities, eating, drinking, and sexual preferences' (Hennessy 1995: 165). Along with other commentators (see, for example, Featherstone 1992) Hennessy notes that consumer practices in late capitalism promise a 'de-centering of identity' (Hennessy 1995: 166) or 'promote a way of thinking about identity as malleable' (Hennessy 1995: 166), since identity is increasingly shaped through consumer choices, rather than through moral codes or rules. This notion of identity, Hennessy claims, resonates strongly with the understanding of identity found in much queer theory and activism. Specifically, for Hennessy, what queer and consumer culture's 'life-stylism' share in common is a separation of identity from the social and historical conditions that enable it.

So strong are the resonances between the notion of identity found in queer theory and consumer culture's 'life-stylism' that Hennessy suggests queer theory itself must be understood as participating in the aestheticization of everyday life.[6] Indeed, it must be recognized that queer identities and queer visibility are themselves enabled by the social relations of consumer capitalism, especially through the reconfiguration of identity as stylized, self-fashioning and malleable in consumer culture. Moreover, given that there is a 'class boundness' to stylization (Hennessy 1995: 166), in that a self-fashioned, stylized, flexible' consumer-orientated identity is only fully available to the new urban middle classes of industrialized economies, then it must be recognized that a performative relation to identity is not fully available to everyone in consumer culture. And it is in this sense that Hennessy suggests that queer theory and activism risk promoting 'an updated, postmodern, reinscription of the bourgeois subject's fetishized identity' (Hennessy 1995: 153).

Further examples abound of the charge of recuperating privileged gendered and classed notions of the subject, subjectivity and selfhood in recent social and cultural theory. John Urry's (2000) recent vision of the reformulation of sociological rules of method has also been subject to this line of critique. At issue here is Urry's argument that the social is materially reconstructing from the 'social as society' to the 'social as mobilities' (Urry 2000: 2) and his related claim that as a consequence of this reconstruction, the discipline which held society as its key methodological focus – sociology – needs to reformulate its methods. Thus, rather than on order, structure and stasis, sociology should focus on movement, mobility and contingency; and rather than on societies, sociologists should focus on the post-societal flows and mobilities of images, information, knowledge, capital, money and people.

What has been claimed about this analysis is similar to the charge levelled at analyses of aesthetic reflexivity – namely, that Urry's sociology of mobilities post-society reinstalls and idealizes a disembodied, disembedded subject who moves unfettered across and within the social realm. As a consequence it focuses sociological analysis on a privileged subject.

In a discussion of Urry's analysis Skeggs (2002), for example, has claimed that the subjectivity assumed in Urry's analysis – a mobile subjectivity – is related to established techniques for knowing and telling the self (such as the technique of confession) which attribute knowledge and epistemological authority to the person. Moreover, she shows how such authority allows certain forms of experimentation in relation to the self, including experimentations (such as specific forms of telling the self) which may appear to de-centre the self, that is, to attribute the property of mobility to the person. Skeggs argues further that these properties (and techniques for knowing and telling) have been historically more available to some than to others and in particular that such experimentations rely on forms of appropriation, which dispossess certain 'selves' of such properties. For example, in the disciplines of sociology and anthropology, telling stories of the subaltern has been a technique through which such appropriation and exclusion has taken place. Specifically, Skeggs shows how such techniques have both dispossessed the subaltern ('the working classes', 'women') of properties of experimentation in relation to the self and classified them as such, while at the same time attributed to storytellers properties of authority and mobility. Skeggs therefore highlights how mobility is an established and privileged mode of subjectivity, connected to forms of socio-cultural classification. Skeggs's analysis thus suggests that a sociology of mobilities will privilege this particular form of subjectivity and make invisible this very privileging.

What seems to be clear is that various forms of recent social and cultural theory appear to reinscribe models of privilege and exclusion associated with classical theorizing even as much of this theory appears to challenge these very models. And this appears to be the case from the social theory of the body, through accounts of reflexive and aesthetic modernity, to theories of sexuality and gender. Indeed it would seem from the kind of commentaries on this theory that I have discussed above, that the legacies of classical social theory continue to shape contemporary visions of the social and socio-cultural. But is this so? Can contemporary social and cultural theory be said to seamlessly reproduce and reinscribe the very same models of the social and of privilege and exclusion as enacted in accounts of the *fin de siècle*? Is this not to presume an epistemological and ontological sameness across time and space? Can such universalizing assumptions be upheld? In what follows I argue that to suggest that contemporary social theory simply reproduces the legacies of the classical tradition may be to sidestep the contemporary politics of classification, privilege and exclusion. In particular, in what follows, and with reference to recent debates in social theory on reflexivity and gender, I suggest that this is the case since contemporary forms of social and cultural theory work with a rather different set of assumptions to that of the classical tradition. More specifically, via attention to understandings of both women and gender in recent literature on reflexivity, I shall indicate how such recent social theory operates not with a tradition/modern or pre-modern/modern dualism but with a modernity/late modernity or more accurately with a social/post-structural social dualism. I shall claim further that this dualism operates not to exclude women from and include men within the social as in the classical tradition but to locate women as *overdetermined* by the social and men as freed from the constraints of the social, or at least from the constraints of socio-structural forms of determination. In short, I shall show how the narrative of gender found in the classical traditional social theory is not operative within contemporary theorizing. As such the question of how and if such theory enacts relations of privilege and exclusion needs to be explored rather than assumed.

The figure of woman in reflexive modernity

One of the most influential ideas in contemporary sociology is the afore-mentioned notion that social life is increasingly characterized by increased capacities for reflexivity. Such intensified capacities towards reflexivity are generally understood to be linked to – and constituted by – a decline in the significance of structural forms of determination. As a consequence of the retrocession of the structural, agency is understood as being progressively 'freed' or unleashed from structure. This is encapsulated in the theory of reflexive modernization as 'a theory of the ever-increasing powers of social actors, or "agency" in regard to structure' (Lash 1994: 111). Such increased capacities towards reflexivity are understood to concern the constitution of new life forms and modes of sociality within late modernity. Thus, 'family' ties are now understood less in terms of obligations constituted by fixed 'ties of blood' and more in terms of negotiated commitments and bonds (Beck and Beck-Gernsheim 1995; Beck-Gernsheim 1998); and labour market positions are constituted less by determinants such as class or gender location and more by self-design, self-creation and individual performances (Beck 1992; Bauman 1998). Thus one reading of the reflexively organized social is 'what the social is and does has to be involved with individual decisions' (Beck 1992: 90). Many of modernity's key abstract collective categories of belonging, such as class and gender, are therefore now less a matter of external forms of determination and more a matter of individual decisions. Indeed, according to Beck and Beck-Gernsheim: 'Life, death, gender, corporeality, identity, religion, marriage, parenthood, social ties – all are becoming decidable down to the small print; once fragmented into options, everything must be decided' (1995: 29).

Thus the 'freeing' of agency from structure is often held to mean that 'traditional' forms of social regulation and organization are disintegrating and that agents are increasingly free from the rules, expectations, and forms of authority associated with modernity.

A parallel may be drawn here between the idea that traditional modes of life, interaction and organization are being challenged or destabilized, and the more classical view that the onward march of modernity is destructive or incites the collapse of tradition, as, for example, in Giddens' description of how 'the capitalistic market, with its "imperatives" of continuous expansion destroys tradition' (1992: 197). But in analyses of reflexive modernity what is at issue is not the destruction of the pre-modern by the modern as in much classical social thought, but rather the collapse and undercutting of the traditions of modernity itself by a new modernity, another modernity (Lash 1999).

It is clear that the changes at issue in the reflexive modernization/ modernity thesis are far reaching. Indeed so profound are these changes that it has been suggested that sociology must reinvent itself in order to come to grips with these shifts: it must become 'a bit of art, a bit playful, in order to liberate itself from its own intellectual blockades' (Beck 1994: 24). And many sociologists have found in the reflexive modernization thesis precisely the kind of tools that allow this kind of creativity and movement away from some of the assumptions that have characterized the discipline. For example, in (aspects of) the reflexive modernization thesis an important corrective to overly structuralist understandings of social process has been found (Lash and Urry 1994).

However, and as noted above, it is these and related ideas around reflexivity which have been understood to recuperate the privileged, disembodied, rational, masculine subject, particularly in the emphasis found in such analyses on increased capacities for the self-fashioning of identities and biographies – a self-fashioning made possible via the freeing of agency from structure. Indeed a number of writers have indicated what they see to be the *limits* of reflexivity, limits that suggest that analyses of reflexivity may indeed be guilty of such a recuperation. Discussing the development of reflexive accumulation (or what is sometimes referred to as flexible specialization), involving knowledge-intensive production, chronic innovation and self-regulation on the part of workers, Lash (1994) has, for example, indicated such limits to reflexivity. He asks why is such reflexivity found in some economic sectors and not in others? And why do writers such as Giddens and Beck pay so little attention to these questions even to the extent that these do not even register within their frameworks? To highlight the significance of this point, Lash contrasts on the one hand the massive increases in the number of reflexive producers, and on the other, the post-Fordist creation of millions of 'junk jobs'. For example, reflexive producers populate business services, the software sector and computer production, alongside the creation of a 'McDonalds proletariat' in the service sector. He also discusses the situation of women in regard to reflexive accumulation. Specifically he points to 'the systemic exclusion of women from knowledge intensive occupations' (Lash 1994: 133). Thus he comments on the tendencies towards an exclusion of women from places in, and access to, the mode of information, including access to knowledge and information-intensive occupations and to informational, knowledge and communication goods outside of work life in the household. In neo-liberal labour markets such as those of the UK and the US, for example, women 'are shunted away from the information intensive end of the labour force and disproportionately into the new lower class positions' (Lash 1994: 133; Adkins 1999). All of these new labour market positions, Lash argues, make it clear that alongside what he terms 'reflexivity winners' there are millions of 'reflexivity losers'.

Lash's point in all of this is to suggest that to be able to account for such systematic inequalities it is urgent to consider the 'structural conditions of reflexivity' (Lash 1994: 120). Yet, as Lash himself makes clear, herein lies an apparent paradox. If reflexivity – as he agrees – involves the freeing of agency from structure, indeed the retreat of social structure, how can inequality have a structural explanation (Lash 1994: 120)? The structures to which Lash refers are, however, not *social* structures, such as the familiar Marxist social structures – the economic, the political and the ideological – but are new non-social *cultural* information and communication structures, 'an articulated web of global and local networks of information and communication structures' (Lash 1994: 120–1; Castells 1996). For Lash, in reflexive modernity, life chances depend not on place or access to the mode of production, but rather place in and access to the mode of information. Moreover, to ignore these new information and communication structures is to be unable to account for 'systematic inequalities in our globalized informational capitalism, as well as the systematic inequalities between core and peripheral nations' (Lash 1994: 120).

However, reflecting on this exclusion from the new reflexive classes, and especially the exclusion of women, Lash suggests that women may be part of a new lower class or underclass. Although this for Lash is a new class category he argues that 'the personnel filling these class positions are typically determined by more particularistic, "ascribed" characteristics – by race, country of origin and gender' (Lash 1994: 134). But Lash does not attend to how such processes of ascription relate to the new cultural information and communication structures of reflexive modernity. Indeed we might ask how this exclusion works and how processes of ascription relate to the new structural conditions of reflexivity. How is it that many women end up being 'reflexivity losers'?

The answer to this issue seems to lie in the broader theoretical apparatus Lash draws upon in his analysis. Specifically Lash situates his analysis of the shift from a mode of production to a mode of information in Bourdieusian terms as involving the emergence of a new field of action – the information and communication field – or what at times Lash terms the emergence of the cultural field. Thus Lash draws on Bourdieu's understanding of the 'social' world as comprising differentiated, but overlapping, fields of action, for example, the economic, the political and the legal field. Moreover, Lash extends Bourdieu's contemporary social theory further, especially Bourdieu's account of embodied social action or practice, to understand the reflexivity operating in the cultural field as reflection on the unconscious categories of our thought (Bourdieu 1977; Wacquant 1992). This reflexivity is not cognitive – where agents reflect on structures in a realist fashion – but rather is hermeneutic or aesthetic, involving subject–subject rather than subject–object relations. Thus, by drawing on Bourdieu's social theory to explicate the features of reflexive modernity – especially his understanding of fields of action – Lash's analysis not only suggests that women are reflexivity losers, but also implies that women are excluded from what he conceives as the post- (social) structural cultural field where both (non-social) structure and action are reflexive in character. In short, in Lash's analysis women are reflexivity losers as they are excluded from the cultural field and hence from the very modes of action-embodied reflexivity constituted in the context of a freeing of agents from structure – which secure a position and an identity within reflexive modernity.[7]

What is so interesting about this account from the point of view of my concerns here is that it by no means recuperates the legacies of classical sociology and social theory vis-à-vis gender but presents an entirely different vision. Specifically, in this account women are not excluded from the social field and sociality as in classical accounts, but instead tend to be excluded from the cultural field. Thus, in this account, hermeneutic or aesthetic reflexivity is overwhelmingly masculinist. Indeed we may ask how it is that Lash's account – even though it offers such an important corrective to the scientism of Beck and Giddens – ends up making reflexivity so masculinist. Does contemporary social theory exclude women from the field of reflexivity as classical sociology excluded women from the field of the social? But what perhaps is more significant about this vision is that while in classical social theory women were excluded from sociality, here woman is *overdetermined* by the social, indeed cannot escape the social. Thus, while those working in knowledge intensive production, that is, participating in the post-structural cultural field, are no longer subject to forms of socio-structural determination and indeed are freed from social structure, women continue to be positioned as subject to these forces. Thus in this analysis women and women's positions are determined by external *social* forces – by an ascribed 'gender' – that is, by the very socio-structurally organized system of classification, ordering and regulation which feminist sociologists have theorized in their various attempts to socialize women (and thus correct overly masculine conceptions of the social). And this is the case even though these socio-structural forces are posited in this account as historically receding. Indeed in the post-structural social 'women' cannot free themselves or be set free from structure since their positions are (over) determined by (a socially organized) gender.

While I have singled out these tendencies in Lash's analysis, this is by no means to imply that this vision is only at play in this account, for a similar set of assumptions may be found in Beck's analysis of reflexive modernization. Here there is a general emphasis on the release of people from the socio-structural traditions of modernity, including those of class, gender and sexuality. He writes 'people are being removed from the constraints of gender, from its quasi-feudal attributes and givens' (Beck 1992: 105). But alongside this reference is also made to the continuing relevance of these traditions. Thus Beck discusses their ongoing relevance as bases for identification, in the development of social bonds, and as sources of conflict and inequality. But much like in Lash's account 'gender', 'class' and 'sexuality' are understood as 'particularistic' 'ascribed' characteristics (Beck 1992: 101). Hence Beck at once defines gender as a *social* tradition of modernity and indeed argues that 'the ascription of gender characteristics is the *basis* of the industrial society, and not some traditional relic that could be easily be dispensed with' (Beck 1992: 104, emphasis in original). He then goes on to posit a theory of reflexive modernity in which people are being released from these very social traditions – to the extent that 'the individual himself or herself becomes the reproduction unit of the social in the lifeworld' (Beck 1992: 90). Yet while he does so he simultaneously stresses the ongoing significance of these traditions including those of gender, class and sexuality. Thus while Beck argues that to some extent women are being 'liberated' from the traditions of modernity – indeed he argues there is a strong degree of 'liberation of women from the dictates of their modern, female status fate, which can no longer be altered' (Beck 1992: 111) – he goes on to suggest that individualization (I am I) for women is very often confounded by processes which reconnect women 'to the old ascribed roles' (Beck 1992: 111–12). Beck discusses the socio-political organization and regulation of paid labour and childcare as examples of processes which reconnect women to the ascribed roles of modernity, especially since both tend to underscore the idea that women exist for others.

In Beck's analysis of reflexive modernity, as in Lash's, the position of women is therefore understood to be predominately determined by *social* forces, and more generally the social organization of gender (including the organization and regulation of paid labour and childcare). Indeed, in the insistence that gender is a constitutive feature of industrial society, Beck clearly acknowledges his debt to the labour of feminist sociologists, especially their critiques of the classical legacy and the various excursions which have socialized women. However, Beck's concurrent insistence that such a social arrangement of gender is part of an older modernity and moreover that women find it difficult to remove themselves from these social traditions and become individualized subjects belies his apparent acknowledgement and debt to feminist sociology. For, much like the vision found in Lash's analysis of reflexive modernity, in Beck's account women are presented as being trapped in and determined by the social and hence as unable to achieve the form of personhood required to participate in the new modernity, that is in reflexive modernity. Thus in Beck's account, individualization for women is often confounded by socio-structural or institutional processes which continue to produce the norms and expectations associated with industrial society. Put another way 'women' are unable to escape a socially organized ascriptive order to become individualized subjects who may participate in reflexive modernity. Women remain caught up in the socially organized and regulated first industrial modernity and the best they can seem to hope for is to live with the contradictory forces of individualization on the one hand and processes which reconnect women to the familiar expectations of industrial modernity on the other.

Conclusions

The examples of contemporary sociological theorizing I have discussed here clearly indicate that far from reinscribing the legacies of the classical tradition vis-à-vis gender, contemporary social and cultural theory is offering a rather different vision. For while in classical accounts (whether this was a cause for condemnation or celebration) women were located as outside of socio-historical time – for instance as pre-modern, pre-industrial, undifferentiated figures or as figures who remained in a highly ambivalent relation to the modern (see Chapter 3, this volume) – this is by no means the case for the kinds of contemporary social theory I have examined here. On the contrary, in this social theory women are firmly located in the sociological time of (first) modernity, and indeed are often located as such via the very feminist social theory that exposed the limits and assumptions of classical theorizing. Yet despite this recognition of the limits of the classical tradition via the socialization of women, such contemporary social theory only then goes on to suggest that this very socialization sets a limit to women's participation in the contemporary post-structural social since women cannot overcome a previous mode of social organization, and indeed are overdetermined by the social. Thus the very project with which feminist sociologists have concerned themselves and more specifically the product of this project – fully socialized women in sociological discourse – is now presented as the very stumbling block for women's participation in contemporary modes of sociality. And this is the case even though such contemporary social and cultural theory not only ostensibly appears to challenge the legacies of the classical tradition, but also declares such forms of sociological determination both theoretically and substantively bankrupt.

As well as suggesting a very problematic slippage in the contemporary theoretical imaginary between women and feminism, what this also suggests is that instead of focusing attention on classical models of privilege and exclusion and its alleged recuperation in sociological discourse, feminist sociologists may do better to focus on the ways in which contemporary social and cultural theory offers up a socially determined view of woman, and of a masculine view of a post-structural social. Indeed it suggests that feminist sociologists should now talk, for example, not of natural women and social men as they did in their parodies of classical sociology, but of social women and reflexive men. But this vision of the post-structural social also prompts a series of compelling questions. Perhaps one of the most interesting of these concerns the impetus that is shaping this vision of woman. What impulse is at play that locates woman firmly (even traps women) in industrial society or first modernity even though in earlier forms of sociological discourse the symbols of this society – the machine, the industrial worker, class and status hierarchies – were so overwhelmingly masculine? Indeed in contemporary social theory woman is not just located in industrial society but may be said to act as a powerful symbol of that society. Thus in contemporary social theory woman is strongly associated with those characteristics and properties which sociologists (including feminist sociologists) have attributed to industrial society, including socio-structural ordering and regulation, social determination, economic, political and ideological structures, collective categories of belonging, and the traditions of class and gender. That is, woman appears to stand in for the properties of industrial society, even though in the classical tradition these properties were overwhelmingly associated with men. What accounts for this extraordinary reversal in sociological discourse?

Felski may provide us with some clues here. In her analysis of accounts of the *fin de siècle*, Felksi located a nostalgic impulse as fuelling classical visions of woman, a yearning for a non-differentiated and non-alienated identity which positioned woman as the explicit object of nostalgic desire and located women as symbols of pre-modernity. As the symbol of first modernity or industrial society the impulse fuelling visions of woman in contemporary social theory is clearly not a desire for a non-differentiated or non-alienated identity. But given the overwhelming association of woman with industrial society, not only in contemporary social theory but also in the charge that this social theory reinstates classical legacies, we may well ask if there is a yearning not for the pre-modern but for the modern itself, for industrial society? Or perhaps a yearning for the sociological certainties that appeared to go alongside that society? Does this yearning account for this vision of woman? Whatever the case it seems that woman must now free herself from the burdens of industrial society.

Notes

1   See, for example, Wolff (1983); Sydie (1987); Marshall (1994); Felski (1995); Witz (2000; 2001); see also Chapter 1, this volume.

8 Rethinking the revival of social capital and trust in social theory: possibilities for feminist analysis

o (innister

Anne Kovalainen

This chapter will focus on two specific aspects of contemporary social theory where the apparent non-existence of gender in the theoretical corpus will be analysed. Social capital and trust have within a short time become hugely influential, truly global, theoretical concepts in analyses of current social and economic development, change and cohesion in various societies. While the term 'social capital' features in much scholarly and interdisciplinary discourse, it also has parallels with political agendas, large-scale social and economic development and, in particular, social policy development. This is visible in the influence of the World Bank and International Monetary Fund, both in the defining of research areas and the framing of discussion on social issues.[1] The assumption of a positive relationship between democracy, participation and social capital and trust prevails in much of the research literature. The intuitive appeal seems clear: the analytical concepts of social capital and trust do not seem burdened by the rigidity of classical sociological conceptual schemes, such as social class, power or stratification.

Despite their appeal, this chapter raises the following questions about the new conceptual schemes of social capital and trust. Have these been able to extract the masculinity from sociological agency, or is the concept of agency in the newly rediscovered ideas of social capital and trust still predominantly masculine, as remains the case with much sociological theorizing? Is this also the case in economics, which has had a substantial influence on sociological discussions of social capital theory (Coleman 1990; Dasgupta 2000; Solow 2000)? The feminist call for the rewriting of economics in terms of gender seems to have had little impact on mainstream economics (for example, Folbre 1994). The inadequacy of economic gender theorizing and the treatment of gender in economics could also be seen as a metaphor for a larger set of problems within the discipline. For example, it has been noted that emphatic emotional connections between individuals are emphasized within the family, whereas they are totally denied in the analysis of market relations that focus on formal transactions (for example, England 1993: 37; Kovalainen 1994: 19). In similar manner, the question of how economic development interacts with families shifts the emphasis away from market analysis alone (Folbre 1994), and more in the direction of social networks and reciprocities that are crucial in the analysis of social capital. Clearly, gender has affected the construction of disciplines in terms of the viewpoint from which society and economy are analysed (see, for example, Ferber and Nelson 1993).

The elasticity of the term 'social capital' across disciplinary fields has led to a situation where it is used very differently, depending on the context and research purpose in question. What is common to much research in political science and sociology is the use of the concept of 'social capital' to refer to a set of norms, networks, institutions and organizations through which access to specific elements such as power or resources embedded within or available through these elements is gained. According to Coleman (2000: 23), 'all social relations and social structures facilitate some forms of social capital; actors establish relations purposefully and continue them when they continue to provide benefits'. Coleman introduces social capital into social theory as paralleling the concepts of financial capital, physical capital and human capital – 'but embodied in relations among persons' (2000: 36). In a rather similar fashion, trust is defined as 'confidence or expectation . . . that an event or action will or will not occur, and such faith is expected to be mutual in repeated exchanges' (Lin 2001: 147). Trust, defined as one of the three crucial components of social capital, has caught the interest of sociology, and especially social theory, in a new and appealing way. This contrasts with the earlier ways of referring to trust as either saving society from disintegration (Simmel 1978) or as a basis for legitimating power to achieve collective goals and social integration (Parsons 1963). These ways of defining social capital and trust are not unique, as the fluidity of the notion of social capital has given rise to several definitions, captured through social relations as well as through economic structures (Lin 2001).

The uneasy relationship between sociological theorizing and feminism has manifested itself in many ways in sociological research and analyses. While feminist analysis of social theory in general has worked to unsettle rigid and established categories and concepts, ranging from class stratification to identity theories, most mainstream sociological theorizing still ignores the questions posed by considerations of gender. Attempts to rethink sociological concepts and theories to include gender have often led to 'adding' gender, along with other categories such as 'race/ethnicity', to describe a variety of social dimensions of life.

The general argument of this chapter is that the assumed gender neutrality of contemporary social theory and its new tenets should be challenged at many levels. The assimilation of gender into the dominant sociological dis-courses often changes the reproduction of sociological knowledge and the ways research is being done, but questions of an epistemological nature may remain untouched. Many feminist sociologists, such as Marshall (1994); Jackson (1998); Jackson and Scott (2002); and Stanley (2002); and feminist philosophers (for example, Longino 1990) have pointed to this problem.

My intention in the first section of this chapter is to describe some of the reasons why social capital has appealed across disciplinary fields and why it has become such an influential concept in social theorizing. In the first two sections of the chapter I discuss both sociological and economic variations of social capital, and relate the different measures and definitions of social capital to one another. In the final section of the chapter I discuss the reasons as to why social capital theory has – even if considered as a new theoretical agenda – been immune to a rethinking of the androcentric concept of agency. Rather, it has reinforced the kind of social theory where gender is disentangled and invisible, and yet written into the theory in various ways. I delineate where feminist analysis might be possible and where it would make a difference in the theoretical corpus of social capital, and relate these questions to some key epistemological assumptions.

Social capital and trust – reciprocation between social theory, sociology and economics

The inherent appeal of social capital rests on the idea of its being at one and the same time an economic, political and sociological concept, thus having interdisciplinary prominence and potential. Similarly, the concept of trust extends beyond economics and sociology to philosophical and political fields, describing the creation and maintenance of interaction between individuals and institutions, for example. Studies of social capital and trust do not form a coherent paradigm. On the contrary, they attempt to expand the disciplinary boundaries in a variety of directions. However, in the attempt to create an interdisciplinary field, the concepts of social capital and trust are given differ-ent positions in explanations of social, cultural and economic phenomena by different disciplines. Yet, the elusive nature of both concepts seems to have led to generalizations that are far from clear, and to the omission of both theor-etical and historically specific insights (Fine 2000; Lin *et al.* 2001).

In the social sciences, discussion of the overall theoretical attachment of social capital and trust is dispersed. The body of theoretical discussion could be presented as condensed within two extremes of social theory discourses: the search for a solution to the 'collective action dilemma' on one hand, and to 'inequalities of different kinds' on the other. These two directions open up diverse perspectives and intangibles, ranging from rational action theory to social construction of social capital, as fields for discussion covered by research on social capital and trust. Two prominent authors, Bourdieu (1986) and Coleman (1988, 1990), differ fundamentally in the ways they describe the development of social capital 'accumulation'. For Bourdieu, social capital develops through the economic infrastructure. For Coleman social capital manifests itself through a process of negotiation of contracts between individuals. Whatever the origins of social capital are, there seems to be widespread agreement that the notion of social capital incorporates both the social and the economic into a single explanatory framework (Fine 2000; Lin 2001). To some extent, the theoretical question at stake here could also be expressed as the classical problem of rational choice theory, that is, how to show how 'interdependent individual actions produce collective-level outcomes' (Abell 1992: 186).

The concept of social capital encapsulates a wide range of social mechanisms, individuals, networks and institutions, and their actions, from the perspectives of social cohesion and struggle, economic activity and generalized exchange. The wide variation of interest in the concept is partly evident in early works by Pierre Bourdieu (1980), Bourdieu and Louis Wacquant (1992), James Coleman (1990) and Robert Putnam (1993, 2000) but some references to Jane Jacobs' (1961) classic work can be found. Even if the nature of these works is seen to be relatively similar, as argued by Burt (2001), calling attention to the similarity of approaches glosses over the different theoretical commitments. They all address the notion of social capital from quite different perspectives, developing the idea further from two opposing sociological traditions, that of integration (Putnam) and that of struggle (Bourdieu). Recognizing the contextual nature of these discourses means acknowledging that the viewpoints of the abovementioned authors diverge in important ways. (see, for example, Siisiäinen 2000). To develop the key argument of this chapter, I will briefly present some of the main developments in the theorization of social capital and trust.

Social capital as social relation

The fleeting appearance of social capital in Bourdieu's *Reproduction in Education, Society and Culture* (1977) laid out the conceptual grid upon which the definition of social capital was later based. Bourdieu's definition and analysis of 'social capital' is strongly related to the idea of networks and resources. His main idea could be formulated in terms of how cultural reproduction fosters the social reproduction of durable relations between groups and classes, culminating in social capital. To a large extent this contrasts with sociologically defined economic capital as the main source of inequality and class division. Through a variety of connections, capital is used as a collective 'asset' within and outside of the group (see also Schuller *et al.* 2000).

Bourdieu's text distinguishes between different forms of capital: *cultural capital, social capital* (which he describes as social connections), *symbolic capital* (understood as prestige or fame), *economic capital* and '*distinction*'. All forms of capital that Bourdieu presents are interconnected, and they become meaningful and socially effective through the process of symbolic translation. For Bourdieu, social capital remains at the level of connectedness, even if it is part of symbolic power. He defines social capital as 'the aggregate of the actual or potential resources which are linked to possession of a durable network of more or less institutionalised relationships of mutual acquaintance and recognition' (Bourdieu 1986: 248). Bourdieu's use of social capital varies between the realist and the metaphorical, and remains, at least when thinking of the possibilities for empirical analysis, relatively 'sketchy' (Schuller *et al.* 2000).

The logic of economic and cultural capital grows in different directions and becomes objectified as measures (money, exams), while symbolic capital exists only immaterially. For Bourdieu, social capital lies between the economic and cultural forms of capital on the one hand, both of which can be objectified, and symbolic form of capital, which is immaterial, on the other. In his analysis, the 'volume of social capital possessed by a given agent . . . depends on the size of the network of connections that he can effectively mobilize' (Bourdieu 1986: 249). According to Bourdieu, these networks in themselves do not create or accumulate social capital, but their usefulness does (see, for example, Moi 1999a; Burt 2001).

How does an agent gain knowledge of the social capital he or she possesses? How is the usefulness measured? These questions are left unanswered in Bourdieu's texts. Bourdieu does not respond to his critics who suggest that the networks are usually built for purposes other than their potential usefulness in the future. Much of the reward from networks might also be intrinsic, thus conflating some of the analytical power of Bourdieu's definition of social capital. Even if Bourdieu discusses the plurality of subject identifications in his theory, and his definition of social capital is based on mutual cognition and recognition, gender is not part of agency, nor part of the idea of networks in the theory.

Coleman, Putnam and the consensus view on social capital

Work which more explicitly pinpoints the definition and limits of the analytical power of social capital has been published by James Coleman and Robert Putnam, whose theories seem to be the most influential in developing and directing the discussions of social capital within the field of economics. Putnam's work on the decline of social capital in the United States (2000) has become as influential as his earlier work on Italy (1993). Originally interested in the concept of social capital as a regional level shoring-up of democratic institutions and economic development, Putnam defined it as 'trust, norms and networks' that facilitate cooperation for mutual benefit (1993: 167). The question of trust is inherently part of social capital. While Bourdieu's idea of the *recognition* of symbolic capital resembles the concept of trust in Coleman's or Putnam's theoretical framework, the concept of trust as such does not exist in Bourdieu's texts (see, for example, Hollis 1998; Stzompka 2000).

For Putnam, the dense networks of horizontal interactions among relative equals (neighbourhood associations, football clubs, bowling leagues, PTAs) produce norms of reciprocity, work as information channels and create a culturally favourable atmosphere for future collaboration between those who participate. Putnam's definition of social capital is strongly influenced by Coleman. Putnam focuses on complex community, regional and national level outcomes of social capital, which are related to political and economic development taking place at that level. Networks of civic engagement are the key to the existence of social capital, as they foster norms of reciprocity. These norms in turn sanction those individuals who are not part of the reciprocal system.

Putnam's way of measuring social capital emphasizes participation in voluntary associations, which has never been the most common form of social participation in many countries, compared with the US. The problem here is that a causal link, between participation in voluntary organizations and improved democratic institutions, is simply assumed (for example, Harriss and de Renzio 1997). An additional and problematic assumption in Putnam's theory is that both reciprocity and trust will follow from participation in such associations. Margret Levi (1998) has outlined several problems with the way social capital is produced and maintained in Putnam's work. Levi argues that football clubs, bowling leagues or churches may not be the types of organizations that are able to produce the trust needed to facilitate collective action, and that this type of trust would not enhance collaboration among a diverse set of stakeholders. They are also gender-biased in composition: football clubs and bowling leagues are generally not representative of women's participation, whereas church going is based on more than just gender, encompassing generational, cultural and class differences.

For Putnam, social capital consists of a set of horizontal associations among people who have an effect on the *productivity* of the community. These associations include networks of civic engagement and social norms (Putnam 2000). Furthermore, it is also important that networks and norms are empirically associated and that they have important economic consequences. The ends, and not so much the means – in other words the use-value of social capital – seems to be thus one of its defining criteria. This is naturally a very problematic way of defining a concept, as, among other things, structural inequalities are not included. Do we get a good job because of the existing social or human capital (networks, education) or is the lack of social capital (not knowing the right people) the reason for not getting the job, despite having good social/human capital (in other words, education)? Also, voting should be an *outcome* of social capital, not part of its empirical measurement, as noted by Paxton (1999), who analysed the change in the level of social capital in the US over a 20 year period. The inherent discrepancies between a theoretical definition of said capital and measurements of it are evident. The reliance on single indicators poses a problem of measurement: can a general, multidimensional concept be captured in a single variable? In empirical research, this has resulted in a variety of ways of measuring social capital.

Putnam's thesis has been challenged as both theoretically gender-biased and empirically problematic (Skocpol 1996; Paxton 1999). Gender in Putnam's theory appears to be a middle class orientated bipolar category of men and women. According to Putnam, women who moved out from the home into the paid employment have, at least partially, been responsible for the decline in the accumulation of commodified social capital (Putnam 1995, 2000: 312), even if he disclaims the view 'that working women are "to blame" for our civic disengagement' (Putnam 2000: 201). Putnam largely ignores the idea that social capital can also accumulate at paid work, and even more so, in comparison to having women as homemakers. Putnam's insensitivity to gender is visible in the fact that not all gender contracts have changed in the way exemplified by the white middle class in the US. In Nordic countries women have 'never' been at home only, but 'always' at the labour market. Adopting Putnam's theory as it has been done in many countries, to measure up social capital, would provide faulty results in the Nordic national contexts. The visibility of women's active citizenship is absent in Putnam's analysis. Gender is defined as a rigid, stereotypically female quality. The text focuses on the activity of men, while women exist mainly in relation to family.

In comparison with Putnam, Coleman brings economics closer to sociology in his theorization and measurement of social capital. In Coleman's theory of social capital, economic prosperity follows from human capital, and not necessarily from social capital. Coleman (1988) differentiates between two broad intellectual streams in discussions of social capital. One argues for a socialized actor, whose actions are governed by social norms, rules and obligations. The other stems from economics, where the actor is traditionally defined as seemingly neutral, having achieved goals independently and being fully self-interested (for a critique of this see, for example, Folbre 1994).

Even if Coleman's characterization is a somewhat simplified and time-bound analysis of social and economic theories, it carves out the essential question of existing tensions in the interdisciplinary project of social capital. Coleman's answer is to introduce rational action theory into the sociological analysis of social capital and trust. For Coleman, this means that social capital exists in 'the *relations* between actors and among actors' (1988: 100). Coleman argues that in contrast with other forms of capital, social capital is '*embodied in relations among persons*' (p. 120). These persons are individuals, who act rationally within specific, given constraints and on the basis of the information that they have.

What elements do these relations consist of? Coleman argues for two key elements: the trustworthiness of the social environment (obligations to be met) and the extent of obligations held. The idea of trust as an integral part of social capital, together with norms and social networks, can receive different emphasis: trust can be seen as a rational way of dealing with exchange, as Diego Gambetta (1990) defines it (similar to Coleman's definition), while the more Durkheimian tradition sees trust arising out of the internalization of collective values, as Francis Fukuyama (1995) defines it. Annette Baier (1995) calls for dependency and trust to be discussed as a question of reliance, in other words, feeling trust that something will be entrusted to others. In caring and dependency relations, trust also always involves power and inequality embedded in caring and dependency. Within relationships of trust bad things also happen, such as abuse and misbehaviour. The feminist notion of relations within trust becomes visible only in Baier's (1995) and Sevenhuijsen's (1998) texts, compared to those mentioned earlier. Baier considers the ways trust generalizes moral features of binding obligations and moral virtues, and criticizes the contractarian ways of viewing individuals as autonomous and free from all obligations. This is elaborated further by Sevenhuijsen (1998), in relation to care work. According to Sevenhuijsen, with the acknowledgement of dependency comes that of vulnerability, which specifies the form of trust in relations in which we are dependent on others; what do we entrust to those others? Sevenhuijsen argues that care should be seen as a democratic practice, and that democratic citizenship supposes that everybody would be guaranteed equal access to the giving and receiving of care. Care implies responsibility, trust and reliance, and insists on the ethical salience of another person's condition, according to Sevenhuijsen (1998).

Social capital and the renewal of social theory?

The introduction of rational action theory and rational choice into the debates within sociological theory predates theorizations of social capital. The debate on rational action theory – its applicability and limitations – also has a history within economics. Even if economics is partly based on the idea of rational agency, agency as such does not have a specific role in economic theory other than in decision making. The feminist critique of this notion has been twofold. The inadequacy of economic analyses of gendered issues such as invisible work and the wage gap is one line of critique. Another line of critique focuses on the more theoretical set of problems within economics which call for the redefinition of the subject of a discipline. It is this second line of critique which I will take up here, as it goes to the heart of the issue of gendered agency in economics and calls for the redefinition of agency within the discipline.

In economics, the critique of 'rational economic man' as one modification of rational action theory's conception of agency has also taken a variety of forms, ranging from philosophical arguments criticizing the simplified idea of rational economic man (for example, Hollis and Nell 1975) to feminist critique extending from the pre-eminence of mathematical modelling 'to its congruence with a particular image of masculinity, one created in the gender structure of dualisms' (Longino 1993: 160; see also, for example, England and Kilbourne 1990; Nelson 1993). The main point of feminist critique within economics of rational action theory has focused on the missing links within the theory propositions and 'reality' on the one hand, and the theoretically problematic idea of '*homo economicus*' as it is defined within neo-classical economics on the other. The way economics treats rationality is based on the idea of an autonomous self, independent from other individuals or persons, a conception remarkably similar to the stereotype of ideal masculinity (see, for example, Longino 1993). This notion is central to the self-understanding of economics, as noted by Strassman (1993), and thus uneasily changed.

However, rational action theory extends beyond the disciplinary borders of economics. Economic theories are concerned with the ways in which the production, distribution and consumption of goods and services is organized through exchange and market mechanisms, and rational choice theorists have argued that the same general principles can be used to understand individual interactions in any disciplinary field where a form of exchange takes place. Rational choice theories hold that individuals must anticipate the outcomes of alternative courses of action and calculate what is best for them. Rational individuals choose alternatives likely to give them the greatest satisfaction (Coleman 1990). The rational individual does not have any ties or dependencies, which need to be taken into account in decision making. The actor is general, abstract, detached from ties and dependencies, an omnipotent agent. The problematic nature of this perspective for sociology is obvious: the agent is not only without social ties but also presented as a socially atomic, abstract masculinity.

If the actions of individuals form the starting point for the analysis, then all other social phenomena are reducible to individual actions. Neo-classical economics is fundamentally asocial, as are most of the rational action theory applications in other disciplinary fields. The core of methodological individualism is expressed in Coleman's definition, even if he acknowledges the role of social structure as facilitating social capital: 'Actors establish relations purposefully and continue them when they continue to provide benefits' (Coleman 1988: 105). Furthermore, the functionalist definition – social capital as a means to increase an individual's resources – places more emphasis on the individual than the societal level. Coleman's empirical work was focused more on norms and sanctions, which together with networks facilitated the accumulation of human capital at the individual level. From a feminist point of view, the adoption of rational action theory as the starting point for social capital theory, includes several problematic notions, starting from the idea of atomic agency and ranging to conflation of moral and structural issues into individual level questions.

To summarize the above discussion, the contrast between the social capital theorists examined is between the emphases put on the level of analysis: for Bourdieu, it is individuals in struggle; for Putnam it is community, region or even nation; while for Coleman it is individuals in a variety of structural settings (mainly family or community). For all theorists the distinction and relationship between agency and structure is central. Flyvbjerg (2001: 138) argues that for Bourdieu, the use of the notion of habitus can be understood as a way of escaping from the choice between 'a structuralism without a subject and the philosophy of the subject', as Bourdieu himself claimed.[2] In their earlier work on Italy, Putnam *et al.* (1993) similarly combine individual and structural analysis in an attempt to explain democracy in Italy. This model of theorizing follows the path of asking which structural factors influence individual actions, how these actions are constructed and what their structural consequences are (Flyvbjerg 2001). The notion of the individual is left untouched, however: the individual is mostly assumed – in the realist tradition – to be a rational decision maker who works within the given framework, that is, within the existing structures.

But is the structure/agency problem, in the way it has been understood in sociology, the same problem that Coleman takes up? While Coleman follows more clearly the tradition of economics in his strong programme for social capital, he also restricts his analytical perspective to rational action theory, more so than do his followers.[3] Attempts by some economists, such as Dasgupta and Serageldin (2000), to treat social capital as a measurable entity, functioning as a relationship between the market and social interactions and having positive implications for efficiency, are numerous. The application of social capital to mainstream economic theory might prove difficult, however. Conventional economic theory is highly formalized and consists mainly of mathematical models containing few 'residual' variables, which is one of the explicit 'places' for social capital in regression models or other explanatory models used. This form of economics, the neo-classical, is not only non-gendered but also fundamentally asocial. The asociality of neo-classical economic agency was exposed through the critique associated with social scientists such as Elster (1982), Sen (1995) and Granovetter (1985, 1988), among others, who make no reference to feminist theories. Feminist critique has further clarified and elaborated this critique and made specific comments not only on the agency/structure problem, but also on the notions of dependency and connectedness of agencies, the contextuality of knowledge and boundaries of explanatory power of neoclassical economics (see, for example, Ferber and Nelson 1993; Folbre 1994; Carruthers and Babb 2000).

The influence of economic theory in sociology is also visible, for example, in the works of Gary Becker (1996), who explicitly subsumes his concept of social capital as part of the theory of the utility-maximizing individual. It is also evident in the work of other theorists, too numerous to mention here. Within social theory, social capital is, or should be, a sociological concept, not an individually orientated, psychological one. Thus, social capital is not reducible to the individual, as it can only operate at the shared and collective level (Furstenberg 1998: 296). Here, shortcomings to some extent in Bourdieu's, but particularly in Coleman's, definitions of social capital are evident.

Several factors can be considered when we are analysing the emergent interest in economics within sociology. One influential and pioneering discussion concerns the notion of 'risk society' (Beck 1992). Perhaps more influential has been fluctuating and changing economies and labour markets, and the 'corrosion of character' of the workforce (Sennett 1998). In related work, notions of globalization have shifted interest away from cultural sociology and closer to economic sociology. This does not signify that there is only one way or level of analysing economics sociologically, as the economy and its functioning can be seen as socially constructed phenomena or fully embedded in society (Granovetter 1985).[4] According to Fine and Green (2000: 89), part of the attraction derives from the quantifiable nature of the economy: the result is, as they argue, an 'expanding list of studies that show, in some way or other, a non-economic factor having a substantive impact on economic performance'. This is the issue of the embeddedness of the economic in the social. The discussions and studies of social capital and trust show, for their part, the increase in sociological analysis of the economy, despite possible limitations and related criticism. The underlying dilemma of the juxtaposition of sociology and economics is that the social cannot be identified as an independent factor separate from individual activities. In the social sciences, this dilemma is overshadowed or made to disappear specifically in those fields of sociological theorizing where rational choice is the meta-level theoretical choice.

In summary, the views on social capital include informal and local horizontal networks, hierarchical associations and institutions, ranging from informal to formal national and transnational organizations. According to Misztal (1996), many arguments about social capital have extended the idea of cooperation from an individual characteristic to one of societies. As Portes remarked (1998: 107) 'Social capital has come to be applied to so many events and in so many different contexts, that it has lost its distinct meaning'. Although I do not agree that simply using the concept in different contexts reduces its meaning as such, the point is important. Since there is an existing definitional diversity among those doing research on social capital, there is also a justified reason for asking whether we can talk about social capital as a single conceptual category or entity.

Possibilities for considering gender in social capital theory

Just as Habermas's 'peculiar blindness to gender issues' (Cohen 1995: 54) has been criticized by feminists (Fraser 1989; Cohen 1995), so too has Coleman's: 'Coleman's interest in equity issues was combined with a curious blindness to gender, ethnicity and disability' (Field et al. 2000: 248). The confidence in abstract rationality as the general logic of the underlying agency becomes visible in the role of the social in the analysis. Social capital theories seem to epitomize Oakley's reflections on developments in the social sciences more generally: 'The masculinisation of science underwrites the methodological paradigm divisions of the late twentieth century' (Oakley 2000: 76). But, just as importantly, she argues that 'it was not simply the case that women were excluded from the processes of intellectual development (although most of them were) but rather that "science" was absorbed into, and in turn helped to infuse, a cultural division of labour, which opposed masculinity and scientific activity to the passivity of feminine nature' (Oakley 2000: 76).

Despite criticism targeted at functionalist or even tautological ways of defining social capital, the concept has found its field. This is a key reason why the study of gender in the theoretical foundations of social capital is crucially important. The questions of the influence of economics on social theory, the adoption of rational action theory and, most of all, the realist epistemology of social theory makes finding space for gendered analysis difficult. For both Putnam and Coleman, the social actor, in the process of creating, using and recreating social capital, is of crucial importance. This social actor is inherently male and in this sense the theoretical assumptions of social capital theorists differ hardly at all from those of rational choice theorists, where the actor is omnipotent, without formal or informal ties to other actors other than those that are contract related.

In the texts of Coleman, Putnam and Fukuyama, where exactly does the notion of gender become visible? It is at home, within the family, where agency acquires its explicitly gendered bodily expression as a mother or a father? In Coleman's analysis – less so than in Putnam's – social structure is a mere facilitator for social capital: the closure of social networks suggests the existence of norms, and it is through this idea that Coleman inserts the explicitly gendered agent into his theory. Coleman defines the importance of social capital taking place within the family, in the creation of human capital. For Coleman, family is generalized, as is the aim in economics, and the contextual element is lacking. For both Putnam and Coleman, the birth and the origin of social capital reside within the family, which comprises 'the most fundamental form of social capital' (Putnam 1995: 73). What the definition of family is and how it functions is not explicitly stated in any of these theories. However, a heteronormative matrix with a gender-specific division of labour and inequalities is apparent in the texts. The idealization of the family as the core of civic engagement and social capital rests on the assumption that families will provide good models for relationships and civic virtues (see, for example, Cox 1995: 28–9).

According to Putnam, even children who are at risk (for example, those from low-income families) 'can succeed in life if their mothers have sufficient social capital' (2000: 306). It is thus the mother's task to transfer the abilities central to social capital to their children, no matter what social and societal conditions they are living in. Even if the division of work at home is clear, the causal links between family activities, the labour of love at home and social capital are not: do children have high social capital because their parents (in other words, mothers) supervise their schoolwork? Is that a sign of a close family network? And, following from that, is interaction (supervision of homework) within a family a sign of social capital? Or is the supervision a sign of lack of trust within the family, suggesting that high school grades do not result from social capital at home but from something else?

The core of the concept of social capital rests with the household, and the key components of this concept are the least known, defined and debated by theorists. The definition of gender as a binary biologically determined variable recalls the idea of gender prevalent in earlier theory. The manner in which social theory has treated gender is illuminated in a somewhat old quotation from Anthony Giddens, who defends structuration theory from critiques posed by several feminist authors, including Linda Murgatroyd (1989), as follows: 'Not all aspects of social life are gender-divided, and precisely one of the issues which has to be faced in social theory is how far, and in what ways, the difference that is gender "makes a difference" ' (Giddens 1989: 282). To a large extent this is reflected in the treatment of gender in mainstream social theory literature: gender is discussed as a pre-existing, binary distinction. Clearly, in social capital theory, the gender difference *is* making a difference in terms of the transmission and acquisition of social capital, yet gendered agency remains completely untheorized.

The crucial questions of power, dominance or indeed of dependence and vulnerability are left aside. For Putnam, gender is explicitly present only when he discusses women, their role and their contribution to the increase or decrease in social capital. While he acknowledges that in the US, the movement of women into the labour force is not the *main* reason for the basic decline in American civic engagement, women are still culpable: according to Putnam (2000: 202), 'the long-term movement of women out of the category of affluent housewife into other social categories has tended to depress civic engagement'. What Putnam fails to acknowledge is that social capital might take forms which fall outside his definition, that social capital can possibly accumulate at work, and that the measurements he uses, such as 'entertaining, club going, community projects, etc' are all empirical measures attached to time and place, and that other kinds of measures (emails, mobile phones) have replaced his ideal of the accumulation of social capital.

Questions central to sociological theory, such as those of embodied agency and gender, become visible in texts on social capital solely through discussions which are reserved for women: that is, family-related issues. Although many sociological truisms may now be under close scrutiny, there still seem to be some areas where naturalistic assumptions exist. Undoubtedly, this is partly due to realist assumptions about knowledge in social capital theories. Gender can be found via a variety of ways and levels – existing as empirically identified 'women' or as an invisible element – in theories of social capital. Yet, there are strong links in the knowledge base of social capital to empiricism and rationalism, thus giving less theoretical space and possibilities for gendering the theoretical basic assumptions within the theories. Normative assumptions about the nature of good in social capital accumulation are strong. One example can be seen in the way Coleman (1990: 590–5) argues that women's participation in paid employment has been highly destructive to family life and children's social capital, as in the similar argument he uses for single parenthood (see also Fine 2000: 75). Another example of this is the way Putnam (2000: 201–2) argues that women's voluntary part-time work is a practical solution for the increase of community engagement in America. According to him, if women are able to work part-time, if they so wish, they will directly engage themselves more in community activities. In these theoretical directions, gender is taken up as a 'naturally' occurring role of a mother for women. There is no place for the gendering of social capital theory itself, as discussed earlier. Gender might remain here as an added category, while the theoretical ideas remain untouched.

However, I think we need to make a distinction here between theoretical debate stemming from economics and debates with closer links to sociology. With respect to economics, two points are important. First, the idea of social capital is poorly dealt with in contemporary economic thinking, largely because of social capital's elusive nature. It is not easily defined as an economic good, or as a measurable variable. Thus, it tends to assume a so-called 'residual' role in economic modelling. When all measurable variables, which can be classified in modelling national development and so on, are accounted for, the residue remains. This residue consists of, for example, skills and knowledge or other forms of unmeasurable dimensions such as caring, dependencies, power imbalances and inequalities. Second, being able to see social capital as a productive asset in economics means that the whole notion would have to be built upon problematic and deeply gendered assumptions about such things as the division of labour, invisible work and social networks. Third, economic analysis skirts a fundamental problem when trying to use the concept of social capital: is social capital a public good, such as shared knowledge, or more of a private good, such as human skills? This question too, calls up deeply rooted assumptions about gender, which beg a more sociological analysis.

In conclusion, my proposal for analysing gender in social capital theory refers to both making visible the implicit gendered theoretical claims, by explicating the gendered assumptions operating within the theoretical discussions encompassing social capital theories. The questions of seeing gender as a variable, or as a bipolar category of women and men with specific functional roles in society (woman as the mother: man as a citizen and breadwinner), calls for further and more elaborated feminist analysis of social capital theories. Otherwise the threat is that the explanatory power and appeal of social capital theories disappear, or lose their relevance, in sociology. New forms of civic engagement, changes in the labour market positions and development, changing ideas of citizenship and roles of families, and the gendered categories we use to understand them, all need to be analysed anew. Additionally, discussion of social capital theory must relate it to the epistemological assumptions of such debate. While the dominant voice in discussions of social capital at present comes from the Putnam–Coleman tradition, the subject is inherently and explicitly orientated towards economics and rational action theory. The epistemological assumptions in theories where formalism reigns allow little margin for gender and/or feminist epistemological or social epistemological orientation. I have argued here that knowledge on social capital is in fact very much a socially created and constructed knowledge, which is shaped by gendered social relations and interactions. Therefore, the 'capital' of social capital research and theories of social capital cannot be conflated with the knowledge or possession of an atomic individual, and thus cannot be understood as deriving from solely individualistic processes.

Notes

1   See, for example, http://worldbank.org/poverty/scapital
2   Margaret Archer (2000: 172) sees this avoidance of division by Bourdieu as 'a central conflation of subject and object'. She distinguishes and analyses the relations between embodied, practical and discursive knowledge and presents a solution for avoiding this two-fold distinction within the realist approach.
3   Francis Fukuyama (1995, 1999) argues, following Coleman, that social capital creates prosperity. Fukuyama's thesis on the relationship between social

9 Situated intersubjectivity

Lois McNay

Numerous social and feminist theorists have commented on the changing nature of gender relations in the last 30 years or so. However, in assessing the nature and significance of these changes, there is little consensus. Feminists have often been more cautious about the emancipatory implications of these shifts than social theorists, who have often made quite naive claims about the increasing fluidity of social identity and the 'transformation of intimacy' (for example, Bauman 1991b; Giddens 1992; Beck and Beck-Gernsheim 1995). Women have undoubtedly benefited from greater economic, civil and political freedoms since the late 1960s, yet discrimination persists in systemically maintained gender inequalities such as segregation in employment and unequal pay. Thus, against some of the ungrounded naive claims of social theory, many feminists would insist that changes within gender relations are indicative of the emergence of new forms of oppression as well as new types of freedom (see, for example, Chapter 7, this volume).

Yet, despite the argument that changes within gender norms and practices are complex and uneven, feminist theory itself often seems stuck in a series of conceptual disagreements that prevent it from developing a differentiated analysis of new dimensions of autonomy and dependence. One key division is that between cultural and materialist feminisms over what constitutes the most significant determinants of women's freedom.

In this chapter, I will sketch out an idea of *situated intersubjectivity*, arguing that it may overcome certain divisions between material and cultural feminisms and that it contributes to the development of a social theory of gender.

The force of the idea of situated intersubjectivity is that it presents a sociological alternative to the concern with the dynamics of desire that currently occupies much cultural feminism. At the same time, the hermeneutic dimension inherent to the idea corrects the structural perspective of materialist feminism that tends to lack categories for examining subjective experience. In elaborating the idea of situated intersubjectivity, I discuss the work of Jürgen Habermas and Pierre Bourdieu. Feminists have long recognized the contribution that Habermas's concept of communicative intersubjectivity may make to a sociological understanding of gender. While it undoubtedly initiates a valuable shift towards a dialogical and pragmatic conception of subjectivity, I argue that it forecloses an adequate examination of the way in which cultural issues of identity formation are linked to material issues of exploitation and oppression. It thus reinforces the split between material and cultural feminisms. The opposition Habermas posits between system and life-world prevents an analysis of how gender inequalities are central to the reproduction of wider power relations. Although Bourdieu's work lacks an adequate theory of intersubjectivity, his idea of the field provides a way of examining the imbrications of symbolic and material power relations and of situating a cultural politics of identity within materialist concerns with systemic exploitation. In other words, the idea of the field opens up a way of exploring how intersubjective relations of daily life bear within them the presence of more abstract systems of power. In conclusion, I indicate how the idea of situated intersubjectivity might contribute to a more explicit analysis of the differentiated power relations that render change within gender norms and practices uneven and discontinuous.

Cultural and material feminisms

Over the last ten years, one of the key debates within feminist theory has been that between material and cultural feminists about how to conceptualize the nature of gender oppression and, by implication, the possibilities for change. As Nancy Fraser (2000: 207–24) has observed, this debate has often engendered a host of 'false antitheses' where economic accounts of subordination are opposed to discursive accounts of identity construction, where 'exclusionary' accounts of subject formation are opposed to 'inclusionary' ones or where a politics of desire is opposed to a politics of redistribution. Such antitheses have served to defer a more constructive exploration of how the insights of cultural and material feminist theory may be combined rather than endlessly opposed. Here, I argue that an idea of *situated intersubjectivity* may serve as a way of more securely integrating cultural feminist work on the linguistic construction of gender identity with an analysis of power relations suggested by materialist feminism. In sum, the idea of intersubjectivity provides a category through which the intertwinement of symbolic and material power relations can begin to be thought.

Cultural feminism, of course, developed out of the 'linguistic turn' initiated by post-structural theory and used key ideas of discourse, difference and resistance to overcome what were seen to be the theoretical rigidities of first wave feminism, in particular, its a historical and simplified concepts of patriarchy and oppression. As a result of this critique, a sophisticated form of feminist theory has emerged which understands gender identity as an effect of culturally variable processes through which the body is discursively shaped. The work of Judith Butler (1990, 1993) is often taken as a paradigm of this kind of cultural feminism. Her idea of the performative construction of gender identity expresses a dialectical process where, on the one hand, the ceaseless and repeated ways in which cultures inscribe gender norms upon the body are indicative of the deeply entrenched and inescapable nature of this type of identity. On the other hand, the self-same compulsion to reiterate gender norms points to the arbitrary and unstable nature of these norms. It is by prising open these instabilities through subversive gender practices ('resignification') that changes to dominant heteronormativity can be wrought.

Butler's work on the performative construction of gender identity has been enormously influential, yet the critical pendulum seems to have come full circle. Just as her work emerged from the critique of the simplifications of first wave feminism so now this type of cultural feminist theory has been criticized for a symbolic determinism which effects a 'reduction upwards' where all issues of gender oppression are treated in the narrow terms of positionality within language (Hall 1997: 33). This reduction of society to language lacks a sufficiently differentiated analysis of power relations within which to analyse new formations of gender autonomy and dependence. For example, Butler's idea of performative resignification relies on an etiolated idea of agency that has little to do with historically specific practices because it is understood primarily as a structural property of language, namely, the inherent indeterminacy of meaning. Similarly, social transformation is understood in terms of the fetishized ideas of non-identity and marginality, which again have little to do with the discrete dynamics of social action and remain caught up within simplistic dualisms of domination and resistance, the normal and the abject, the central and the marginal (McNay 2000: 31–73). A further problem of this symbolic determinism is that the focus on resistance as libidinal activity or a 'style of the flesh' (Butler 1990: 139) remains caught within a privatized and individualist conception of activity whose radical political status is open to question in so far as it is complicit with, rather than disruptive of, capitalism. As Rosemary Hennessey puts it:

> These more open, fluid, ambivalent sexual identities . . . are quite compatible with the mobility, adaptability, and ambivalence required of service workers today and with the new more fluid forms of the commodity. While they may disrupt norms and challenge state practices that are indeed oppressive, they do not necessarily challenge neoliberalism or disrupt capitalism
>
> (Hennessey 2000: 108–9)

In criticizing the symbolic determinism of cultural feminism, materialist feminists argue that by absorbing society into language, the former fail to understand the complex and uneven ways in which gender inequalities are produced. In particular, cultural feminists underestimate the intractability of systemic forms of oppression and overestimate changes that can be brought about by a cultural identity politics. Nicola Field, for example, criticizes the connections between queer politics and the commodification of social life: 'gay lifestyle is visible as a specialised form of middle-class lifestyle and therefore is second nature to some, completely unattainable and meaningless to many' (Field 1997: 260). Materialist feminists tend to offer more cautious accounts of change asserting that, if gender relations are transforming at all, then it is in a gradual and complex fashion where the emergence of new forms of autonomy coincides with new forms of dependency and subordination. The emphasis placed by cultural feminists on discursive instabilities within gender norms is countered by a stress on the regular and predictable features of gender relations, as Walby argues: 'while gender relations could potentially take an infinite number of forms, in actuality there are some widely repeated features' (Walby 1990: 16). This stress by materialist feminists on an entrenched regularity within the reproduction of gender relations involves drawing attention to economic and other material conditions that form the condition of possibility of identity politics. For instance, transformations in the gender division of labour and the access it gives to material resources are regarded as more crucial determinant of levels of emancipation or subordination than shifts within gender ideologies and norms. Janet Saltzman Chafetz asserts that, although issues pertaining to sexual orientation are not irrelevant to gender system maintenance, compulsive and exclusive heterosexuality is not a fundamental bulwark of systemic reproduction. In contrast to the prevailing focus in cultural feminism on sexuality, lesbianism, in her view, is only harshly sanctioned when it is tied to social rebellion; it is against rebellion, not sexual preference *per se*, that societal repression is most strongly directed (Saltzman Chafetz 1990: 90). Similarly, Rosemary Hennessey argues that cultural feminist work on the indeterminacies of desire reifies identity by abstracting sexuality from the historical and sexual relations that produce and sustain them. The preoccupation with a certain notion of ambivalent lesbian desire in the work of thinkers such as Elizabeth Grosz (1994), Judith Butler (1990, 1993) and Teresa de Lauretis (1994) rests on an unexamined perspective of middle-class privilege. The celebration of the lesbian 'as a figure of unfettered lust' fails to examine the social conditions which allow it to arise at the same time as 'welfare reform debates in which the sexuality and needs of unmarried poor women and their children have become the punitive targets of state mandated "personal responsibility"' (Hennessey 2000: 197). Ultimately, this fetishization of 'dead identities' freezes experience, blocks the establishment of connections with other types of 'outlawed need', and narrows the field of possible action and collective agency (Hennessey 2000: 228–9).

Mediating the material and the symbolic

The materialist feminist stress on the deep-rooted nature of gender inequalities and on the gradual and uneven nature of any possibility of their restructuring is undoubtedly very powerful. However, in its opposition to the discursive framework of cultural feminism, it often borders on a countervailing systemic reductionism where the determining priority of economic structures is unambiguously asserted over other types of social and cultural experience. What is often lost is any kind of hermeneutic notion of self or coherent account of subjectivity and agency through which the daily experiences of economic, social and cultural oppression might be thought and through which these dimensions of oppression might be conceived of as co-extensive rather than crudely determining of each other (McNay 2000: 74–116). While cultural feminisms do tend to disconnect the discussion of identity from a social and material context, they nonetheless draw attention to processes of self-formation and dimensions of lived experience that materialist analysis overlooks.

Raymond Williams (1977) has drawn attention to the importance of theorizing lived social experience in his important but neglected idea of 'structures of feeling'. The categories and relations of social analysis tend to be construed in the past tense, as finished and explicit forms that stand in opposition to the uncertain and often confused present of lived experience understood as 'elements of impulse, restraint, and tone; specifically affective elements of consciousness and relationships: not feelings against thought, but thought as felt and feeling as thought: practical consciousness of a present kind, in a living and interrelating continuity' (Williams 1977: 132). This type of lived experience – social experience 'in solution' – transcends that of the merely personal or idiosyncratic, although, in its nascent stages, it may be experienced as private and isolating. It is a form or quality of social experience that is indicative of the emergence of new practices and norms that may be in an embryonic phase but will become recognizable at a later historical stage. In this sense, although they may not be explicitly articulated, structures of feeling are not simply flux but should be conceived as structured formations that can 'exert palpable pressures and set effective limits on experience and on action' (Williams 1977: 132).

Williams's work underscores the importance of a hermeneutic or interpretative perspective for social analysis. In particular, it demonstrates how, without any category of experience, an understanding of change would be rendered one dimensional because it would neglect the active, interpretative role played by social agents. It may be difficult to plot a direct causal link between attitudinal shifts and structural transformation. Nonetheless, the former may equally contribute to a gradual alteration in shared social practices that, in turn, may have a transforming impact on systemic tendencies in the manner of the so-called new social movements. In this respect, change is not the result of 'the vague tendency of the system, nor the undefined drive of change-oriented collectivities . . . but [of] the everyday conduct of common people, often quite far removed from any reformist intentions that are found to shape and reshape human societies' (Stzompka 1994: 39). The materialist emphasis on objective structures at the expense of ideas of agency and experi-ence may not detect such attitudinal shifts that contribute to social transform-ation. An act that may seem conformist, from a structural perspective, may in fact entail either a non-propositional content or, conversely, high levels of self-consciousness, both of which may be indicative of slow but far-reaching cultural shifts. For example, in *Having None of It*, Suzanne Franks (1999) docu-ments a growing discrepancy between young women's expectations of social equality and the persistence of discriminatory practices and inequalities at work and in the domestic sphere. On one level, this disjunction endorses a materialist insistence on placing the analysis of identity within the context of other power relations. However, on another level, this semi-articulated disjunction between expectations and actuality illustrates how the non-propositional or pre-rational content of agency may contribute to a trans-formation in social relations. It underscores the importance of adopting an interpretative perspective in the analysis of social change in so far as persistent and widespread dissatisfaction experienced by social actors may eventually catalyse moves towards reform.

The split between material and cultural feminisms – between what Nancy Fraser (1997) has called an understanding of gender oppression in terms of a logic of recognition and a logic of redistribution – has hindered the develop-ment of mediatory categories through which the interconnections between different regimes of power, between the material and symbolic realms of experience, can be thought. Feminists have long recognized the need to develop analytical tools capable of mapping these kinds of social complexity; as Judith Butler has noted, issues of material redistribution are inevitably caught up in a politics of cultural recognition (Butler 1998). This may be the case but, as Fraser points out, material and cultural inequalities have different dynamics and they have also become decoupled from each other disrupting clear patterns of determination: 'cultural value patterns do not strictly dictate economic allocations (contra the culturalist theory of society), nor do eco-nomic class inequalities simply reflect status hierarchies' (Fraser 2000: 118). In this respect, Rosemary Hennessey's *Profit and Pleasure* (2000) constitutes a notable attempt to overcome the oppositions between material and cultural feminisms and to produce concepts that are capable of linking some of the lived historical realities of sexual identity to global structures of oppression. She draws on E.P. Thompson's concept of experience to explain the primacy of capitalist economic structures in determining social existence but not in an absolute or mechanical sense. Thompson's idea of experience rests on a notion of class, not as an objective position, but as a 'structured process' that is always present, in an explicit or latent form, in the antagonisms and conflicts of daily experience. Class relations remain the 'kernel of human relationships' in so far as they structure emotions and legitimate or 'outlaw' need, but in ways that are indirect rather than causal. Thus, against the cultural feminist concern with the ambivalences of desire, the concept of experience allows a systematic examination of the contradictory forms of identification and affective force that underlie these ambivalences and it also makes visible the fundamental social structures from which identities emerge.

Hennessey's remarks on how it is possible to connect even the most intimate experiences of daily life to global structures of capital are very suggestive but they are also rather elliptical. Moreover, her assertion of the centrality of class would not only be problematic for many feminists but also it raises, rather than resolves, well-known difficulties with class analysis, notably the problem of determination, in the last instance. Instead of Thompson's class-based notion of experience, I want to suggest here the alternative concept of situated intersubjectivity as an analytical tool through which some of the insights of cultural and materialist perspectives on gender might be integrated.

Intersubjectivity

The force of the concept of intersubjectivity is that, on the one hand, its recognition of the essential sociality of human identity leads away from the ego-logical concern with the dynamics of desire that underlies much cultural feminist work on identity. Indeed, one of the central paradoxes of such discursive theories of identity is that, although they present themselves as a critique of the unitary individual, their narrow focus on the intra-psychic dynamics of desire tacitly reinstalls the primacy of the individual. The idea of intersubjectivity undermines this monological emphasis by asserting the embeddedness of the subject within social relations. On the other hand, the hermeneutic notions of recognition, intention and agency inherent in the idea of intersubjectivity counteract the functionalist emphasis of materialist theory that asserts the priority of structures and systems over experience. In other words, the idea of intersubjectivity contains within itself a way of connecting experience to the power relations that sustain and structure it. If, as Jean-Paul Sartre has observed, 'human relations are a mediation between different sectors of materiality' then the idea of intersubjectivity is one way of examining the coexistence and interconnections between these different levels of materiality (Sartre 1976: 94).

The work of Jürgen Habermas has been a fruitful source from which feminists have developed an account of intersubjectivity. The 'turn to Habermas' among feminists (for example, Meehan 1995) was a response in part to the economism of orthodox Marxism which, as is well-known, does not offer a satisfactory analysis of the centrality and pervasiveness of gender inequality in captialist social relations. Habermas's reorientation of Marxist thought towards the recognition of the primacy of an intersubjective rationality immanent in the practical interactions of the lifeworld overcomes the productivist emphasis that an exclusive focus on instrumental rationality yields. The uncovering of a relational dynamic inherent to the development of modernity opens up a space in which to explore the symbolic generation of gender relations. Some feminists have also used Habermas's thought because it provides a materialist antidote to what are seen as the relativism and aestheticizing tendencies of the post-structuralist tradition (Meehan 1995). From an analytical point of view, the post-structuralist dissolution of the subject abruptly forecloses an examination of dimensions of women's experience which depend on some notion of agency. Habermas's uncovering of an interactionist logic governing social action is seen to provide a more pragmatic and dialectical framework in which to examine the dynamics of gender relations. From a normative point of view, Habermas's championing of the emancipatory content of modernity in the form of undistorted communication resonates much more closely than a post-structural relativism with the feminist concern to liberate women and men from oppressive gender regimes.

In a recent exchange with Judith Butler, Selya Benhabib (1999) has made such points in arguing for the greater relevance of a theory of intersubjectivity for an analysis of gender and agency than a theory of performative identity. Benhabib maintains that a primarily discursive understanding of the subject does not distinguish sufficiently between different modes of subjectivation; between, for example, 'subjectivity, selfhood and agency'. The primacy accorded to linguistic processes of signification does not adequately differentiate between structural processes and dynamics of socialization and individuation on the one side, and historical processes of signification and meaning constitution on the other. Discursive accounts of identity do not have sufficiently strong concepts of human intention or sufficiently developed ideas of the communicative pragmatic abilities of everyday life. The possibility of linguistic agency in Derrida, for example, is linked to the reiterative structure of language itself. When this essentially structural account of agency is generalized, as it is in Butler's idea of performative resignification, it is unable to answer the question 'how does anyone know, that such resignification and reinterpretation have taken place?' (Osborne and Segal 1994; Benhabib 1999: 340). The abstract account of agency in terms of the reiterative structure of speech does not provide adequate accounts of intention or associated ideas of validity claims against which the political impact of a speech act can be assessed. The idea of instability within meaning systems provides a necessary but not sufficient condition for understanding agency (McNay 2000: 44–5). In so far as it involves the configuration of meaningful constellations of attitudes, intersubjective communication reveals an active dimension to subject forma-tion as self-interpretation. Ideas of intention associated with the communica-tive pragmatic abilities of daily life yield a fuller account of subjectivity and agency than discourse theory because they explain how 'speech acts are not only iterations but also innovations and reinterpretations' (Benhabib 1999: 339). For Habermas, the surplus of meaning that forms the condition of possi-bility of agency cannot be understood as a purely structural capacity but is the product of pragmatic communication or 'language-in-use': 'this "more" in language comes about through the communicative competence of social act-ors in generating situational interpretations of their lifeworld through com-municative acts oriented to validity claims' (Benhabib 1999: 339–40).

Yet, despite the emphasis both Habermas and Benhabib place on their idea of intersubjectivity as a pragmatic relation, the way in which they link this idea to a highly normative notion of communication forecloses an adequate analysis of power relations. There is not space here to go into Habermas's or Benhabib's work in any detail, suffice to say that the normative force invested in the idea of communicative intersubjectivity retroactively limits their socio-logical analysis of the power relations that overdetermine social interaction (see McNay 2002, forthcoming). The communicative paradigm remains too closely wedded to notions of community as a co-presence of subjects or as face to face relations and, in this stress on immediacy, it misses the temporally and spatially distantiated ways in which gender inequalities are reproduced. In the final analysis, the unyoking of the idea of intersubjecivity from an analysis of power can be traced to a culturalist or 'associational' mode of thinking where gender inequalities are considered primarily as lifeworld issues of identity and recognition and not as systemically perpetuated forms of discrimination (Sayer 2000).

It is obviously not the case that the Habermas's work lacks a theory of power. Rather the problem lies with a series of dualisms in his thought which block an analysis of the connections between identity formations and under-lying structures. A key dualism here is his account of social power as system and lifeworld where the instrumental rationality of the former has distorting effects on the communicative rationality of the latter. The dualist account of power confines an understanding of gender inequalities to the cultural realm, neglect-ing the systemic and material dimensions in their construction (Fraser 1989; Meehan 1995). For example, as Nancy Fraser argues, Habermas regards the family solely as an institution of the lifeworld and thereby misses its 'dual aspect', in other words, the family perpetuates systemic relations of oppression as much as it reproduces values and cultural norms. Money and power do not have only an extrinisic and incidental relation to the family but are constitu-tive of its core dynamics. In Fraser's view, such a one-sided conception occludes an understanding of families as 'thoroughly permeated with . . . the media of power and money. They are sites of egocentric, strategic, and instrumental calculation as well as sites of usually exploitative exchange of services, labour, cash and sex – and, frequently, sites of coercion and violence' (Fraser 1989: 119–20). In an analogous fashion, Habermas understands gender only as a type of identity formation (lifeworld) and not as a structuring principle of social division (system). Furthermore, the unidirectional dynamic of distortion of the lifeworld by systems posited by Habermas is too simplified a model with which to analyse the uneven phenomenon of gender oppression. For example, the intrusion of an economic dynamic into the affectual relations of the family can not be regarded as simply distorting but may be empowering for women in that it gives them a greater potential capacity for exit from oppressive marriages (Fraser 1997: 228–9).

In short, in an era of increasingly formal equality, gender inequalities are often reproduced in a discontinuous and uneven way. Systemically maintained oppression does not necessarily manifest itself through explicit discrimination or, in Habermas's terms, through the unremittingly negative distortions imposed upon the lifeworld by the imperatives of money and power. As feminists like Carol Brown (1981) and Sylvia Walby (1990) have pointed out, there has been a shift in the last hundred or so years from private to public patriarchy; gender inequalities are no longer perpetuated so much through arbitrary and direct sanctions confining women to the domestic sphere but rather through indirect forms of economic exploitation and state inertia. These indirect and impersonal forms of structural discrimination render gender inequality less visible because formal equality between men and women, at the level of civil and social freedoms, appears to be upheld. The distinction between private and public patriarchy is analogous to a distinction made by Iris Marion Young (1990) between oppression and domination. Domination refers to constraints upon oppressed groups to follow rules set by others, whereas oppression refers to inequalities maintained at a structural and non-intentional level where 'an oppressed group need not have a correlate oppressing group' (Young 1990: 41). If we apply this distinction to the idea of communicative rationality, we can see that while it might identify forms of gender domination in terms of explicit patriarchal sanctions, it does not so readily capture types of systemic and impersonal gender oppression associated with public patriarchy. In short, Habermas's dualism of system and lifeworld compounds a 'cultural turn' where systems are reduced to the lifeworld and gender is considered almost entirely from within the paradigm of identity issues (Ray and Sayer 1999).

In sum, despite Benhabib's claim that Habermas's pragmatic conception of intersubjectivity overcomes discursive abstraction, it in fact replicates a 'linguistic universalism' similar to that of cultural feminism which separates the consideration of identity from the analysis of power relations. In order to indicate how the idea of intersubjectivity may be situated more centrally within an analysis of power relations, I will now discuss Bourdieu's concept of the field.

Bourdieu and the field

In *Pascalian Meditations*, Pierre Bourdieu criticizes Habermas for subjecting social relations to a two-fold de-politicization: 'He [Habermas] reduces political power relations to relations of communication . . . that is, to relations of "dialogue" from which he has in practice removed the power relations that take place there in a transfigured form' (Bourdieu 2000: 66). Bourdieu believes that power relations are immanent within all social relations and that, even as a regulative ideal, Habermas's idea of a reciprocal intersubjectivity is untenable: 'It is only in exceptional cases (in the abstract and artificial situations created by experimentations) that symbolic exchanges are reduced to relations of pure communication, and that the informative content of the message exhausts the content of the communication' (Bourdieu 1991: 107). Like Foucault, Bourdieu regards the ubiquitous presence of power relations, absorbed and naturalized within the body, as the condition of possibility of social existence. Inequalities of power are an inevitable feature of social interaction and cannot be escaped in the way that Habermas's communicative ethics assumes. Bourdieu uses the concepts of habitus and the field to explain the way in which the body and its dispositions are insidiously shaped and determined to ensure accommodation to dominant power relations (McNay 1999).

Many commentators have argued that Bourdieu's assertion of the inexorable and ubiquitous nature of power relations pushes his work into a crude form of material determinism (for example, Alexander 1994). Judith Butler (1999) claims, for example, that the concepts of habitus and the field are determinist in so far as they deny the possibility of radical change and, in the final analysis, reassert a reductionist base–superstructure model. This is because, despite Bourdieu's claim that there exists a relation of double conditioning between habitus and field, it is in fact the field that is attributed a pre-given objectivity and enshrined, therefore, as an 'unalterable positivity' (Butler 1999: 117). Whereas habitus adapts to the objective demands of the field, there is no sense of a countervailing alteration of the field by habitus. The unidirectional causality ascribed to the field undermines any idea of the instabilities and resistances inherent to the process through which social norms are inscribed upon the body. This is compounded by Bourdieu's deployment of a rather functionalist notion of adaptation where habitus – the physical and psychological dispositions of the individual – are always calibrated to the exigencies of social structure (the field) rather than having their own determining effect. By producing an account of power that is structurally committed to the status quo, Bourdieu allegedly forecloses the possibilities of resistance and agency emerging from the margins in the way that Butler envisages in her idea of performative resignification.

There is undoubtedly a tendency in some of Bourdieu's work to over-estimate the accommodation between symbolic codes and the reproduction of social structures (McNay 2000: 51–3). However the concept of the field in fact expresses a complex and differentiated notion of power where the relation between material practices and symbolic relations are not conceived as straightforwardly causal and oriented towards social reproduction. In the space that remains I will argue that the idea of the field provides a nonreductionist way of situating social experience, and categories for its analysis such as intersubjectivity, within the context of systemic power relations. The field expresses a double principle of differentiation understood as both movement across fields and as the internal complexity of material and symbolic relations within any given field. It is the latter that I will concentrate on here, but it is worth mentioning that the first Weberian principle of differentiation means, (*contra* Butler and other critics) that Bourdieu does not understand social position as fixed but as entailing movement across fields which may involve contradictory and dissonant power relations. I have argued elsewhere that this idea of differentiation replaces dualisms of the public and the private with a more complex notion of society as an uneven and open structure, against which it is possible to analyse unfolding patterns of gender autonomy and dependence (McNay 2000: 71).

It is the second principle of differentiation internal to the field, however, which is of most relevance here. Bourdieu understands the field as a complex imbrication of material and symbolic relations of power, expressed as the intertwinement of the structure of 'positions' within the 'space of possibles'. The tendencies of the field may be absorbed within the body in the form of dispositions but, in a countervailing logic, they can react and modify behaviour within the field: 'through the cognitive and motivating structures that it brings into play . . . habitus plays its part in determining the things to be done, or not to be done, the urgencies, etc., which trigger action' (Bourdieu 2000: 148). In other words, there is an 'affective transaction' between habitus and field which may reinforce or dislodge objective tendencies and which disrupts the unidirectional determinism that flows from what Butler claims is the inert positivity of the field.

Bourdieu illustrates the interaction between the space of possibles and the structures of positions in a discussion of hope. On the one hand, there is an alignment between symbolic and material relations in that subjective structures of hope are aligned with objective structures of probability. In other words, there is a tendency for hope to increase proportionally with social power that enables an agent to manipulate the potentialities of the present in order to realize some future project. The most oppressed groups in society often oscillate between fantasy and surrender; reflecting how, below a certain threshold of objective chances, the strategic and anticipatory dimension diminishes. For example, the appeal of national lotteries lies partly in the extent to which they re-inject expectation into the negated or non-time of life in which nothing happens. Yet, Bourdieu goes on to argue that systemic tendencies towards social complexity and uncertainty lead increasingly to a more general experience of mismatches between expectations and objective chances: 'the lack of a future, previously reserved for the "wretched of the earth" is an increasingly wide-spread, even modal experience' (Bourdieu 2000: 234).

Bourdieu only discusses the way in which this disjunction between the experience of hope and social position may engender despair or 'destabilized habitus, torn by contradiction and internal division, generating suffering' (Bourdieu 2000: 160). Yet, it is possible to imagine the inverse, where the disjunction between hope and social position might produce an active and anticipatory disposition towards the future. This might be the case in the example already considered of the disjunction between women's experience of discrimination in some realms of social life and their heightened expectation of freedom in others. The dissatisfaction with the present may engender a more hopeful and motivated orientation towards the future that may eventually contribute towards social change in the way that Williams speaks about with his idea of structures of feeling.

In short, I am arguing that Bourdieu's conceptualization of the discontinuity between the space of possibles and the structure of positions produces a more nuanced understanding of the relation between structures and experience than is available in much theory at the moment. I will conclude with a concrete illustration of how Bourdieu's idea of the field can be used to situate notions of intersubjectivity, by which I mean how it can be used to unpack the overdetermined complex of material and symbolic power relations that are immanent within social experience giving it both its unfinished and predictable character.

Marriage as situated intersubjectivity

Marriage and the family have always been pivotal to the feminist analysis of the subordination of women but, with the shift of concern over the last ten or so years to the analysis of desire, it has become much less central. This change in focus signals, to a degree, an analytical weakness in discursive theories of identity construction, because the emphasis placed on abject and marginalized sexualities often entails the assumption that the reproduction of hegemonic 'heteronormativity' is unproblematic. It is an error to assume that hegemonic heterosexuality passively exists as a form of dominance, rather it 'has continually to be renewed, recreated, defended, and . . . also continually resisted, limited, altered, challenged by pressures not at all its own' (Williams 1977: 112). The reproduction of heterosexual relations has become increasingly complex and unstable in the last 20 years, resulting in what Beck and

Beck-Gernsheim (1995) have called the 'normal chaos of love'. The reasons for these transformations in the reproduction of heterosexuality involve the interaction between a multiplicity of macro structural transformations – such as the expansion of higher education and the 'flexibilization' of labour that have pulled more women into the workforce – and changes within subjective dispositions involving conflicting expectations and experiences of marriage and intimacy. By placing the relation between husband and wife within the framework of situated intersubjectivity, it is possible to begin to unpack the complex co-existence of positions and possibles, of material and symbolic relations, that interact with each in a variable fashion and contribute to the appearance of an increasing uncertainty within intimate relations.

Bourdieu does not address such questions directly, but his article 'On the family as a realized category' (1996) provides an interesting if sketchy attempt to analyse the ambivalent relation that exists between symbolically con-structed dynamics of affect and material interests. Here, the family is understood as both an objective and subjective social category that plays a fundamental role in the ordering of social practice and the perception of experience. Thus, on the one hand, the structure of the family and its legitimacy is determined by the objective role it plays in the accumulation and transmission of eco-nomic, cultural and symbolic privileges, such as property, the family name and social capital. On the other hand, in its subjective function as a tacitly internalized principle of perception (habitus), the family is marked by an intense emotional logic involving the symbolic inculcation of obliged affec-tions and affective obligations of family feeling. The family is characterized by a constant and intense maintenance work that turns the nominal bonds of the family group ('she's your sister . . .') into intense and uniting affective bonds. Through an endless practical and symbolic labour comprising a myriad of ordinary and continuous exchanges – exchange of gifts, service, help, atten-tion, visits – the 'obligation to love' is transformed into a 'loving disposition' that tends to endow each member with family feeling and generates solidarity. This emotional labour of integration is especially important in that it may serve as a counter to the potentially disintegrative effects of struggle over other power relations both within and beyond the field of the family. Thus, the family is both an immanent and transcendent structure: '[it] is both immanent in individuals (as an internalized collective) and transcendent to them, since they encounter it in the form of objectivity in all other relations' (Bourdieu 1996: 21).

A significant implication of this article is that it alludes to the ways in which affectual ties and motivations may have an ambivalent relation with material and instrumental interests, sometimes reinforcing them, sometimes running counter to them. Although the family is a primary site where indi-viduals are accommodated to the social system, the bonds that it generates may be orthogonal to any socializing function. The family may engender conformity among its members but it may equally engender idiosyncratic, asocial and even resistant dispositions. Against determinist analyses, the family is seen, therefore, as internally contradictory: 'it does not form its own dynamic, nor is it part of the dynamic of capitalist production' (German 1997: 153). Bourdieu does not pursue the implications of this ambivalent relation between symbolically engendered relations of affect and material interests, but I will finish by drawing out a few of its implications for an understanding of certain gendered dynamics within marriage.

Feminist analyses of marriage have often examined the husband–wife relation in terms of Hegel's logic of recognition. Indeed, it is the Hegelian struggle for recognition that constitutes the basic paradigm for Habermas's idea of communicative intersubjectivity. A classic example of this type of analysis is Carole Pateman's (1988) use of the master–slave dynamic to explain how gender inequalities are established in familial relations. The unwritten sexual contract within marriage perpetuates a dynamic of masculinity as sexual mastery and femininity as sexual subjection. This master–slave relation has both social and symbolic effects in that it subordinates women to their husbands in a real sense and sustains patriarchal sexual norms. Nancy Fraser has shown, however, that this analysis of marriage in terms of a structural isomorphism of social and symbolic subordination is too simplistic because it obscures the analysis of structural or systemic processes that undergird hierarchical social relations. For example, within marriage, power has less to do with an implicit sexual contract and 'male sex right', and more to do with the ability to exit defined by structural factors such as inferior labour market opportunities and childcare demands. Moreover, *contra* Pateman, the relations between these symbolic and material relations are not straightforwardly isomorphic. Structural asymmetries may reinforce inequalities within the marriage contract. However, the mediation of the marriage contract through systemic and non-congruent relations may create the potential for trade-offs and new forms of autonomy:

> even as the wage contract establishes the worker as subject to the boss's command in the employment sphere, it simultaneously constitutes that sphere as a limited sphere. "The outside" here both includes a market in consumer commodities into which the wage buys entry and a noncommodified domestic sphere in which much of the work of social reproduction is performed without pay by women. In those arenas, which are themselves permeated by power and inequality, the wage functions as a resource and a source of leverage. For some women, it buys a reduction in vulnerability through marriage
> (Fraser 1997: 230)

These resources may not be simply material but may also take the form of symbolic or emotional compensations. Bourdieu (1996), for example, speaks of the 'symbolic capital of normalcy' within marriage that may engender a sufficiently strong bond to counter other types of subordination and exploitation within the family. Rosemary Hennessey (2000) describes a similar phenomenon of 'compensation' in terms of the overdetermination of class dynamics by cultural categories. Thus, embracing heteronormativity in the form of marriage can offer many non-white workers an 'imaginary compensatory psychological wage of normalcy' which may offset economic exploitation and racial discrimination. Compensations may be imaginary or material, but they 'keep those who benefit and those who lose from seeing their wider common interests' (Hennessey 2000: 92). The point is that these multiple dynamics may be simultaneously present within the intersubjective relation between husband and wife, influencing their actions in a systematic but not necessarily predictable fashion.

Conclusion

The analysis of marriage as a complex ensemble of material and symbolic dynamics yields a determinate and complex notion of intersubjective relations. Social theorists from Godelier through Williams to de Certeau have all established the importance of acknowledging the co-existence and determining force of both material and symbolic factors in the analysis of social action and change (Williams 1977; De Certeau 1984; Godelier 1984). Feminist theory, however, has tended to separate the analysis of material from cultural relations and this has resulted in one-sided accounts of changes in gender relations either as an indefinable indeterminacy of meaning systems or as variations in the inertness of capitalist structures. I have suggested the idea of situated intersubjectivity as a way of reconnecting certain aspects of the symbolic and materialist analysis of gender. My development of the idea of intersubjectivity runs counter to many feminist formulations of the concept in so far as they tend to view it primarily as a dyadic, psychological and primarily linguistically mediated relation of recognition. Against this, intersubjectivity needs to be conceived in sociological terms as ineluctably situated in differentiated power relations ranging from structures of affect to systemic material interests. Intersubjective relations are the point at which the generality of power relations become visible in everyday life – often as an absent presence – giving the latter its both unfinished and predictable quality and against which shifts within gender relations might be examined.

References

Abell, P. (1992) Is rational choice theory a rational choice of theory? in J. Coleman and T. Fararo (eds) *Rational Choice Theory: Advocacy and Critique*. Newbury Park: Sage.

Abrams, P. (1968) *The Origins of British Sociology 1834–1914*. Chicago: University of Chicago Press.

Adam, J. (1904) *Mes premières armes littéraires et politiques*. Paris: A. Lemerre.

Adams, B.N. and Sydie, R.A. (2001) *Classical Sociological Theory*. Thousand Oaks, CA: Pine Forge Press.

Adkins, L. (1999) Community and economy: a retraditionalization of gender? *Theory, Culture and Society*, 16(4): 119–39.

Adkins, L. (2002) *Revisions: Sex and Gender in Late Modernity*. Buckingham: Open University Press.

Albisetti, J. (1986) Women and the professions in imperial Germany, in R.E.B. Joers and M.J. Mayns (eds) *German Women in the Eighteenth and Nineteenth Centuries. A Social and Literary History*. Bloomington: Indiana University Press.

Alexander, J. (1994) *Fin de Siècle Social Theory: Relativism, Reduction and the Problem of Reason*. London: Verso.

Allen, A.T. (1991) *Feminism and Motherhood in Germany, 1800–1914*. New Brunswick: Rutgers University Press.

Alway, J. (1995) The trouble with gender: tales of the still-missing revolution in sociological theory, *Sociological Theory*, 13(3): 209–28.

Ansart, P. (1967) *La sociologie de Proudhon*. Paris: Presses Universitaires.

Archer, M. (2000) *Being Human. The Problem of Agency*. Cambridge: Cambridge University Press.

Atkinson, M. (1914) *The Economic Foundations of the Women's Movement*, Fabian Tract no. 175. London: Fabian Society.

Baier, A.C. (1995) *Moral Prejudices. Essays on Ethics*. Cambridge: Harvard University Press.

Barrett, M. (1980) *Women's Oppression Today*. London: New Left Books.

Bauman, Z. (1991a) Ideology and the *Weltanschauung* of the intellectuals, *Canadian Journal of Political and Social Theory*, 15(1,2,3): 107–20.

Bauman, Z. (1991b) *Modernity and Ambivalence*. Cambridge: Polity Press.

Bauman, Z. (1998) *Work, Consumerism and the New Poor*. Buckingham: Open University Press.

Bäumer, G. (1901) Die Geschichte der Frauenbewegung in Deutschland, in H. Lange and G. Bäumer (eds) *Handbuch der Frauenbewegung*. Berlin: Moeser.

Bäumer, G. (1904) *Die Frau in der Kulturbewegung der Gegenwart*. Wiesbaden: J.F. Bergmann.

Bäumer, G. (1921) *Die Geschichte des Bundes Deutscher Frauenvereine*. Berlin: Teubner.

Bebel, A. ([1879] 1964) *Die Frau und der Sozialismus*. Berlin: Dietz.

Beck, U. (1986) *Risikogesellschaft. Auf dem Weg in eine andere Moderne*. Frankfurt a.m.: Suhrkamp.

Beck, U. (1992) *Risk Society: Towards a New Modernity*. London: Sage.

Beck, U. (1993) *Die Erfindung des Politischen: zu einer Theorie reflexiver Modernisierung*. Frankfurt a.M.: Suhrkamp.

Beck, U. (1994) The reinvention of politics: towards a theory of reflexive modernization, in U. Beck, A. Giddens and S. Lash (eds) *Reflexive Modernization: Politics, Tradition and Aesthetics in the Modern Social Order*. Cambridge: Polity.

Beck, U. (1996) Das Zeitalter der Nebenfolgen und die Politisierung der Moderne, in U. Beck, A. Giddens and S. Lash (eds) *Eine Kontroverse*. Frankfurt a.M.: Suhrkamp. Reflexive Modernisierung.

Beck, U. (ed.) (2002) *Riskante Freiheiten. Individualisierung in modernen Gesellschaften*. Frankfurt a.M.: Suhrkamp.

Beck, U. and Beck-Gernsheim, E. (1990) *Das ganz normale Chaos der Liebe*. Frankfurt a.M.: Suhrkamp.

Beck, U. and Beck-Gernsheim, E. (eds) (1994) *Riskante Freiheiten. Individualisierung in modernen Gesellschaften*. Frankfurt a.M.: Suhrkamp.

Beck, U. and Beck-Gernsheim, E. (1995) *The Normal Chaos of Love*. Cambridge: Polity Press.

Beck, U. and Beck-Gernsheim, E. (2002) *Individualization. Institutionalized Individualism and its Social and Political Consequences*. London: Sage.

Beck, U., Giddens, A. and Lash, S. (eds) (1996) *Reflexive Modernisierung: Eeine Kontoverse*. Frankfurt a.M.: Suhrkamp.

Beck-Gernsheim, E. (1980) *Das halbierte Leben. Männerwelt, Beruf, Frauenwelt, Familie*. Frankfurt a.M: Fischer.

Beck-Gernsheim, E. (1983) Vom 'Dasein für andere' zum Anspruch auf ein Stück 'eigenes Leben': Individualisierungsprozesse im weiblichen Lebenszusammenhang, *Soziale Welt*, 34(3): 307–40.

Beck-Gernsheim, E. (1998) On the way to a post-familial family: from a community of needs to elective affinities, *Theory, Culture and Society*, 15(3–4): 53–70.

Beck-Gernsheim, E. (2002) From 'living for others' to 'a life of one's own': individualism and women, in U. Beck and E. Beck-Gernsheim (eds) *Individualization. Institutionalized Individualism and its Social and Political Consequences*. London: Sage.

Becker, G. (1996) *Accounting for Tastes*. Cambridge, MA: Harvard University Press.

Becker-Schmidt, R., Knapp, G-A. and Gadrar-Axeli (2000) *Feministische Theorien zur Einfuhrung*. Hamburg: Junius.

Beer, U. (1990) *Geschlecht, Struktur, Geschichte. Soziale Konstituierung des Geschlechterverhältnisses*. Frankfurt a.M.: Campus.

Behr, W.J. (1804) *System der allgemeinen Staatslehre zum Gebrauche für seine Vorlesungen*, Vol. 1. Bamberg: Goebhardt.

Benhabib, S. (1982) Die Moderne und die Aporien der Kritischen Theorie, in W. Bonss and A. Honneth (eds) *Sozialforschung als Kritik*. Frankfurt a.m: Suhrkamp.

Benhabib, S. (1999) Sexual difference and collective identities: the new global constellation, *Signs: Journal of Women in Culture and Society*, 24: 335–61.

Benhabib, S., Butler J., Cornell, D. and Fraser, N. (1993) *Der Streit um Differenz: Feminismus und Postmoderne in der Gegenwart*. Frankfurt a.M.: Fischer.

Benjamin, J. (1982) Die Antinomien des patriarchalen Denkens. Kritische Theorie und Psychoanalyse, in W. Bonss and A. Honneth (eds) *Sozialforschung als Kritik*. Frankfurt a.M.: Suhrkamp.

Berg, M. (1992) The first women economic historians, *Economic History Review*, 45.

Bernard, J. (1973) My four revolutions: an autobiographical history of the ASA, *American Journal of Sociology*, 78(4): 773–91.

Bertilsson, M. (1991) Love's labour lost? A sociological view, in M. Featherstone, M. Hepworth and B. Turner (eds) *The Body: Social Processes and Cultural Theory*. London: Sage.

Bock, G. (1998) *Women in European History*. Oxford: Basil Blackwell.

Bock, G. and Thane, P. (eds) (1991) *Maternity and Gender Policies. Women and the Rise of the European Welfare States 1880s–1950s*. London: Routledge.

Bologh, R.W. (1990) *Love or Greatness: Max Weber and Masculine Thinking – A Feminist Inquiry*. London: Unwin Hyman.

Bosanquet, B. (1899) *The Philosophical Theory of the State*. London: Macmillan.

Bosanquet, H. (1902) *The Strength of the People: A Study in Social Economics*. London: Macmillan.

Bosanquet, H. (1911) Letter to *The Times*, 12 December.

Bosanquet, H. (1923) *The Family*. New York: Macmillan.

Bosanquet, H. (1924) *Bernard Bosanquet: A Short Account of His Life*. London: Macmillan.

Bosanquet, T. (1927) *Harriet Martineau. An Essay in Comprehension*. London: Etchels & MacDonald.

Both, W. (1993) Zur Sozialen und politischen Situation von Frauen in Hessen und zur Frauenpolitik der Amerikanischen Besatzungsmacht, in U. Wischermann, in E. Schuller and U. Gerhard (eds) *Staatsbürgerinnen zwischen Partei und Bewegung. Frauenpolitik in Hessen 1945 bis 1955*. Frankfurt a.M.: Ulrike Helmer.

Bourdieu, P. (1977) *Outline of a Theory of Practice*. Cambridge: Cambridge University Press.

Bourdieu, P. (1980) Le capital social: notes provisoires, *Actes de la Recherche en Sciences Sociales*, 3: 2–3.

Bourdieu, P. (1986) The forms of capital, in J. Richardson (ed.) *Handbook of Theory and Research for the Sociology of Education*. New York: Greenwood Press.

Bourdieu, P. (1991) *Language and Symbolic Power*. Cambridge: Polity Press.

Bourdieu, P. (1996) On the family as a realised category, *Theory, Culture and Society*, 13(3): 19–26.

Bourdieu, P. (1997) Die männliche Herrschaft, in I. Dölling and B. Krais (eds) *Ein alltägliches Spiel. Geschlechterkonstruktion in der sozialen Praxis*. Frankfurt a.M.: Suhrkamp.

Bourdieu, P. (2000) *Pascalian Meditations*. Cambridge: Polity Press.

Bourdieu, P. and Passeron, J-C. (1977) *Reproduction in Education, Society and Culture*. Beverly Hills, CA: Sage.

Bourdieu, P. and Wacquant, L.J.D. (1992) *An Invitation to Reflexive Sociology*. Chicago: University of Chicago Press.

Brand, K-W. (1982) *Neue soziale Bewegungen. Entstehung, Funktion und Perspektive neuer Protestpotentiale. Eine Zwischenbilanz*. Opladen: Westdeutscher Verlag.

Branford, V. (1903) On the origins and use of the word sociology and on the relation of sociology to other studies and to practical problems, *American Journal of Sociology*, 9(2): 145–622.

Branford, V. (1914) *Interpretations and Forecasts: A Study of Survivals and Tendencies in Contemporary Society*. London: Duckworth and Company.

Branford, V. (1927) Letter to G. Sandeman, 30 April, Institute of Sociology papers, University of Keele, S. Gurney box.

Branford, V. (1930) An appeal to university women, *Sociological Review*, 22.

Braun, L. (1895) *Die Bürgerpflicht der Frau*. Berlin: Dümmler.

Brown, C. (1981) Mothers, fathers and children: from private to public patriarchy, in L. Sargent (ed.) *Women and Revolution: A Discussion of the Unhappy Marriage of Marxism and Feminism*. London: Pluto Press.

Browne, A. (1987) *The Eighteenth Century Feminist Mind*. Sussex: Harvester Press.

Buechler, S.M. (1990) *Women's Movement in the United States: Women Suffrage, Equal Rights and Beyond*. New Brunswick: Rutgers.

Bulmer, M. *et al.* (eds) (1991) *The Social Survey in Historical Perspective 1880–1940*. Cambridge: Cambridge University Press.

Bundestags-Drucksache (1966) Bericht der Bundesregierung über die Situation der Frauen in Beruf, *Familie und Gesellschaft*, 5: 909.

Burkart, G. (1995) Zum Strukturwandel der Familie. Mythen und Fakten, *Politik und Zeitgeschichte*, 52–3: 3–15.

Burt, R.S. (1980) Autonomy in a social topology, *American Journal of Sociology*, 85: 892–925.

Burt, R.S. (2001) Structural holes versus network closure as social capital, in N. Lin, K. Cook and R.S. Burt (eds) *Social Capital. Theory and Research*. New York: Aldine de Gryuter.

Bussemer, H.U. (1985) *Frauenemanzipation und Bildungsbürgertum. Sozialgeschichte der Frauenbewegung in der Reichsgründungszeit*. Weinheim: Beltz.

Butler, J. (1990) *Gender Trouble: Feminism and the Subversion of Identity*. London: Routledge.

Butler, J. (1991) *Das Unbehagen der Geschlechter*. Frankfurt a.M.: Suhrkamp.

Butler, J. (1993) *Bodies that Matter: On the Discursive Limits of Sex*. London: Routledge.

Butler, J. (1997) *Excitable Speech: A Politics of the Performative*. London: Routledge.

Butler, J. (1998) Marxism and the merely cultural, *New Left Review*, 227: 33–44.

Butler, J. (1999) Performativity's social magic, in R. Schusterman (ed.) *Bourdieu: A Critical Reader*. Oxford: Blackwell.

Calhoun, C. (1995) 'New social movements' of the early nineteenth century, in M. Traugott (ed.) *Cycles and Repertoires of Collective Action*. Durham: Duke University Press.

Canguilhem, G. (1981) Auguste Comtes Philosophie der Biologie und ihr Einfluss im Frankreich des 19. Jahrhunderts, in W. Lepenies (ed.) *Geschichte der Soziologie. Studien zur kognitiven, sozialen und historischen Identität einer Disziplin*, vol. 3. Frankfurt a.m.: Suhrkamp.

Carruthers, B.G. and Babb, S.L. (2000) *Economy/Society. Markets, Meanings and Social Structure*. London: Pine Forge Press.

Castells, M. (1996) *The Rise of Network Society*. Oxford: Blackwell.

Cavana, M.L. (1991) *Der Konflikt zwischen dem Begriff des Individuums und der Geschlechtertheorie bei Georg Simmel und José Ortega y Gasset*. Pfaffenweiler: Centaurus.

Chafetz, J.S. (ed.) (1999) *Handbook of Sociology of Gender*. New York: Kluwer Academic/Plenum Publishers.

Chodorow, N. (1985) *Das Erbe Der Mutter. Psychoanalyse und Soziologie der Geschlechter*. München: Frauenoffensive.

Clark, B.R. (ed.) (1987) *The Academic Profession. National, Disciplinary, and Institutional Settings*. Berkeley: California University Press.

Clarke, J.F. (1877) Art. VII – Harriet Martineau, *The North American Review*, 124(256): 435–50.

Cobbe, F.P. (1861) Social science congresses and women's part in them, *Macmillans Magazine*, December.

Cohen, J.L. (1995) Critical social theory and feminist critique: the debate with Jürgen Habermas, in J. Meehan (ed.) *Feminists Read Habermas: Gendering the Subject of Discourse*. New York: Routledge.

Coleman, J.S. (1988) Social capital in the creation of human capital, *American Journal of Sociology*, 94: S95–S120.

Coleman, J.S. (1990) *Foundations of Social Theory*. Cambridge, MA: Harvard University Press.

Coleman, J.S. (2000) Social capital in the creation of human capital, in P. Dasgupta and I. Serageldin (eds) *Social Capital. A Multifaceted Perspective*. Washington: The World Bank.

Collini, S. (1979) *Liberalism and Sociology: L.T. Hobhouse and Political Argument in England 1880–1914*. Cambridge: Cambridge University Press.

Comte, A. (1816–28) *Écrits de jeunesse*. Paris/La Haye: Mouton.

Comte, A. (1852) *Catéchisme positiviste ou Sommaire exposition de la religion universelle de l'humanité*. Paris: Carilian-Goeury et V. Dalmont.

Comte, A. (1975) in G. Lenzer (ed.) *Auguste Comte and Positivism: The Essential Writings*. Chicago: University of Chicago Press.

Condorcet, J.A. ([1789] 1979) Über die Zulassung der Frauen zum Bürgerrecht, in H. Schröder (ed.) *Die Frau ist frei geboren*, Vol. 1. München: C.H. Beck.

Connell, R.W. (1997) Why is classical theory classical? *American Journal of Sociology*, 102: 1511–57.

Coser, L.A. (1977a) *Masters of Sociological Thought*, 2nd edn. New York: Harcourt Brace Jovanovich.

Coser, L.A. (1977b) Georg Simmel's neglected contribution to the sociology of women, *Signs*, 2: 869–76.

Coser, L.A. (1984) Georg Simmels vernachlässigter Beitrag zur Soziologie der Frau, in H. J. Dahme and O. Rammstedt (eds) *Georg Simmel und die Moderne. Neue Interpretationen und Materialien*. Frankfurt a.M.: Suhrkamp.

Cott, N. (1987) *The Grounding of Modern Feminism*. New Haven: Yale University Press.

Coward, R. (1983) *Patriarchal Precedents: Sexuality and Social Relations*. New York: Routledge.

Cox, E. (1995) *Truly Civil Society*. Sydney: ABC Books.

Crossley, N. (2001) The phenomenological habitus and its construction, *Theory and Society*, 30: 81–120.

Curtis, R.F. and MacCorquodale, P. (1990) Stability and change in gender relations, *Sociological Theory*, 8(2): 136–52.

D'Héricourt, J.P. (1855) Le catéchisme positiviste de M. Auguste Comte, *Revue philosophique et religieuse*, 3: 47–61.

D'Héricourt, J.P. (1860) *La femme affranchie. Réponse à MM. Michelet, Proudhon, E. de Girardin, A. Comte et aux autres novateurs modernes*, 2 vols. Brussels: Fr. van Meenen et Cie, A. Bohné.

D'Héricourt, J.P. ([1864] 1981) *A Woman's Philosophy of Woman; Or Woman Affranchised. An Answer to Michelet, Proudhon, Girardin, Legouvé, Comte, and other Modern Innovators*. New York: Carleton (Hyperion reprint edition 1981).

Dahme, H.J. (1986) Frauen- und Geschlechterfrage bei Herbert Spencer und Georg Simmel. Ein Kapitel aus der Geschichte der 'Soziologie der Frauen', *Kölner Zeitschrift für Soziologie und Sozialpsychologie*, 38: 490–509.

Dahme, H.J. (1988) Der Verlust des Fortschrittglaubens und die Verwissenschaftlichung der Soziologie. Ein Vergleich von Georg Simmel, Ferdinand Tönnies und Max Weber, in O. Rammstedt (ed.) *Simmel und die frühen Soziologen. Nähe und Distanz zu Durkheim, Tönnies und Max Weber*. Frankfurt a.M.: Suhrkamp.

Dahme, H.J. and Köhnke, K.C. (1985) Einleitung, *Georg Simmel: Schriften zur Philosophie und Soziologie der Geschlechter*. Frankfurt a.M.: Suhrkamp.

Dahme, H.J. and O. Rammstedt (eds) (1984) *Georg Simmel und die Moderne. Neue Interpretationen und Materialien*. Frankfurt a.M.: Fischer.

Dahrendorf, R. ([1965] 1994a) *Homo Sociologicus*, Köln: Westdeutscher Verlag.

Dahrendorf, R. (1994b) Deutsche Forschungsgemeinschaft, *Sozialwissenschaftliche Frauenforschung in der Bundesrepublik Deutschland*. Berlin: Akademieverlag.

Dasgupta, P. (2000) Economic progress and the idea of social capital, in P. Dasgupta and I. Serageldin (eds) *Social Capital. A Multifaceted Perspective*. Washington: The World Bank.

Dasgupta, P. and Serageldin, I. (2000) Preface, in P. Dasgupta and I. Serageldin (eds) *Social Capital. A Multifaceted Perspective*. Washington: The World Bank.

Davies, E. ([1866] 1973) *The Higher Education of Women*. New York: AMS.

De Certeau, M. (1984) *The Practice of Everyday Life*. Berkeley: University of California Press.

De Lauretis, T. (1994) *The Practice of Love: Lesbian Sexuality and Perverse Desire*. Bloomington: Indiana University Press.

Deegan, M.J. (1981) Early women sociologists and the American Sociological Society, *American Scholar*, 1(6): 14–34.

Deegan, M.J. (1988) Women in sociology: 1890–1930, *Journal of the History of Sociology*, 1: 11–34.

Deegan, M.J. (ed.) (1991) *Women in Sociology. A Bio-Bibliographical Sourcebook*. New York: Greenwood Press.

Delanty, G. (1999) *Social Theory in a Changing World: Conceptions of Modernity*. Cambridge: Polity.

Delphy, C. (1984) *Close to Home: A Materialist Feminist Analysis of Women's Oppression*. London: Hutchinson.

Delphy, C. (1993) Rethinking sex and gender, *Women's Studies International Forum*, 16(1): 1–9.

Deutsche Forschungsgemeinschaft (ed.) (1994) *Sozialwissenschaftliche Frauenforschung in der Bundesrepublik Deutschland*. Berlin: Akademieverlag.

Dodd, N. (1999) *Social Theory and Modernity*. Cambridge: Polity.

Dohm, H. (1876) *Der Frauen Natur und Recht. Zwei Abhandlungen über Eigenschaften und Stimmrecht der Frauen*. Berlin: Wedekind & Schwieger.

Dölling, I. and Krais, B. (eds) (1997) *Ein alltägliches Spiel. Geschlechterkonstruktion in der sozialen Praxis*. Frankfurt a.M.: Suhrkamp.

Durkheim, E. (1951) in G. Simpson (ed.) *Suicide*, trans. by J.A. Spaulding with Introduction by G. Simpson. New York: The Free Press.

Durkheim, E. (1956) *Education and Sociology*. New York: The Free Press.

Durkheim, E. (1960) The dualism of human nature and its social conditions, in K.H. Wolff (ed.) *Emile Durkheim, 1858–1917: A Collection of Essays*. Columbus: Ohio State University Press.

Durkheim, E. (1963) Incest: the nature and origin of the taboo, in E. Sagarin (ed.) *Incest*. New York: L. Stuart.

Durkheim, E. ([1933] 1964a) *The Division of Labor in Society*, trans. by G. Simpson. New York: The Free Press.

Durkheim, E. (1964b) in K.H. Wolff (ed.) *Essays on Sociology and Philosophy*. New York: Harper Torchbooks.

Durkheim, E. (1979). A discussion on sex education, in W.S. Pickering and H.L. Sutcliffe (eds) *Durkheim: Essays on Morals and Education*. London: Routledge and Kegan Paul.

Durkheim, E. (1980) in Y. Nandan (ed.) *Contributions to L'Annee Sociologique*, with Introduction by Y. Nandan. New York: The Free Press.

Durkheim, E. ([1895] 1982) in S. Lukes (ed.) *Rules of Sociological Method and Selected Texts on Sociology and Its Method*, trans. by W.D. Halls. New York: The Free Press.

Durkheim, E. (1992) *Professional Ethics and Civic Morals*, Preface by B. Turner. London: Routledge.

Durkheim, E. (1995) *The Elementary Forms of Religious Life*. New York: The Free Press.

Durkheim, E. ([1893] 1996) *Über soziale Arbeitsteilung*. Frankfurt a.M.: Suhrkamp.

Eisenstadt, S.N. and Curelaru, M. (1976) *The Form of Sociology – Paradigms and Crises*. New York: John Wiley & Sons.

Elias, N. (1993) *Was ist Soziologie?* Weinheim: Juventus.

Elster, J. (1982) Marxism, functionalism and game theory: the case for methodological individualism, *Theory and Society*, 11: 453–82.

Empson, W. (1833) *Illustrations of Political Economy*. Mrs Marcet – Miss Martineau, *Edinburgh Review*, 57 (W. Empson).

England, P. (1993) The separative self: androcentric bias in neoclassical assumptions, in M.A. Ferber and J.A. Nelson (eds) *Beyond the Economic Man: Feminist Theory and Economics*. Chicago: University of Chicago Press.

England, P. and Kilbourne, B. (1990) Feminist critiques of the separative model of the self: implications for rational choice theory, *Rationality & Society*, 2(2): 156–72.

Escher, E. (1925) *Harriet Martineaus sozialpolitische Novellen*. Weida: Thomas & Hubert.

Evans, D.T. (1993) *Sexual Citizenship: The Material Construction of Sexualities*. London: Routledge.

Fabian Women's Group (1911) *Three Years' Work, 1908–1911*. London: Fabian Women's Group.

Featherstone, M. (1992) Postmodernism and the aestheticization of everyday life, in Lash, S. and Freidman, J. (eds) *Modernity and Identity*. Oxford: Blackwell.

Felski, R. (1995) *The Gender of Modernity*. Cambridge, MA: Harvard University Press.

Ferber, M.A. and Nelson, J.A. (1993) Introduction, in Ferber, M.A. and Nelson, J.A. (eds) *Beyond Economic Man. Feminist Theory and Economics*. Chicago: University of Chicago Press.

Field, N. (1997) Identity and the lifestyle market, in R. Hennessey and C. Ingraham (eds) *Materialist Feminism: A Reader in Class, Difference and Women's Lives*. London: Routledge.

Field, J., Schuller, T. and Baron, S. (2000) Social capital and human capital revisited, in S. Baron, J. Field and T. Schuller (eds) *Social Capital. Critical Perspectives*. Oxford: Oxford University Press.

Fine, B. (2000) *Social Capital versus Social Theory: Political Economy and Social Science at the Turn of the Millennium*. New York: Routledge.

Fine, B. and Green, F. (2000) Economic, social capital and the colonization of the social science, in Baron, S., Field, J. and Schuller, T. (eds) *Social Capital: Critical Perspectives*. Oxford: Oxford University Press.

Firestone, S. (1975) *Frauenbefreiung und sexuelle Revolution*. Frankfurt a.M.: Fischer-Taschenbuch.

Fitzpatrick, E. (1990) *The Endless Crusade. Women Social Scientists and Progressive Reform*. Oxford: Oxford University Press.

Flyvbjerg, B. (2001) *Making Social Science Matter*. Cambridge: Cambridge University Press.

Folbre, N. (1994) *Who Pays for the Kids? Gender and the Structures of Constraint*. London: Routledge.

Foucault, M. (1980) *The History of Sexuality*. New York: Vintage Books.

Foucault, M. (1983) *Der Wille zum Wissen. Sexualität und Wahrheit 1*. Frankfurt a.M.: Suhrkamp.

Fourier, C. (1966) *Theorie der vier Bewegungen und der allgemeinen Bestimmungen*. Frankfurt a.M.: Europäische Verlagsanstalt.

Fraisse, G. (1992) *La Raison des femmes*. Paris: Plon.

Frank, A.W. (1991) For a sociology of the body: an analytical review, in M. Featherstone, M. Hepworth and B. Turner (eds) *The Body: Social Processes and Cultural Theory*. London: Sage.

Franklin, S. (1996) Introduction, in S. Franklin (ed.) *The Sociology of Gender*. Brookfield, VT: Edward Elgar.

Franks, S. (1999) *Having None of It: Women, Men and the Future of Work*. London: Granta.

Fraser, N. (1989) What's critical about critical theory? The case of Habermas and gender, *Unruly Practices: Power, Discourse and Gender in Contemporary Social Theory*. Cambridge: Polity Press.

Fraser, N. (1993) Pragmatismus, Feminismus und die linguistische Wende, in S. Benhabib *et al.* (eds) *Der Streit um Differenz. Feminismus und Postmoderne in der Gegenwart*. Frankfurt a.M.: Fischer.

Fraser, N. (1997) *Justice Interruptus: Critical Reflections on the Postsocialist Condition*. London: Routledge.

Fraser, N. (1998) Heterosexism, misrecognition and capitalism: a response to Judith Butler, *New Left Review*, 228: 140–9.

Fraser, N. (1999) Classing queer: politics in competition, *Theory, Culture and Society*, 16(2): 107–31.

Fraser, N. (2000) Rethinking recognition, *New Left Review*, 3: 107–20.

Freudenberg, I. (1911) *Die Frau und die Kultur des öffentlichen Lebens*. Leipzig: C.F. Amelangs.

Frevert, U. (1989) *Women in German History: From Bourgeois Emancipation to Sexual Liberation*, trans. Stuart McKinnon Evans *et al*. Oxford: Berg Publishers.

Friedan, B. (1963) *The Feminine Mystique*. New York: Dell.

Friedrichs, J. (1998) Die Individualisierungsthese. Eine Explikation im Rahmen der

Rational-Choice Theorie, in J. Friedrichs (ed.) *Die Individualisierungsthese.* Opladen: Leske & Budrich.

Frisby, D. (1992) *Simmel and Since. Essays on Georg Simmel's Social Theory.* London: Routledge.

Fukuyama, F. (1995) *Trust: The Social Virtues and the Creation of Prosperity.* New York: Free Press.

Fukuyama, F. (1999) *The Great Disruption. Human Nature and the Reconstitution of Social Order.* London: Profile Books.

Furstenberg, F. (1998) Social capital and the role of fathers in the family, in A. Booth and A Creuter (eds) *Men in Families: When Do They Get Involved? What Difference Does It Make?* New Jersey: Lawrence Erbaum.

Gambetta, D. (ed.) (1990) *Trust: Making and Breaking Cooperative Relations.* London: Blackwell.

Gane, M. (1993) *Harmless Lovers? Gender, Theory and Personal Relationships.* London: Routledge.

Gatens, M. (1991) *Feminism and Philosophy: Perspectives on Difference and Equality.* Cambridge: Polity.

Geddes, P. (1905) Civics as applied sociology, *Sociological Papers.* London: Macmillan.

Geddes, P. and Thomson, J.A. ([1889] 1901) *The Evolution of Sex.* London: Williams and Norgate.

Geddes, P. and Thomson, J.A. (1911) *Evolution.* London: Williams and Norgate.

Geddes, P. and Thomson, J.A. (1914) *Sex.* London: Williams and Norgate.

Gerhard, U. (1978) *Verhältnisse und Verhinderungen. Frauenarbeit, Familie und Rechte der Frauen im 19. Jahrhundert.* Frankfurt a.M.: Suhrkamp.

Gerhard, U. (1990a) *Unerhört. Die Geschichte der deutschen Frauenbewegung.* Reinbek: Rowohlt.

Gerhard, U. (1990b) *Gleichheit ohne Angleichung. Frauen im Recht.* München: Beck.

Gerhard, U. (1990c) Patriarchatskritik als Gesellschaftsanalyse. *Ein nicht erledigtes Projekt, in Arbeitsgemeinschaft Interdisziplinäre Frauenforschung und – studien.* Feministische Erneuerung von Wissenschaft und Kunst. Pfaffenweiler: Centaurus.

Gerhard, U. (1991) 'Bewegung' im Verhältnis der Geschlechter und Klassen und der Patriarchalismus der Moderne, in W. Zapf (ed.) *Die Modernisierung moderner Gesellschaften. Verhandlungen des 25. Deutschen Soziologentages in Frankfurt am Main 1990.* Frankfurt a.M.: Campus.

Gerhard, U. (ed.) (1997) *Frauen in der Geschichte des Recht.* München: C.H. Beck.

Gerhard, U. (1999) *Atempause: Feminismus als demokratisches Projekt.* Frankfurt a.M.: Fischer.

Gerhard, U. (2001) *Debating Women's Equality. Toward a Feminist Theory of Law from a European Perspective.* New Brunswick, NJ: Rutgers University Press.

Gerhard, U., Schwarzer, A. and Slupik, V. (1988) *Sozialstaat auf Kosten der Frauen: Frauenrechte im Sozialstaat.* Weinheim: Beltz.

German, L. (1997) Theories of the family, in R. Hennessey and C. Ingraham (eds) *Materialist Feminism: A Reader in Class, Difference and Women's Lives*. London: Routledge.

Giddens, A. (1989) A reply to my critics, in D. Held and J.B. Thompson (eds) *Social Theory of Modern Societies*. Cambridge: Cambridge University Press.

Giddens, A. (1991) *Modernity and Self-Identity*. Cambridge: Polity.

Giddens, A. (1992) *The Transformation of Intimacy: Sexuality, Love and Eroticism in Modern Societies*. Cambridge: Polity Press.

Giddens, A. (1995) *Konsequenzen der Moderne*. Frankfurt a.m.: Suhrkamp.

Gilcher-Holtey, I. (1988) Max Weber und die Frauen, in C. Gneuss and J. Kocka (eds) *Max Weber. Ein Symposium*. München: dtv.

Gildemeister, R. and Wetterer, A. (1992) Wie Geschlechter gemacht werden. Die soziale Konstruktion der Zweigeschlechtlichkeit und ihre Reifizierung in der Frauenforschung, in G.A. Knapp and A. Wetterer (eds) *Traditionen Brüche. Entwicklungen feministischer Theorie*. Freiburg i.Br.: Kore.

Godelier, M. (1984) *The Mental and the Material: Thought, Economy and Society*. London: Verso.

Goldman, L. (1987) A peculiarity of the English? The Social Science Association and the absence of sociology in nineteenth-century Britain, *Past and Present*, 114.

Gouges, O. de ([1791] 1990) Erklärung der Rechte der Frau und Bürgerin, in U. Gerhard (ed.) *Gleichheit ohne Angleichung. Frauen im Recht*. Munich: Beck.

Granovetter, M. (1985) Economic action and social structure: the problem of embeddedness, *American Journal of Sociology*, 91(3): 481–519.

Granovetter, M. (1988) The sociological and economic approaches to labor markets: a social structural view, in G. Farkas and P. England (eds) *Industries, Firms and Jobs*. New York: Plenum.

Green, M. (1974) *The von Richthofen Sisters*. New York: Basic Books.

Greven, M.T. (1991) Geschlechterpolarität und Theorie der Weiblichkeit in 'Gemeinschaft und Gesellschaft' von Tönnies, in L. Clausen and C. Schlüter (eds) *Hundert Jahre 'Gemeinschaft und Gesellschaft'*. Opladen: Leske und Budrich.

Grosz, E. (1994) Refiguring Lesbian Desire, in L. Doan (ed.) *The Lesbian Postmodern*. New York: Columbia University Press.

Habermas, J. (1979) *Stichworte zur 'Geistigen Situation der Zeit'*. Frankfurt a.m.: Suhrkamp.

Habermas, J. (1982) *Theorie des kommunikativen Handelns*. Frankfurt a.m.: Suhrkamp.

Habermas, J. (1990) *Stukturwandel der Öffentlichkeit. Untersuchungen zu einer Kategorie der bürgerlichen Gesellschaft*. Frankfurt a.m.: Suhrkamp.

Habermas, J. (1992) *Faktizität und Geltung. Beiträge zur Diskurstheorie des Rechts und des demokratischen Rechtsstaates*. Frankfurt a.m.: Suhrkamp.

Haensch, D. (1969) *Repressive Familienpolitik*. Reinbeck: Rowohlt.

Hall, S. (1997) Interview on culture and power, *Radical Philosophy*. 86: 24–41.

Halstead, R. (1926) Letter to V. Branford, 16 June, Institute of Sociology papers, University of Keele.

Harriss, J. and de Renzio, P. (1997) Missing link or analytically missing? The concept of social capital, *Journal of International Development*, 5(7): 919–37.

Hausen, K. (1976) Die Polarisierung der 'Geschlechtscharaktere' – Eine Spiegelung der Dissoziation von Erwerbs- und Familienleben, in W. Conze (ed.) *Sozialgeschichte der Familie in der Neuzeit Europas*. Stuttgart: Klett-Cotta.

Hausen, K. (1986) Patriarchat. Von Nutzen und Nachteil eines Koncepts für Familiengeschichte und Familienpolitik, *Journal für Geschichte*.

Hawthorne, G. (1987) *Enlightenment and Despair*. Cambridge: Cambridge University Press.

Heilbron, J. (1990) Auguste Comte and Modern Epistemology, *Sociological Theory*, 8(2): 152–62.

Hekman, S. (1990) *Gender and Knowledge*. Cambridge: Polity.

Hennessy, R. (1995) Queer visibility in commodity culture, in L. Nicholson and S. Seidman (eds) *Social Postmodernism: Beyond Identity Politics*. Cambridge: Cambridge University Press.

Hennessey, R. (2000) *Profit and Pleasure: Sexual Identities in Late Capitalism*. London: Routledge.

Hennessey, R. and Ingraham, C. (eds) (1997) *Materialist Feminism: A Reader in Class, Difference and Women's Lives*. New York: Routledge.

Hill, M.R. (1989) Introduction to the Transaction Edition, in H. Martineau (ed.) *How to Observe Morals and Manners*. New Brunswick, NJ: Transaction Publishers.

Hill, M.R. (1991) Harriet Martineau (1802–1876), in M.J. Deegan (ed.) *Women in Sociology. A Bio-Bibliographical Sourcebook*. New York: Greenwood.

Hobhouse, L.T. ([1904] 1972) *Democracy and Reaction*. Brighton: Harvester Press.

Hoecker-Drysdale, S. (1992) *Harriet Martineau: First Woman Sociologist*. Oxford: Berg Publishers.

Hollis, M. (1998) *Trust Within Reason*. Cambridge: Cambridge University Press.

Hollis, M. and Nell, E. (1975) *Rational Economic Man: A Philosophical Critique of Neo-Classical Economics*. Cambridge: Cambridge University Press.

Honegger, C. (1991a) *Die Wissenschaften vom Menschen und das Weib, 1750–1850*. Frankfurt a.M.: Campus.

Honegger, C. (1991b) *Die Ordnung der Geschlechter. Die Wissenschaft vom Menschen und das Weib 1750–1850*. Frankfurt a.M.: Campus.

Honegger, C. and Wobbe, T. (eds) (1998) *Frauen in der Soziologie. Sieben Porträts*. München: C.H. Beck Verlag.

Horkheimer, M. (1988) Autorität und Familie. Vol. III. Familie, in A. Schmidt and G. Schmid Noerr (eds) *Max Horkheimer: Gesammelte Schriften*. Frankfurt a.M.: Suhrkamp.

Hutchins, B. ([1915] 1978) *Women in Modern Industry*. Wakefield: EP reprint.

Jackson, S. (1998) Feminist social theory, in S. Jackson and J. Jones (eds) *Contemporary Feminist Theories*. Edinburgh: Edinburgh University Press.

Jackson, S. and Scott, S. (1997) Gut reactions to matters of the heart: reflections on rationality, irrationality and sexuality, *Sociological Review*, 45(4): 551–75.

Jackson, S. and Stanley, S. (2002) Introduction: the gendering of sociology, in S. Jackson and S. Scott (eds) *Gender. A Sociological Reader*. London: Routledge.

Jacobs, J. (1961) *The Death and Life of Great American Cities*. New York: Vintage Books.

Jaggar, A.M. (1990) Love and knowledge: emotion in feminist epistemology, in A.M. Jaggar and S.R. Bordo (eds) *Gender/Body/Knowledge*, New Brunswick, NJ: Rutgers University Press.

Jay, N. (1981) Gender and dichotomy, *Feminist Studies*, 7(1): 38–56.

Jordanova, L.J. (ed.) (1986) *Languages of Nature*. New Brunswick, NJ: Rutgers University Press.

Jordanova, L. (1989) *Sexual Visions: Images of Gender in Science and Medicine Between the Eighteenth and Nineteenth Centuries*. New York: Harvester Wheatsheaf.

Kaern, M. *et al.* (eds) (1990) *Georg Simmel and Contemporary Sociology*. Dordrecht: Kluwer Academic Publishers.

Kandal T.R. (1988) *The Woman Question in Classical Sociological Theory*. Miami: Florida International University Press.

Kanter, R.M. (1977) *Men and Women of the Corporation*. New York: Basic Books.

Katscher, L. (1884) Harriet Martineau, in L. Katscher (ed.) *Charakterbilder aus dem neunzehnten Jahrhundert. Biographisch-kritische Essais*. Berlin: Dümmler.

Kettler, M. and Meija, V. (1993) Their own particular way: Karl Mannheim and the rise of women, *International Sociology*, 8: 5–55.

Kimmel, M.S. (1990) After fifteen years: the impact on sociology of masculinity on the masculinity of sociology, in J. Hearn and D. Morgan (eds) *Men, Masculinities and Social Theory*. London: Unwin Hyman.

Klein, V. ([1946] 1971) *The Feminine Character. The History of an Ideology*. London: Routledge.

Klinger, C. (1988) Georg Simmels 'Weibliche Kultur' wiedergelesen – aus Anlaß des Nachdenkens über feministische Wissenschaftskritik, *Studia philosphica*, 47: 141–66.

Knüpper, M-T. (1984) *Feminismus, Autonomie, Subjecktivität. Tendencen und Widersprüche in der neuen Frauenbewegung*. Bochum: Germinal.

Kofman, S. (1978) *Aberrations. Le devenir-femme d'Auguste Comte*. Paris: Aubier Flammarion.

König, R. (1974) *Materialien zur Soziologie der Familie*. Köln: Kiepenheuer & Witsch.

Kovalainen, A. (1994) *The Invisibility of Gender in Economics*, Turku: Turku School of Economics and Business Administration. Series A-2: 1994.

Kreckel, R. (1991) Geschlechtssensibilisierte Soziologie. Können askriptive Merkmale eine vernünftige Gesellschaftstheorie begründen? in W. Zapf (ed.) *Die Modernisierung moderner Gesellschaften. Verhandlungen des 25. Deutschen Soziologentages in Frankfurt am Main 1990*. Frankfurt a.M.: Campus.

Lange, H. (1908) *Die Frauenbewegung in ihren modernen Probleme*. Leipzig: Quelle & Meyer.

Lange, H. ([1897] 1928) Intellektuelle Grenzlinien zwischen Mann und Frau, in H. Lange (ed.) *Kampfzeiten. Aufsätze und Reden aus vier Jahrzehnten*, Vol. 1. Berlin: Herbig.

Laqueur, T. (1990) *Making Sex: Body and Gender from the Greeks to Freud*. Cambridge, MA: Harvard University Press.

Lash, S. (1988) Discourse or figure: postmodernism as a regime of signification, *Theory, Culture and Society*, 5(2–3): 311–36.

Lash, S. (1990) *Sociology of Postmodernism*. London: Routledge.

Lash, S. (1994) Reflexivity and its doubles: structure, aesthetics, community, in U. Beck, A. Giddens and S. Lash (eds) *Reflexive Modernization: Politics, Traditions and Aesthetics in the Modern Social Order*. Cambridge: Polity.

Lash, S. (1999) *Another Modernity: A Different Rationality*. Oxford: Blackwell.

Lash, S. and Urry, J. (1994) *Economies of Signs and Space*. London: Sage.

Leach, W. (1980) *True Love and Perfect Union: The Feminist Reform of Sex and Society*. New York: Basic Books.

Lehmann, J.M. (1990) Durkheim's response to feminism: prescriptions for women, *Sociological Theory*, 8: 163–87.

Lehmann, J.M. (1991) Durkheim's women: his theory of the structures and functions of sexuality, *Current Perspectives in Social Theory*, 11: 141–67.

Lehmann, J.M. (1994) *Durkheim and Women*. Lincoln: University of Nebraska Press.

Lehmann, J.M. (1995a) Durkheim's theories of deviance and suicide: a feminist reconsideration, *American Journal of Sociology*, 100: 904–30.

Lehmann, J.M. (1995b) The question of caste in modern society: Durkheim's contradictory theories of race, class, and sex, *American Social Review*, 60: 566–84.

Lengermann, P.M. and Neibrugge-Brantley, J. (1998) *The Woman Founders: Sociology and Social Theory, 1830–1930*. Boston: McGraw-Hill.

Lepenies, W. (1981a) Einleitung. Studien zur kognitiven, sozialen und historischen Identität der Soziologie, in W. Lepenies (ed.) *Geschichte der Soziologie. Studien zur kognitiven, sozialen und historischen Identität einer Disziplin*, vol. 1. Frankfurt a.M.: Suhrkamp.

Lepenies, W. (1981b) Normalität und Anormalität. Wechselwirkungen zwischen den Wissenschaften vom Leben und den Sozialwissenschaften im 19. Jahrhundert, in W. Lepenies (ed.) *Geschichte der Soziologie. Studien zur kognitiven, sozialen und historischen Identität einer Disziplin*, vol. 3. Frankfurt a.M.: Suhrkamp.

Lepenies, W. (1988) *Between Literature and Science. The Rise of Sociology*. Cambridge: Cambridge University Press.

Lepsius, M.R. (1992) Das Bildungsbürgertum als ständische Vergesellschaftung, in M. Rainer Lepsius (ed.) *Bildungsbürgertum im 19. Jahrhundert. Part III: Lebensführung und ständische Vergesellschaftung*. Stuttgart: Clett Cotta.

Levi, M. (1998) State of trust in Braithwaite, in V. and Levi, M. (eds) *Trust and Governance*. New York: Russell Sage Foundation.

Levine, D.N. (ed.) (1971) *Georg Simmel on Individuality and Social Forms*. Chicago: University of Chicago Press.

Levy, A. (1991) *Other Women: The Writings of Class, Race, and Gender 1832–1898*. Princeton: Princeton University Press.

Lewis, J. (1992) Gender and the development of welfare regimes, *Journal of Social Policy*, 2: 159–173.

Lichtblau, K. (1989/90) Eros and culture. Gender theory in Simmel, Tönnies and Weber, *Telos*, 82: 89–110.

Lichtblau, K. (1992) Eros und Kultur. Zur Geschlechterproblematik in der Deutschen Soziologie der Jahrhundertwende, in I. Ostner and K. Lichtblau (eds) *Feministische Vernunftkritik. Ansätze und Traditionen*. Frankfurt a.M.: Campus.

Lichtblau, K. (1996) *Kulturkrise und Soziologie um die Jahrhundertwende. Zur Genealogie der Kultursoziologie in Deutschland*. Frankfurt a.M.: Suhrkamp.

Lichtblau, K. (1997) *Georg Simmel*. Frankfurt a.M.: Campus.

Lin, N. (2001) *Social Capital. A Theory of Social Structure and Action*. Cambridge: Cambridge University Press.

Lin, N., Cook, K. and Burt, R.S. (2001) *Social Capital. Theory and Research*. New York: Aldine de Gruyter.

Lipset, S.M. ([1837] 1962) Harriet Martineau's America, in H. Martineau (ed.) *Society in America*. Gloucester: Peter Smith.

Lloyd, G. (1985) *Das Patriarchat der Vernunft. 'Männlich' und 'Weiblich' in der westlichen Philosophie*. Bielefeld: Daedalus.

Longino, H. (1990) *Science as a Social Knowledge: Values and Objectivity in Scientific Inquiry*. Princeton: Princeton University Press.

Longino, H. (1993) Economics for Whom? in M.A. Ferber and J.A. Nelson (eds) *Beyond Economic Man. Feminist Theory and Economics*. Chicago: University of Chicago Press.

Luhmann, N. (1981) Wie ist soziale Ordnung möglich? in N. Luhmann (ed.) *Gesellschaftsstruktur und Semantik*, vol. 2. Frankfurt a.M.: Suhrkamp.

Luhmann, N. (1988) Frauen, Männer und George Spencer Brown, *Zeitschrift für Soziologie*, 1: 47–71.

Luhmann, N. ([1893] 1996) Arbeitsteilung und Moral. Durkheims Theorie, in E. Durkheim (ed.) *Über soziale Arbeitsteilung. Studie über die Organisation höherer Gesellschaften*. Frankfurt a.M.: Suhrkamp.

McDonald, L. (1994) *The Woman Founders of the Social Sciences*. Ottawa: Carleton University Press.

McDonald, L. (1997) Classical social theory with the woman founders included, in C. Camic (ed.) *Reclaiming the Sociological Classics: The State of the Scholarship*. Maldon, MA: Blackwell.

McLaren, A. (1981) A prehistory of social sciences: phrenology in France, *Comparative Studies in Society and History*, 23: 3–22.

McNay, L. (1994) *Foucault. A Critical Introduction*. Cambridge: Polity Press.

McNay, L. (1999) Gender, habitus and the field: Pierre Bourdieu and the limits of reflexivity, *Theory, Culture and Society*, 16: 95–117.

McNay, L. (2000) *Gender and Agency: Reconfiguring the Subject in Feminist and Social Theory*. Cambridge: Polity Press.

McNay, L. (2002) Communitarians and feminists: the case of narrative identity, *Literature and Theology*, 16(1): 1–15.

McNay, L. (forthcoming) Having it both ways: the incompatibility of communicative ethics and narrative identity, *Theory, Culture and Society*.

Maffesoli, M. (1996) *The Time of the Tribes*. London: Sage.

Marcet, J. (1816) *Conversations on Political Economy*. London: Longman, Hurst *et al.*

March, A. (1982) Female invisibility in androcentric social theory, *Insurgent Sociologist*, 11: 99–107.

Marshall, A.M. and Paley, M. (1879) *The Economics of Industry*. London: Macmillan.

Marshall, B.L. (1994) *Engendering Modernity. Feminism, Social Theory and Social Change*. Cambridge: Polity Press.

Marshall, B.L. (2000) *Configuring Gender: Explorations in Theory and Politics*. Peterborough: Broadview Press.

Marshall, B.L. (2002) 'Snips and Snails and Theorists' tales: classical sociological theory and the making of sex, *Journal of Classical Sociology*, 2(2): 135–55.

Marshall, M.P. (1947) *What I Remember*, Introduction by G.M. Trevelyan. Cambridge: Cambridge University Press.

Martineau, H. (writing as Discipulus) (1822) Female writers on practical divinity, *Monthly Repository*, 17: 593–6, 746–50.

Martineau, H. (1830) *Traditions of Palestine*. London: Longman *et al.*

Martineau, H. (1832–34) *Illustrations of Political Economy*, 9 vols. London: Charles Fox.

Martineau, H. (1833–34) *Poor Laws and Paupers Illustrated*, 4 parts. London: Charles Fox.

Martineau, H. (1834) *Illustrations of Taxation*, 5 parts. London: Charles Fox.

Martineau, H. (1837) *Society in America*, 2 vols. Paris: Baudry's European Library.

Martineau, H. (1838) *Retrospect of Western Travel*, 2 vols. London: Saunders & Otley.

Martineau, H. (1838–39) *The Guide to Service: The Maid of All Work. The Housemaid. The Lady's Maid. The Dressmaker*. London: Charles Knight.

Martineau, H. (1839) *Deerbrook. A Novel*, 3 vols. London: Moxon.

Martineau, H. (1841) *The Playfellow: Settlers at Home. The Peasant and the Prince. Feats on the Fjord. The Crofton Boys*, 4 vols. London: Charles Knight.

Martineau, H. (1848) *Eastern Life, Present and Past*, 3 vols. London: Edward Moxon.

Martineau, H. (1849) *Household Education*. Philadelphia: Lea and Blanchard.

Martineau, H. (1849–50) *The History of England During the Thirty Years' Peace 1816–1846*, 2 vols. London: Charles Knight.

Martineau, H. (1853) *The Positive Philosophy of Auguste Comte*. Trans. and condensed by H. Martineau, 2 vols. New York: Appleton, Chapman.

Martineau, H. (1877) *Autobiography*, with Memorials by Maria Weston Chapman, 3 vols. London: Smith, Elder & Co.

Martineau, H. ([1838] 1989) *How to Observe Morals and Manners*, Introduction by M.R. Hill. New Brunswick, NJ: Transaction Publishers.

Marx, K. (1975) *Das Kapital. Kritik der politischen Ökonomie*. Marx-Engels-Werke vol. 23. Berlin: Dïetz Verlag.

Maynard, M. (1990) The re-shaping of sociology? Trends in the study of gender, *Sociology*, 24: 260–2.

Meehan, J. (ed.) (1995) *Feminists Read Habermas: Gendering the Subject of Discourse*. London: Routledge.

Merton, R.K. (1968) *Social Theory and Social Structure*. New York: Free Press.

Meurer, B. (1991) Die Frau in 'Gemeinschaft und Gesellschaft', in L. Clausen and C. Schlüter (eds) *Hundert Jahre 'Gemeinschaft und Gesellschaft'*. Opladen: Leske & Budrich.

Meurer, B. (1992) Geschlecht als soziologische Kategorie. Das 'Männliche' und das 'Weibliche' in der deutschen Kulturgeschichte und die Bedeutung der Kategorie 'Geschlecht' für die theoretische Begründung der Sozialwissenschaften durch Tönnies, Simmel und Weber, *Ethik und Sozialwissenschaften. Streitforum für Erwägungskultur* 3: 343–57.

Meurer, B. (1997) Geschlechtsfeudale 'Ständegesellschaft' oder 'Gesellschaft der Individuen', in G. Klein and K. Liebsch (eds) *Zivilisierung des weiblichen Ich*. Frankfurt a.M.: Suhrkamp.

Meurer, B. (ed.) (2003) *Marianne Weber: Leben und Werk*. Tübingen: Mohr Siebeck.

Mill, J. (1835) *A Fragment on Mackintosh*. London: Baldwin and Cradock.

Mill, J.S. ([1848] 1891) *Principles of Political Economy with Some of their Applications to Social Philosophy*. London: George Routledge and Sons.

Mill, J.S. ([1819] 1978) *An Essay on Government*, in J. Lively and J. Rees (eds) *Utilitarian Logic and Politics*. Oxford: Clarendon Press.

Mill, J.S. ([1873] 1989) *Autobiography*. London: Penguin.

Mill, J.S. and Mill, H.T. ([1869] 1976) *Die Hörigkeit der Frau und andere Schriften zur Frauenemanzipation*. Frankfurt a.M.: Syndikat.

Millet, K. (1974) *Sexus und Herrschaft. Die Tyrannei des Mannes in unserer Gesellschaft*. Reinbek: Rowohlt.

Millman, R. and Kanter, R. (1975) Editorial introduction, *Another Voice: Feminist Perspectives on Social Life and Social Sciences*. Garden City, NY: Anchor/Doubleday.

Milz, H. (1994) *Frauenbewußtsein und Soziologie. Empirische Untersuchungen von 1910–1990*. Opladen: Leske & Budrich.

Misztal, B. (1996) *Trust in Modern Societies: The Search for the Bases of Social Order*. Cambridge: Polity Press.

Mitzman, A. (1970) *The Iron Cage: An Historical Interpretation of Max Weber*. New York: Alfred A. Knopf.

Möhrmann, R. (1977) *Die andere Frau. Emanzipationsansätze deutscher Schriftstellerinnen im Vorfeld der Achtundvierziger-Revolution*. Stuttgart: Metzler.

Moi, T. (1999a) Appropriating Bourdieu: feminist theory and Pierre Bourdieu's sociology of culture, *New Literary History*, 22: 1017–49.

Moi, T. (1999b) *What is a Woman? – And Other Essays*. Oxford: Oxford University Press.

Morgan, D. (1981) Men, masculinity and sociological enquiry, in H. Roberts (ed.) *Doing Feminist Research*. London: Routledge and Kegan Paul.

Morgan, D. (1992) *Discovering Men*. London: Routledge.

Morgan, D. (1993) You too can have a body like mine: reflections on the male body and masculinities, in S. Scott and D. Morgan (eds) *Body Matters: Essays on the Sociology of the Body*. London: Falmer Press.

Moses, C. (1993) 'Difference' in historical perspective: Saint-Simonian feminism, in C. Moses and L. Rabine (eds) *Feminism, Socialism, and French Romanticism*. Bloomington: Indiana University Press.

Mülder-Bach, I. (1987) 'Weibliche Kultur' und 'stahlhartes Gehäuse'. Zur Thematisierung des Geschlechterverhältnisses in den Soziologien Georg Simmels und Max Webers, in S. Anselm and B. Beck (eds) *Triumph und Scheitern in der Metropole. Zur Rolle der Weiblichkeit in der Geschichte Berlins*. Berlin: Reimer.

Müller, H-P. and Schmid M. ([1893] 1996) Arbeitsteilung, Solidarität und Moral. Eine werkgeschichtliche und systematische Einführung in die 'Arbeitsteilung' von Emile Durkheim, in E. Durkheim *Über soziale Arbeitsteilung. Studie über die Organisation höherer Gesellschaften*. Frankfurt a.M.: Suhrkamp.

Mumford, L. (1982) *Sketch from Life: The Autobiography of Lewis Mumford. The Early Years*. New York: Dial Press.

Murgatroyd, L. (1989) Only half of the story: some blinkering effects of 'malestream' sociology, in D. Held and J.B. Thompson (eds) *Social Theory of Modern Societies*. Cambridge: Cambridge University Press.

NAPSS (National Association for the Promotion of Social Science) (1868a) Meeting on wages and capital, *Sessional Papers*, 20 August. London: NAPSS.

NAPSS (National Association for the Promotion of Social Science) (1868b) *Transactions*. London: NAPSS.

Neckel, S. (1993) *Macht der Unterscheidung. Beutezüge durch den modernen Alltag*. Frankfurt a.M.: Fischer.

Neidhardt, F. (1985) Einige Ideen zu einer allgemeinen Theorie sozialer Bewegungen, in S. Hradil (ed.) *Sozialstruktur im Umbruch*. Opladen: Leske & Budrich.

Nelson, J. (1993) The study of choice or the study of provisioning? in M.A. Ferber and J.A. Nelson (eds) *Beyond Economic Man. Feminist Theory and Economics*. Chicago: University of Chicago Press.

Newnham College Register ([1871–1971] 1971) Cambridge: Newnham College.

Nunner-Winkler, G. (1994) Begründungen für die Bedeutsamkeit von Frauenforschung, in D. Forschungsgemeinschaft (ed.) *Sozialwissenschaftliche Frauenforschung in derBundesrepublik Deutschland*. Berlin: Akademieverlag.

Oakes, G. (1984a) *Georg Simmel: On Women, Sexuality and Love*. New Haven: Yale University Press.

Oakes, G. (1984b) The problem of women in Simmel's theory of culture, in G. Oakes (ed.) *G. Simmel: On Women, Sexuality and Love*. New Haven: Yale University Press.

Oakley, A (1989) Women's studies in British sociology: to end at our beginning? *British Journal of Sociology*, 40: 442–70.

Oakley, A. (2000) *Experiments in Knowing. Gender and the Method in Social Sciences*. London: Polity Press.

Offe, C. (1985) New social movements: challenging the boundaries, *Social Research*, 52(4): 817–68.

Offen, K. (1987) A nineteenth-century French feminist rediscovered: Jenny P. d'Héricourt, 1809–1875, *Signs*, 13(1): 145–58.

Offen, K. (1993) Feminismus in den Vereinigten Staaten und in Europa. Ein historischer Vergleich, in H. Schissler (ed.) *Geschlechterverhältnisse im historischen Wandel*. Frankfurt a.M.: Campus.

Okin, S.M. (1979) *Women in Western Political Thought*. Princeton: Princeton University Press.

Orazem, C. (1999) *Political Economy and Fiction in the Early Work of Harriet Martineau*. New York: P. Lang.

Osborne, P. and Segal, L. (1994) Gender as performance: an interview with Judith Butler, *Radical Philosophy*, 67: 32–9.

Parsons, T. (1963) On the concept of influence, *Public Opinion Quarterly*, 27: 37–62.

Pateman, C. (1988) *The Sexual Contract*. Stanford: Stanford University Press.

Pateman, C. (1992) Gleichheit, Differenz, Unterordnung, *Feministische Studien*, 10(1): 54–69.

Paxton, P. (1999) Is social capital declining in the United States? A multiple indicator assessment, *American Journal of Sociology*, 105(1) (June): 88–127.

Pedersen, J. (2001) Sexual politics in Comte and Durkheim: feminism, history and the French sociological tradition, *Signs*, 27(1): 229–63.

Peyser, D. (1958) *Alice Salomon. Die Begründerin des sozialen Frauenberufs in Deutschland*. Köln: Heymanns.

Pichanick, V.K. (1980) *Harriet Martineau. The Woman and Her Work, 1802–1876*. Ann Arbor: University of Michigan Press.

Pickering, M. (1993) *Auguste Comte. An Intellectual Biography*, vol. I. Cambridge: Cambridge University Press.

Pope, B.C. (1987) The influence of Rousseau's ideology of domesticity, in M. Boxer, J. Quataert and J. Scott (eds) *Connecting Spheres*. New York: Oxford University Press.

Portes, A. (1998) Social capital: its origins and applications in modern society, *Annual Review of Sociology*, 24: 1–24.

Portes, A. and Landolt, P. (1996) The downside of social capital, *The American Prospect*, 26 (May–June).

Pross, H. (1975) *Die Wirklichkeit der Hausfrau. Die erste repräsentative Untersuchung über nichterwerbstätige Ehefrauen. Wie leben sie? Wie denken sie? Wie sehen sie sich selbst?* Reinbek: Rowohlt.

Proudhon, P.J. (1857) Lettre à Madame J. d'Héricourt, *Revue philosophique et religieuse,* 6: 164–8.

Putnam, R.D. (1993) The prosperous community, *The American Prospect,* 4, March.

Putnam, R.D. (1995) Bowling alone: America's declining social capital, *The Journal of Democracy,* 6(1): 65–78.

Putnam, R.D. (2000) *Bowling Alone. The Collapse and Revival of American Community.* New York: Simon and Schuster.

Putnam, R.D., Leonardi, R. and Nanetti, R.Y. (1993) *Making Democracy Work. Civic Traditions in Modern Italy.* Princeton, NJ: Princeton University Press.

Rafferty, A. ([1833] 1996) Miss Martineau's monthly novels, *The Politics of Nursing Knowledge.* London: Routledge.

Rammstedt, O. (1988) Die Attitüden der Klassiker als unsere soziologischen Selbstverständlichkeiten. Durkheim, Simmel, Weber und die Konstitution der modernen Soziologie, *Otthein Rammstedt: Simmel und die frühen Soziologen. Nähe und Distanz zu Durkheim, Tönnies und Max Weber.* Frankfurt a.M.: Suhrkamp.

Ramp, W.J. (2001) Durkheim and the unthought: some dilemmas of modernity, *Canadian Journal of Sociology,* 26(1): 89–115.

Raschke, J. (1985) *Soziale Bewegungen. Ein historisch-systematischer Grundriß.* Frankfurt a.M.: Campus.

Ray, L. (1999) *Theorizing Classical Sociology.* Buckingham: Open University Press.

Ray, L. and Sayer, A. (eds) (1999) *Culture and Economy after the Cultural Turn.* London: Sage.

Redfield, J. (1975) *Nature and Culture in the Iliad: The Tragedy of Hector.* Chicago: University of Chicago Press.

Reinharz, S. (1989) Teaching the history of women in sociology. Or Dorothy Swaine Thomas, wasn't she the woman married to William I.? *The American Sociologist,* 20: 87–94.

Ridgeway, L.C. (1997) Interaction and the conversation of gender inequality: considering employment, *American Sociological Review,* 62: 218–35.

Riehl, W.H. (1855) *Die Naturgeschichte des Volkes als Grundlage einer deutschen Social-Politik,* Vol. 3. *Die Familie.* Stuttgart: Cotta.

Riley, D. (1988) *'Am I that Name?' Feminism and the Category of 'Women' in History.* London: Macmillan.

Ringer, F. (1969) *The Decline of the German Mandarins.* Cambridge: Cambridge University Press.

Rojek, C. and Turner, B.S. (2000) Decorative sociology: towards a critique of the cultural turn, *Sociological Review,* 48: 629–48.

Roper, L. (1990) *The Holy Household. Women and Morals in Reformation Augsburg.* Oxford: Oxford University Press.

Rosenbaum, H. (1973) *Familie als Gegenstruktur zur Gesell-schaft. Kritik grundlegender theoretischer Ansätze der westdeutschen Familiensoziologie.* Stuttgart: Encke.

Roseneil, S. (1995) The coming of age of feminist sociology: some issues of practice and theory for the next twenty years, *British Journal of Sociology*, 46: 191–205.

Rossi, A. (1973) The first woman sociologist: Harriet Martineau (1802–1876), in A. Rossi (ed.) *The Feminist Papers: From Addams to de Beauvoir.* New York: Bantham Books.

Roth, G. (1988) Marianne Weber and her circle. Introduction. *Marianne Weber. Max Weber. A Biography.* New Brunswick: Transaction.

Roth, G. (1989/90) Durkheim and the principles of 1789: the issue of gender equality, *Telos*, 82: 71–88.

Roth, G. (1992) Emile Durkheim und die Prinzipien von 1789. Zum Problem der Geschlechtergleichheit, in I. Ostner and K. Lichtblau (eds) *Feministische Vernunftkritik. Ansätze und Traditionen.* Frankfurt a.M.: Campus.

Roth, G. (2001) *Max Webers deutsch-englische Familiengeschichte 1800–1950 mit Briefen und Dokumenten.* Tübingen: Mohr Siebeck.

Rucht, D. (1994) *Modernisierung und neue soziale Bewegungen. Deutschland, Frankreich und USA im Vergleich.* Frankfurt a.M.: Campus.

Rumpf, M. (1989) *Spuren des Mütterlichen. Die widersprüchliche Bedeutung der Mutterrolle für die männliche Identitätsbildung in kritischer und feministischer Wissenschaft.* Frankfurt a.M: Materialis.

Rupieper, H.J. (1991) Bringing democracy to the Frauleins. Frauen als Zielgruppe der amerikanischen Demokratisierungspolitik in Deutschland 1945–1952, *Geschichte und Gesellschaft*, 17(1): 61–91.

Salomon, A. (1913) *Zwanzig Jahre Soziale Hilfsarbeit.* Karlsruhe: Braun.

Saltzman Chafetz, J. (1990) *Gender Equity: An Integrated Theory of Stability and Change.* London: Sage.

Sanders Arbuckle, E. (ed.) (1994) *Harriet Martineau in the London Daily News. Selected Contributions, 1852–1866.* New York: Garland.

Sartre, J.P. (1976) *Critique of Dialectical Reason*, vol. 1. London: NLB.

Sayer, A. (2000) System, lifeworld and gender: associational versus counterfactual thinking, *Sociology*, 34(4): 707–25.

Sayer, D. (1991) *Capitalism and Modernity.* London: Routledge.

Schelsky, H. (1955) *Wandlungen der deutschen Familie in der Gegenwart. Darstellung und Deutung einer empirisch-soziologischen Tatbestandsaufnahme.* Stuttgart: Enke.

Schmoller, G. (1894) Review of Émile Durkheim's dissertation: De la division du travail social étude sur l'organisation des sociétés supérieures (Paris 1893), *Jahrbuch für Gesetzgebung, Verwaltung und Volkswirtschaft im Deutschen Reich*, 18: 286–9.

Schreiner, O. ([1911] 1978) *Women and Labour.* London: Virago.

Schroer, M. (2001) *Das Individuum der Gesellschaft. Synchrone und diachrone Theorieperspektiven.* Frankfurt a.M.: Suhrkamp.

Schuller, T., Baron, S. and Field, J. (2000) Social capital: a review and critique, in S. Baron, J. Field and T. Schuller (eds) *Social Capital. Critical Perspectives.* Oxford: Oxford University Press.

Schwarzer, A. (1975) *Der kleine Unterschied und seine großen Folgen*. Frankfurt a.M.: Fischer.

Scott, J.W. (1988) Gender: a useful category of historical analysis, in J.W. Scott (ed.) *Gender and the Politics of History*. New York: Columbia University Press.

Scott, J. (1993) Rethinking the history of women's work, Vol. IV, in M. Perrot and Georges (eds) *History of Women*. Cambridge, MA: Harvard University Press.

Scott, J. (1998) *Only Paradoxes to Offer. French Feminists and the Rights of Man*. Cambridge, MA: Harvard University Press.

Seidler, V.J. (1994) *Unreasonable Men: Masculinity and Social Theory*. London: Routledge.

Seidman, S. (1992) *Embattled Eros: Sexual Politics and Ethics in Contemporary America*. New York: Routledge.

Seidman, S. (1997) *Difference Troubles: Queering Social Theory and Sexual Politics*. Cambridge: Cambridge University Press.

Sen, A. (1995) Rationality and social choice, *The American Economic Review*, 85(1): 1–24.

Sennett, R. (1998) *The Corrosion of Character: The Personal Consequences of Work in the New Capitalism*. New York: Norton.

Sevenhuijsen, S. (1998) *Citizenship and the Ethics of Care: Feminist Considerations on Justice, Morality and Politics*. London: Routledge.

Shilling, C. (1993) *The Body and Social Theory*. London: Sage.

Shilling, C. (2001) Embodiment, experience and theory: in defense of the sociological tradition, *Sociological Review*, 49(3): 327–44.

Shope, J. (1994) Separate but equal: Durkheim's response to the woman question, *Sociological Inquiry*, 64: 23–36.

Siisiäinen, M. (2000) Two Concepts of Social Capital: Bourdieu vs. Putnam. Paper presented at ISTR Fourth International Conference 'Third Sector: For What and For Whom'. July 5–8 Trinity College, Dublin, Ireland. http://www.jhu.edu/~istr/conferences/dublin/workingpapers/siisiainen.pdf

Silverberg, H. (ed.) (1998) *Gender and American Social Science. The Formative Years*. Princeton: Princeton University Press.

Simmel, G. (1895) Zur Psychologie der Frauen. Georg Simmel, in H.J. Dahme (ed.) *O Rammst Aufsätze 1887–1890. Über sociale Differenzierung. Die Probleme der Geschichtsphilosophie*. Frankfurt a.M: Suhrkamp.

Simmel, G. (1900) *Philosophie des Geldes*. Leipzig: Duncker & Humblot.

Simmel, G. (1908a) *Soziologie. Untersuchung über die Formen der Vergesellschaftung*. Berlin: Dunker & Humblot.

Simmel, G. (1908c) *Soziologie. Untersuchung über die Formen der Vergesellschaftung*. Berlin: Dunker & Humblot.

Simmel, G. (1950) The stranger, in K.H. Wolff (ed.) *The Sociology of Georg Simmel*. New York: Free Press.

Simmel, G. ([1908b] 1971) The Stranger, in D.N. Levine (ed.) *Georg Simmel. On Individuality and Social Forms. Selected Writings*. Chicago: University of Chicago Press.

Simmel, G. (1978) *The Philosophy of Money*. London: Routledge.

Simmel, G. (1983) Zur Philosophie der Kultur, *Georg Simmel: Philosophische Kultur. Über das Abenteuer, die Geschlechter und die Krise der Moderne*, Gesammelte Essays. Berlin: Wagenbach.

Simmel, G. (1984a) Female culture, in *G. Simmel: On Women, Sexuality, and Love*. New Haven: Yale University Press.

Simmel, G. (1984b) The relative and the absolute in the problem of the sexes, in *G. Simmel: On Women, Sexuality, and Love*. New Haven: Yale University Press.

Simmel, G. ([1896] 1985a) Der Frauenkongreß und die Sozialdemokratie, in H.J. Dahme and K.C. Köhnke (eds) *Georg Simmel: Schriften zur Philosophie und Soziologie der Geschlechter*. Frankfurt a.m.: Suhrkamp.

Simmel, G. ([1911] 1985b) Das Relative und das Absolute im Geschlechter-Problem, in H.J. Dahme and K.C. Köhnke (eds) *Georg Simmel: Schriften zur Philosophie und Soziologie der Geschlechter*. Frankfurt a.M.: Suhrkamp.

Simmel, G. ([1890] 1985c) Zur Psycholgie der Frauen, in H.J. Dahme and K.C. Köhnke (eds) *Georg Simmel: Schriften zur Philosophie und Soziologie der Geschlechter*. Frankfurt a.M.: Suhrkamp.

Simmel, G. ([1898] 1985d) Die Rolle des Geldes in den Beziehungen der Geschlechter, in H.J. Dahme and K.C. Köhnke (eds) *Georg Simmel: Schriften zur Philosophie und Soziologie der Geschlechter*. Frankfurt a.M.: Suhrkamp.

Simmel, G. ([1902] 1985e) *Weibliche Kultur, Schriften zur Philosophie und Soziologie der Geschlechter*, ed. H-J. Dahme and K.C. Köhnke. Frankfurt, a.M.: Suhrkamp.

Simmel, G. ([1895] 1989a) Über sociale Differenzierung, *Simmel*. Frankfurt a.M.: Suhrkamp.

Simmel, G. ([1895] 1989b) Zur Soziologie der Familie, in H.J. Jürgen Dahme and D.P. Frisby (eds) *Aufsätze und Abhandlungen 1894–1900*. Frankfurt a.m: Suhrkamp.

Simmel, G. (1995) in O. Rammstedt (ed.) *Soziologie: Untersuchungen über die Fromen der Vergesellschaftung*, 11. Frankfurt a.M.: Suhrkamp.

Simmel, G. (1997) Female culture, in D. Frisby and M. Featherstone (eds) *Simmel on Culture*. London: Sage Publications.

Skeggs, B. (2002) Mobile selves? Authority, reflexivity and positioning, in T. May (ed.) *Qualitative Research: Issues in International Practice*. London: Sage.

Skocpol, T. (1996) *Social Revolutions in the Modern World*. Cambridge: Cambridge University Press.

Smith, D. (1987a) Women's perspective as a radical critique of sociology, in S. Harding (ed.) *Feminism and Methodology*. Milton Keynes: Open University Press.

Smith, D. (1987b) *The Everyday World as Problematic*. Toronto: University of Toronto Press.

Smith, D. (1990) *Texts, Facts and Femininity*. Toronto: University of Toronto Press.

Smith, D. (1992) Remaking a life, remaking a sociology: reflections of a feminist, in W. Carroll, L. Christiansen-Ruffman, R. Curries and D. Harrison (eds) *Fragile*

Truths: Twenty-five Years of Sociology in Canada. Ottawa: Carleton University Press.

Smith, D. (1999) *Writing the Social: Critique, Theory and Investigations*. Toronto: University of Toronto Press.

Sociological Society Women's Group (1913) 26 September, Victor Branford papers, item 105, Keele University Archives.

Solow, R.M. (2000) Notes on social capital and economic performance, in P. Dasgupta and I. Serageldin (eds) *Social Capital. A Multifaceted Perspective*. Washington: The World Bank.

Spender, D. (1982) Harriet Martineau, in D. Spender (ed.) *Women of Ideas and What Men Have Done to Them*. London: Routledge & Kegan Paul.

Squires, J. (1999) *Gender in Political Theory*. London: Polity Press.

Stacey, J. and Thorne, B. (1985a) The missing feminist revolution in sociology, *Social Problems*, 32: 301–16.

Stacey, J. and Thorne, B. (1985b) Feministische Revolution in der Soziologie? Ein Vergleich feministischer Ansätze in der Geschichte, Literaturwissenschaft, Anthropologie und Soziologie in den USA, *Feministische Studien*, 2: 118–30.

Stanley, L. (2002) Should 'sex' really be 'gender' – or 'gender' really be 'sex'? in S. Jackson and J. Jones (eds) *Contemporary Feminist Theories*. Edinburgh: Edinburgh University Press.

Stanley, L. and Wise, S. (1993) *Breaking Out Again: Feminist Epistemology and Ontology*. London: Routledge.

Stefan, V. (1975) *Häutungen*. Munich: Frauenoffensive.

Steinbrügge, L. (1987) *Das moralische Geschlecht. Theorien und literarische Entwürfe über die Natur der Frau in der französischen Aufklärung*. Weinheim: Beltz.

Strassman, D. (1993) Not a free market: the rhetoric of disciplinary authority in economics, in M.A. Ferber and J.A. Nelson (eds) *Beyond Economic Man. Feminist Theory and Economics*. Chicago: University of Chicago Press.

Strecker, G. (1965) *Frausein – heute*. Weilheim: Barth.

Stzompka, P. (1994) *Agency and Structure: Reorienting Social Theory*. Reading: Gordon and Breach Science Publishers.

Stzompka, P. (2000) *Trust: A Sociological Theory*. Cambridge: Cambridge University Press.

Swedberg, R. (1990) *Economics and Sociology: Redefining their Boundaries. Conversations with Economists and Sociologists*. Princeton: Princeton University Press.

Sydie, R.A. (1987) *Natural Women and Cultured Men. A Feminist Perspective on Sociological Theory*. Toronto: Methuen.

Taylor Mill, H. ([1851] 1983) *Enfranchisement of Women*. London: Virago.

Thompson, W. ([1825] 1983) *Appeal of One Half the Human Race, Women, Against the Pretensions of the Other Half Men, to Retain them in Political and thence in Civil and Domestic Slavery*. London: Virago.

Tönnies, F. (1907) *Die Entwicklung der sozialen Frage*. Leipzig: Goeschen.

Tönnies, F. (1955) *Community and Association (Gemeinschaft und Gesellschaft)*. London: Routledge and Paul Kegan.

Tönnies, F. ([1887] 1963) *Gemeinschaft und Gesellschaft. Grundbegriffe der Reinen Soziologie*. Darmstadt: Wissenschaftliche Buchgesellschaft.

Treibel, A. (1995) *Einführungen in soziologische Theorien der Gegenwart*. Opladen: Leske & Budrich.

Tullborg, R., McWilliams and Marshall, M.P. (1850–1944) Typescript in Newnham College Archive.

Turner, B. (1984) *The Body and Society*. Oxford: Blackwell.

Turner, B. (1992) *Regulating Bodies: Essays in Medical Sociology*. London: Routledge.

Turner, B. (ed.) (1996) *Social Theory and Sociology: The Classics and Beyond*. Cambridge, MA: Blackwell.

Twellmann, M. (1972) *Die Deutsche Frauenbewegung. Ihre Anfänge und erste Entwicklung 1843–1889*, 2 Vol. Meisenheim: Hain.

Tyrell, H. (1986) Geschlechtliche Differenzierung und Geschlechterklassifikation, *Kölner Zeitschrift für Soziologie und Sozialpsychologie*, 38: 450–89.

Tyrell, H. (1992) Unterschätzt/Überschätzt, *Ethik und Sozialwissenschaften. Streitforum für Erwägungskultur*, 3: 308–400.

Urry, J. (2000) *Sociology Beyond Societies: Mobilities for the Twenty-First Century*, London: Routledge.

Urwick, E.J. (1912) *A Philosophy of Social Progress*. London: Methuen.

van Vucht Tijssen, L. (1991) Women and objective culture: Georg Simmel and Marianne Weber, *Theory, Culture & Society*, 8: 203–18.

Vernon, R. (1986) The political self: Auguste Comte and phrenology, *History of European Ideas*, 7(3): 271–86.

von Hippel, T.G. ([1792] 1977) *Über die bürgerliche Verbesserung der Weiber*. Frankfurt a.M.: Syndikat.

von Petzold, G. (1941) *Harriet Martineau und ihre sittlich-religiöse Weltschau*. Bochum-Langendreer: Pöppinghaus.

von Stein, L. (1880) *Die Frau auf dem socialen Gebiete*. Stuttgart: Cotta.

von Stein, L. (1886) *Die Frau auf dem Gebiet der Nationalökonomie*, vol. 3. Stuttgart: Cotta.

von Stein, L. (1890) *Die Frau, ihre Bildung und Lebensaufgabe*. Berlin/Dresden: Dieckmann.

von Stein, L. ([1850] 1921) *Geschichte der sozialen Bewegung in Frankreich von 1789 bis auf unsere Tage*. München: Drei Masken.

von Stein, L. (ed.) ([1848] 1974) *Die socialen Bewegungen der Gegenwart, Schriften zum Sozialismus – 1848, 1852, 1854*. Darmstadt: Wissenschaftliche Buchgesellschaft.

von Sybel, H. (1870) *Über die Emancipation der Frauen*. Bonn: Cohen.

Vromen, S. (1991) Georg Simmel and the cultural dilemma of women, *History of European Ideas*, 8: 563–79.

Wacquant, L. (1992) Toward a praxeology: the structure and logic of Bourdieu's sociology, in P. Bourdieu and L. Wacquant (eds) *An Invitation to Reflexive Sociology*. Cambridge: Polity.

Wagner, P. (1995) *Soziologie der Moderne. Freiheit und Disziplin, Theorie und Gesellschaft 33*. Frankfurt a.m.: Campus.

Walby, S. (1990) *Theorising Patriarchy*. Oxford: Basil Blackwell.

Walters, M. (1976) Mary Wollstonecraft, Harriet Martineau and Simone de Beauvoir, in J. Mitchell and A. Oakley (eds) *The Rights and Wrongs of Women*. Harmondsworth: Penguin.

Wardle, R.M. (1979) *Collected Letters of Mary Wollstonecraft*. Ithaca: Cornell University Press.

Webb, S. and Webb, B. ([1911] 1920) *The Prevention of Destitution*. London: Longmans, Green.

Weber, Marianne ([1907] 1971) *Ehefrau und Mutter in der Rechtsentwickluung: Eine Einfuhrung*. Aalen: Scientia.

Weber, Marianne (1913) Die Frau und die objektive Kultur, *Frauen Fragen und Frauengedanken*. Tübingen: J.C.B. Mohr (Paul Siebeck).

Weber, Marianne (1914a) Die neue Frau, *Frauenfragen und Frauengedanken*. Tübingen: J.C.B. Mohr (Paul Siebeck).

Weber, Marianne (1914b) Eheideal und Eherecht, *Frauenfragen und Frauengedanken*. Tübingen: J.C.B. Mohr (Paul Siebeck).

Weber, Marianne (1926) *Max Weber. Ein Lebensbild*. Tubingen: J.C.B. Mohr.

Weber, Marianne (1948) *Lebenserinnerungen*. Bremen: Johs. Storm.

Weber, Marianne ([1926] 1975) *Max Weber: A Bibliography*, H. Zohn (trans. and ed.). New York: John Wiley and Sons.

Weber, Max (1920) *Gesammelte Aufsatze zur Religionssoziologie*. Tubingen: Paul Siebeck.

Weber, Max ([1919] 1946) Politics as a vocation, *Essays in Sociology*, H.H. Gerth and C.W. Mills (eds). New York: Oxford University Press.

Weber, Max ([1920] 1956a) Asketischer Protestantismus und kapitalistischer Geist, in J. Winckelmann (ed.) *Max Weber: Soziologie. Weltgeschichtliche Analysen. Politik*, 2nd edn. Stuttgart: Kröner.

Weber, Max ([1920] 1956b) Die 'Objektivität' sozialwissenschaftlicher Erkenntnis, *Max Weber: Soziologie. Weltgeschichtliche Analysen. Politik*. Stuttgart: Kröner.

Weber, Max (1958) *The Protestant Ethic and the Spirit of Capitalism*, trans. by T. Parsons. New York: Charles Scribner's Sons.

Weber, Max (1964) *From Max Weber: Essays in Sociology*. New York: Oxford University Press.

Weber, Max ([1922] 1972) *Wirtschaft und Gesellschaft. Grundriss der verstehenden Soziologie*. Tübingen: J.C.B. Mohr.

Weber, Max (1978) in G. Roth and C. Wittich (eds) *Economy and Society*. California: University of California Press.

Weber, Max (1994) Ideal-type constructs, in W. Heydebrand (ed.) *Max Weber: Sociological Writings*. New York: Continuum.

Weeks, J. (1985) *Sexuality and its Discontents*. London: Routledge.

Welsch, W. (1988) *Unsere postmoderne Moderne*. Weinheim: VCH Acta humaniora.

Wiesner, M. (1993) *Women and Gender in Early Modern Europa*. Cambridge: Cambridge University Press.

Williams, R. (1977) *Marxism and Literature*. Oxford: Oxford University Press.

Williams, S. and Bendelow, G. (1998) *The Lived Body: Sociological Themes, Embodied Issues*. London: Routledge.

Winders, J. A. (1991) *Gender, Theory and the Canon*. Madison: University of Wisconsin Press.

Winter, I. (2000) *Towards a Theorized Understanding of Family Life and Social Capital*, working paper no. 21, April. Melbourne: Australian Institute of Family Studies.

Witz, A. (2000) Whose body matters? Feminist sociology and the corporeal turn in sociology and feminism, *Body and Society*, 6(2): 1–24.

Witz, A. (2001) Georg Simmel and the masculinity of modernity, *Journal of Classical Sociology*, 1(3): 353–70.

Witz, A. and Marshall, B.L. (2003) The quality of manhood: gender and embodiment in the classical tradition, *Sociological Review*, 51(3): 339–56.

Wobbe, T. (1995) *Wahlverwandtschaften. Die Soziologie und die Frauen auf dem Weg zur Wissenschaft*. Frankfurt a.M.: Campus.

Wobbe, T. (1996) On the horizons of a new discipline: early women sociologists in Germany, *Journal of the Anthropological Society of Oxford*, 26: 283–97.

Wobbe, T. (1997) *Wahlverwandtschaften. Die Soziologie und die Frauen auf dem Weg zur Wissenschaft*. Frankfurt, a.M.: Campus.

Wobbe, T. (1998a) Ideen, Interessen und Geschlecht. Marianne Webers kultursoziologische Fragestellung, *Berliner Journal für Soziologie*, 8.

Wobbe, T. (1998b) Marianne Weber (1870–1954) Ein anderes Labor der Moderne, *Frauen in der Soziologie. Neun Porträts*. Munich: C.H. Beck Verlag.

Wobbe, T. (1998c) Elective affinities: Georg Simmel and Marianne Weber on differentiation and individuation. Paper presented to ISA World Congress, Montréal.

Wolfer-Melior, A. (1985) Weiblichkeit als Kritik. Über die Konzeption des Gegensatzes der Geschlechter bei Georg Simmel, *Feministische Studien*, 2(4): 62–78.

Wolff, K.H. (ab) (1950) *The Sociology of Georg Simmel*. New York: Free Press.

Wolff, J. (1983) The invisible flaneuse: women and the literature of modernity, *Theory, Culture and Society*, 2: 37–48.

Wolff, J. (2000) The feminine in modern art: Benjamin, Simmel and the gender of modernity, *Theory, Culture and Society*, 17: 33–53.

Wollstonecraft, M. ([1792] 1967) *A Vindication of the Rights of Woman*. New York: W.W. Norton.

Wollstonecraft, M. (1987) in R. Holms (ed.) *A Short Residence in Sweden, Norway, and Denmark*. Harmondsworth: Penguin.

Woolf, V. (1938) *Three Guineas*. London: Hogarth Press.

Yeatman, A. (1987) A feminist theory of social differentiation, in L.J. Nicholson (ed.) *Feminism/Postmodernism*. New York: Routledge.

Yeo, E.J. (1996) *The Contest for Social Science: Relations and Representations of Gender and Class*. London: Rivers Oram.

Young, I.M. (1990) *Justice and the Politics of Difference*. Princeton: Princeton University Press.

Young, I.M. (1994) Gender as seriality: Thinking about women as a social collective, *Signs*, 19: 713–38.

Young, I.M. (1998) Throwing like a girl: twenty years later, in D. Welton (ed.) *Body and Flesh: A Reader*. Oxford: Blackwell.

Zahn-Harnack, A. (1928) *Die Frauenbewegung. Geschichte, Probleme, Ziele*. Berlin: Deutsche Buch-Gemeinschaft.

Zapf, W. (1991) Modernisierung und Modernisierungstheorien, in W. Zapf (ed.) *Die Modernisierung moderner Gesellschaften. Verhandlungen des 25. Deutschen Soziologentages in Frankfurnt am Main 1990*. Frankfurt a.M.: Campus.

Index

THEORIES OF SOCIAL REMEMBERING

Barbara A. Mizstal

- Why does collective memory matter?
- How is social memory generated, maintained and reproduced?
- How do we explain changes in the content and role of collective memory?

Through a synthesis of old and new theories of social remembering, this book provides the first comprehensive overview of the sociology of memory. This rapidly expanding field explores how representations of the past are generated, maintained and reproduced through texts, images, sites, rituals and experiences. The main aim of the book is to show to what extent the investigation of memory challenges sociological understandings of the formation of social identities and conflicts. It illustrates the new status of memory in contemporary societies by examining the complex relationships between memory and commemoration, memory and identity, memory and trauma, and memory and justice.

The book consists of six chapters, with the first three devoted to conceptualising the process of remembering by analyzing memory's function, status and history, as well as by locating the study of memory in a broader field of social science. The second part of the book directly explores and discusses theories and studies of social remembering. The glossary offers a concise and up to date overview of the development of relevant theoretical concepts.

This is an essential text for undergraduate courses in social theory, the sociology of memory and a wider audience in cultural studies, history and politics.

Contents
Series editor's foreword – Introduction – Memory experience – Metamorphosis of memory – Theorizing remembering – The remembering process – Contested boundaries – Studying memory – Epilogue – Glossary – Bibliography – Index.

168pp   0 335 20831 2 (Paperback)   0 335 20832 0 (Hardback)

GENDER AND SOCIAL THEORY

Mary Evans

- What is the most significant aspect of current literature on gender?
- How does this literature engage with social theory?
- How does the recognition of gender shift the central arguments of social theory?

We know that gender defines and shapes our lives. The question addressed by *Gender and Social Theory* is that of exactly how this process occurs, and what the social consequences, and the consequences for social theory, might be. The emergence of feminist theory has enriched our understanding of the impact of gender on our individual lives and the contemporary social sciences all recognise gender differentiation in the social world. The issue, however, which this book discusses is the more complex question of the extent to which social theory is significantly disrupted, disturbed or devalued by the fuller recognition of gender difference.

Mary Evans examines whether social theory is as blind to gender as is sometimes argued and considers the extent to which a greater awareness of gender truly shifts the concerns and conclusions of social theory. Written by an author with an international reputation, this is an invaluable text for students and an essential reference in the field.

Contents
Series foreword – Acknowledgements – Introduction – Enter women – The meaning of work – The world of intimacy – The gendered self – The real world – Now you see it, now you don't – Notes – Bibliography – Index.

160pp   0 335 20864 9 (Paperback)   0 335 20865 7 (Hardback)

ECONOMY, CULTURE AND SOCIETY
A SOCIOLOGICAL CRITIQUE OF NEO-LIBERALISM
Barry Smart

... an authoritative analysis and a definitive defence of sociology as a critical theory of the market, politics and social institutions. A balanced and thorough critique of the neo-liberal revolution.

Professor Bryan Turner, University of Cambridge

- How have economic processes and transformations been addressed within classical and contemporary social thought?
- What impact have the market system and market forces had on social life?
- How has the imbalance between the public and private sectors been felt in contemporary society?

Economic factors and processes are at the heart of contemporary social and cultural life and this book is designed to refocus social theorizing to reflect that fact. The author re-interprets the work of classical theorists and, in the context of the move towards social regulation and protection in the 19th and early 20th centuries, he discusses more recent transformations in capitalist economic life that have led to greater flexibility, forms of disorganization, and a neo-liberal regeneration of the market economy. As our lives have become subject to a process of commodification, market forces have assumed an increasing prominence, and the imbalance in resources between private and public sectors has been aggravated. This illuminating text addresses these central concerns, drawing on the work of key social and economic thinkers.

Contents
Series editor's foreword – Sociological reason and economic life – No alternative? capitalist economic life and the closing of the political universe – Cultures of production and consumption – Without regard for persons: the market economy – Affluence and squalor: the private and public sectors – Conclusion: new economic conditions and their social and political consequences – Further reading – References – Index.

208pp   0 335 20910 6 (Paperback)

ORGANIZATION AND INNOVATION
GURU SCHEMES AND AMERICAN DREAMS
David Knights and Darren McCabe

- What do recent management fads and fashions have in common?
- What are the implications and limitations of the prescriptions on offer for people's working lives?

Managerial fads and fashions, guru panaceas and organisational innovations have proliferated over the last 20 years. Drawing on case studies from the UK manufacturing and financial service sectors, this book argues that the emergence and popularity of a new range of management innovations reflects and facilitates the reproduction of a neo-liberal economics that has dominated Western politics for almost a quarter of a century.

The book contends that current management thinking around 'new' forms of work organization is immersed in a contemporary version of the American Dream. Referring to empirical research, the authors identify numerous difficulties confronting the implementation of this discourse, including:

- Collective and individual forms of resistance
- Unintended consequences and contradictory tensions around the notions of autonomy versus control
- Individualism versus collectivism
- Insecurity versus commitment
- Quality versus quantity.

Organization and Innovation concludes that the contemporary American Dream offers only 'one' dream of a better tomorrow and offers a powerful argument that we should seek other dreams that question rather than simply legitimise current inequalities.

Contents
Series editor's foreword – Introduction – Part one: Management innovation in historical perspective – The false promise of the American Dream: organization, innovation and change management – A research framework; TQM as an illustrative case – Part two: Manufacturing autonomy: re-engineering and culture change – Tales of the unexpected: strategic management and innovation – Teamworking and resistance – A "one team" approach to knowledge management – Part three: Conclusion – Bibliography – Index.

224pp   0 335 20684 0 (Paperback)   0 335 20685 9 (Hardback)

SCIENCE, SOCIAL THEORY AND PUBLIC KNOWLEDGE

Alan Irwin and Mike Michael

- How might social theory, public understanding of science and science policy best inform one another?
- What have been the key features of science-society relations in the modern world?
- How are we to re-think science-society relations in the context of globalization, hybridity and changing patterns of governance?

This topical and unique book draws together the three key perspectives on science-society relations: public understanding of science, scientific and public governance, and social theory. The book presents a series of case studies (including the debates on genetically modified foods and the AIDS movement in the USA) to discuss critically the ways in which social theorists, social scientists, and science policy makers deal with science-society relations.

'Science' and 'society' combine in many complex ways. Concepts such as citizenship, expertise, governance, democracy and the public need to be re-thought in the context of contemporary concerns with globalization and hybridity. A radical new approach is developed and the notion of ethno-epistemic assemblage is used to articulate a new series of questions for the theorization, empirical study and politics of science-society relations.

Contents

Preface – Introducing theory, context and practice – The public understanding of science and technology: from cognition to context – Science and public policy: from government to governance – Social theory and science – Re-conceptualising science, society and governance – Ethno-epistemic assemblages: heterogeneity and relationality in scientific citizenship – Politics and method: governing the assemblage, unearthing the rhizome – Conclusion – Index.

192pp   0 335 20947 5 (Paperback)   0 335 20948 3 (Hardback)

CRITICAL READINGS: MEDIA AND GENDER

Cynthia Carter and Linda Steiner (eds)

Critical Readings: Media and Gender provides a lively and engaging introduction to the field of media and gender research, drawing from a wide range of important international scholarship. A variety of conceptual and methodological approaches is used to explore subjects such as: entertainment; news; grassroots communication; new media texts; institutions; audiences. Topics include:

- Gender identity and television talk shows
- The sexualization of the popular press
- The representation of lesbians on television
- The cult of femininity in women's magazines
- Images of African American women and Latinas in Hollywood cinema
- Pornography and masculine power

This book is ideal for undergraduate courses in cultural and media studies, gender studies, the sociology of the media, mass communication, journalism, communication studies and politics.

Essays by: John Beynon, Mary Ellen Brown, Helen Davies, Elizabeth Hadley Freydberg, Margaret Gallagher, Heather Gilmour, Patricia Holland, Sherrie A. Inness, Robert Jensen, Myra Macdonald, Marguerite Moritz, Carmen Ruíz, Anne Scott, Lesley Semmens, Jane Shattuc, Saraswati Sunindyo, Lynette Willoughby.

Contents
Series editor's foreword – Acknowledgements – The contested terrain of media and gender: editors' introduction – Part one: Gendered texts in context – Readings 1–5 – Part two: (Re)Producing gender – Readings 6–10 – Part three: Gendered audiences and identities – Readings 11–15 – Index.

384pp   0 335 21097 X (Paperback)   0 335 21098 8 (Hardback)